Technology Strategy and the Firm

Technology Strategy and the Firm: management and public policy

Editor: Mark Dodgson

Longman

TECHNOLOGY STRATEGY AND THE FIRM:
management and public policy

First published 1989

Published by Longman Group UK Limited, Professional Reference and
Information Publishing Division, Longman House, Burnt Mill, Harlow,
Essex CM20 2JE, UK.
Telephone: Harlow (0279) 442601

British Library Cataloguing in Publication Data

Technology strategy and the firm: management and public policy
   1. Industries. Technological innovation.
   Management
   I. Dodgson, Mark
   658.5' 77

ISBN 0-582-05057-X

Typeset by P's & Q's Ltd., 18 Harrington Street, Liverpool L2 9QA.

Printed in Great Britain by Bell and Bain Ltd., Glasgow

Preface

The Prussian philosopher Hegel remarked that world history is the 'world court of judgement'. In our day with the contemporary emphasis on market success as the measure of all things his remark might be paraphrased as 'the world market is the world court of judgement'. In these terms the extraordinary success of Japanese firms in the world market over the past 30 years generally gets a favourable verdict from the world court. Indeed, in the opinion of some historians the shift of technological and industrial strength to Asia must ultimately also lead to a redistribution of military and political power.

Be this as it may, there can be no doubt that the extraordinary Japanese success in world markets is exerting a profound influence on management studies and increasingly on firm behaviour and industrial policy in western Europe and North America. This book is not primarily about Japan but the influence of the Japanese 'model' can be seen not only in the very welcome participation of a Japanese colleague, but also in many of the other chapters.

The influence of Japanese corporate success on management thinking elsewhere may be seen in many areas: quality of products, industrial training, devolution of responsibility, horizontal integration of design, development and production, and so forth. But so far as this book is concerned all the main points may be summarised under the heading of long-term strategic thinking about technology, both in firms and in government. Nowhere has this been more apparent than in the extraordinary world market success of Japanese electronic firms described in two chapters of the book. It is apparent also in the automobile industry described in another chapter and in many other industries not dealt with here.

This is an important point for many reasons. Above all it is important as a corrective to some of the simplistic and short-term thinking about 'markets' in the United Kingdom and the United States, which sees 'deregulation' and 'privatisation' as the solution to all economic and social problems. This simplistic approach does violence to the technological sophistication of a century of neo-classical economic theory on market imperfections, market failure, market regulation, social costs and benefits and externalities. Much more seriously, if pushed to extreme limits, it endangers the long-term survival of the British and American manufacturing industry itself. As this book amply demonstrates, competitive survival will depend increasingly on long-term strategic investment in R & D, design, new equipment, marketing networks, and skills, ie on long-term technology strategies.

This long-term orientation depends on social and institutional arrrangements in the capital market, the labour market, the R & D network, the education system and much else which cannot be reduced to short-term profit maximisation on the one hand nor a 'night-watchman' state on the other. To secure a more favourable verdict from the world court in the 21st century (and to deal with their acute trade problems in the 1990s) Britain and America will need to learn many lessons from Japan.

But it is not simply a case of imitating Japanese practices. Several of the chapters in the book deal with European firms who have done just as well through developing their long-term strategies. New understanding and improved performance must come from assimilating the best international experience from whatever source in the world. This book is a very useful contribution to this learning process.

Professor Christopher Freeman   December 1988
Science Policy Research Unit
University of Sussex

Acknowledgements

Keith Pavitt had the original idea to produce this book, and it has benefitted considerably from his continued commitment and support. Its production has been jointly funded by the Leverhulme Trust and the Economic and Social Research Council's Designated Research Centre on Science, Technology and Energy Policy at the Science Policy Research Unit (SPRU). It is very much a SPRU book. I should like to thank Kevin Morgan, Nick von Tunzelmann and Robin Mansell for their helpful comments on various chapters, and I am particularly grateful to Chris Freeman, William Walker, Keith Pavitt, Ian Miles, Margaret Sharp and Roy Rothwell for their comments on the introductory and concluding chapters. Any shortcomings in the book exist despite my colleagues' attempts to prevent them.

A book like this cannot be produced without hours of dedicated secretarial work. Many SPRU secretaries have been involved in its production. I am grateful to them all. In particular I would like to thank Lesley Elliott for all her hard work.

Mark Dodgson   November 1988

Contents

Contents   xi

About the authors

Yasunori Baba Economist, with previous experience at the Industrial Bank of Japan. Currently researching technology, firm behaviour and performance.

Fiorenza Belussi Economist. Current research into the diffusion of technology in traditional sectors.

Tim Brady Mathematician. Earlier work on implications of new technology for manpower and skills in engineering industry. Recent work on the implications of the development and use of new materials for skills and training.

Mark Dodgson Industrial Sociologist. Previously at the Technical Change Centre, London. Past research into work organisation, small firms, industrial relations. Current research on corporate technology strategies.

Paul Gardiner Biologist/physicist. Previously technology consultant. Current work on design and innovation management.

Ken Guy Physicist. Previous SPRU work on technological change and employment. Currently leading team evaluating the Alvey Programme.

Mike Hobday Economist with previous industrial experience in the microelectronics industry. Current work on the evaluation of the Alvey programme and on telecommunications and information technology in the industrialising countries.

Dan Jones Economist. Previously at National Institute of Economic and Social Research, working on technological change, industrial competitiveness and industrial policy. Currently European Research Director of the International Motor Vehicle Programme.

Ian Miles Psychologist/social scientist. Currently leading SPRU work on technology and social change, and project mapping and measuring the information economy.

Keith Pavitt Engineer/economist. Previously at the OECD. Presently Deputy Director of SPRU. Currently Director of ESRC Designated Research Centre on Science, Technology and Energy Policy in British Economic Development.

Mike Robson Physicist. Currently Computer Officer at Brighton Polytechnic, continuing research with SPRU into technology, firm behaviour and performance.

Roy Rothwell Applied Physicist. Previously electronics engineer and materials scientist. Past SPRU work includes research into innovation management and comparative national innovation policies. Currently leading research programme into management of technology.

Jacky Senker Urban and Regional Planner. Current research on a review of the SERC's Biotechnology Directorate.

Peter Senker Economist with previous experience in the electronics industry. Leading SPRU work on new technology, manpower and skills.

Margaret Sharp Economist. Previous experience at LSE, the Civil Service and NEDO, working on industrial policies in UK and Europe. Recent research on evaluation of biotechnology research and on European science and industrial policy.

Graham Thomas Sociologist, with previous experience at the Universities of Konstanz and Ulm. Recent work on technology and social change.

Joe Townsend Historian. Previous experience mainly in teaching and journalism, and in SPRU research concerned with industrial innovation. Current SPRU work on technology, firm behaviour and performance.

Chapter 1

Introduction:
technology in a strategic perspective

Mark Dodgson

1 Introduction

Technology is a core corporate asset and a major source of competitive advantage. In the present period of rapid technological change, firms therefore need to consider technology strategy. A technology strategy involves an understanding within a corporation – manifest amongst senior management, but diffused throughout the organisation – of the importance and potential of technology for its competitive position, how in the future that potential is to be realised, and how this complements the other aspects of strategy, such as finance, marketing and personnel. This involves complex decisions. Foremost amongst these are decisions concerning which technologies are appropriate and necessary for the firm's long-term profitability and growth and how these are to be developed, accessed and diffused.

The term 'strategy' is presently highly fashionable. As with many buzz-words, its excessive use has distorted its meaning. It is commonly used as an antonym of 'tactical'. Thus strategy implies long-term, purposeful and interconnected efforts, and tactics imply action to deal with immediate and specific problems. The relationship between the two – as in their original military sense of movement of troops (tactics) in support of leaders' overall view of how a campaign is to be won (strategy) – is often lost. This book uses 'strategy' in the sense of it determining tactics in the use of resources.

Technology strategy currently has a very high profile in business schools and universities, and increasingly in industry and amongst policy-makers. There exists a growing literature on the need for, and nature and determinants of, technology strategy. Too often, however, little supporting empirical evidence is available. Considerable empirical evidence will be presented in this book to show that technology is a crucial resource in industrial firms, and that its generation, acquisition and diffusion is a strategic concern for firms of all sizes in a wide range of industries.

The raison d'être for the book is simple. The extraordinary range and potential uses of contemporary technology have important consequences for industrial and commercial firms. The industrial and organisational turbulence engendered by technological change and increasing international competitive pressures, provides threats and opportunities for firms. An effective strategic approach to technology allows firms better to cope with these changes, and will reduce the threats and insecurities facing firms and their employees.

The book is structured into five sections. The first, comprising the contributions of Jones, Baba and Pavitt et al sets the scene for what follows. Based on research undertaken in Japan, US and the UK, these chapters provide an introduction to the range of strategic options currently open to manufacturing firms. The second section, the chapters of Hobday and of Thomas and Miles, discusses strategy in two modern industries: semiconductors and New Interactive Services (NIS). The third section by contrast, analyses strategies in two more traditional industries: Belussi on a textile company, and Senker on food retailing. The fourth section considers some specific managerial issues: Dodgson and Rothwell on high-technology small and medium-sized firms, Senker and Brady on human resource development, and Gardiner and Rothwell on design strategies. The final section, in which Guy comments on the UK's Alvey programme and Sharp on the European Community's ESPRIT programme, highlights the interactions between public policies and corporate strategies.

A number of arguments concerning technology strategy, developed throughout the book, are examined in the concluding chapter. These arguments can briefly be summarised:

— The existence of a corporate technology strategy is increasingly necessary for industrial firms and is necessarily long-term. It is appropriate for all companies except the very smallest. Technology strategy should complement other elements of corporate strategy: manufacturing, marketing, investment etc, and should in many cases be international in focus.
— Strategies extend beyond the boundaries of the firm to encompass the behaviour of other companies — suppliers, customers, partners and competitors — and other sources of technology. Public policies can directly affect the technological activities of firms and must be taken into account.
— Strategy formulation, implementation and review are processes which are susceptible to radical change through the intervention of managers. There are benefits to be obtained by basing strategy upon those accumulated competences which provide comparative competitive advantage, and through complementing those competences with external expertise. A crucial factor underlying successful strategy is the ability of managers to adapt and learn from experience.

2 Why technology strategy is important

Before entering into the main text of the book, the question needs to be answered: why is technology strategy important? Five issues which bear on the importance of corporate strategy for technology will now briefly be described: the need to cope with technological uncertainty, complexity and the discontinuous nature of technological development; the need for technology to be viewed in a global context; the need to attain complementarities, internally between different elements of overall corporate strategy, and externally between companies' strategies; the failure of existing strategies which do not integrate technology satisfactorily; and the relationship between corporate technology strategy and public technology policies.

2.1 Technological uncertainty and complexity

The 'new' technologies pervade new and traditional industries. Electronics, for example, has a number of industrial branches in its own right, but significantly affects whole economies through its fusion into wide-ranging applications from manufacturing systems to telecommunications. The pervasiveness of information technology (IT) leads Christopher Freeman and Carlota Perez to describe it as a revolutionary new 'techno-economic paradigm'. The expression 'techno-economic' is used as '...the changes involved go beyond engineering trajectories for specific product or process technologies and affect the input cost structure and conditions of production and distribution throughout the system' (Freeman and Perez, 1988, p47). This period is marked by considerable turbulence and uncertainty for firms. We are currently in a time that Klein (1977) might describe as 'fast history', with firms having rapidly to introduce technological and organisational change in order to remain competitive.

Some argue that technological development is increasingly discontinuous, and that product life cycles are shortening. This has profound consequences for companies' technology strategies (Foster, 1987; Link and Tassey, 1987). There are, however, different interpretations of just how profound these consequences will be for firms. Pisano and Teece argue:

> The frequency of technological discontinuities or technology paradigm shifts seems to have increased. When technological development takes a new trajectory, the direction of technical development is no longer cumulative and self-generating...In short, the logic of previous technical advance is broken; and the capabilities that the firm possesses in house may no longer suffice. (1988, p6)

Tushman and Anderson (1987) in their study of the cement, airline and microcomputer businesses argue that technological change is characterised by periods of continuous incremental change punctuated by more radical discontinuities. These periods of more rapid change can be 'competence-enhancing' (usually derived from, and beneficial to, existing firms) or 'competence-destroying' (usually exogenously sourced, and threatening to existing firms). This distinction has the advantage of at least ascribing some influence to companies in the process of technological change. Pavitt (1987), however, goes further. He contends that the formation of research and development (R&D) laboratories in large firms is in part a means of internalising technological discontinuities, and thereby ensuring institutional stability.

Whatever the source of the technological breakthrough, it is companies with wider-ranging R&D expertise that are more likely to recognise the significance and potential of both incremental and radical technological developments. Broad R&D competences and skills are a method of dealing with discontinuities and turbulence; a way of technology-watching and keeping options open.

The 'new' technologies are enormously complex. Complexity results from the convergence of technologies between, for example, electronics and mechanics to create 'mechatronics' and computers and communications technology to create integrated digital networks. Pavitt et al, in Chapter 4, conjecture that one of the reasons for their finding that companies show greater diversification in their technological activities than in output is because of the complex nature of contemporary technological interdependencies. The sheer complexity of technological systems dictates the inclusion of technology amongst corporate, ie boards of directors' concerns. Strategic decisions need to be made on how to deal with this complexity; on how to match or better the opportunities it provides to existing or potential competitors.

Thomas and Miles's chapter on new interactive services (NIS) highlights just how complex new technologies can be. They distinguish three related aspects to this complexity, including: the 'swarming' of new IT based goods and services associated with its rapid and widespread diffusion; the 'clustering' of infant, and generally unproven products; and the need for comprehensive convergence of differing technologies and skills. Such convergence often requires the merging of previously discrete business interests; through acquisition, joint venture or technological alliance. Decisions on acquisition and collaboration as a means of dealing with technological complexity are an important component in technology strategy.

The development of new technological systems is extremely costly. It is estimated that the UK's System X digital exchange cost $1.5 billion to develop. Sharp, in Chapter 13, shows that a new generation of memory chips has a minimum 'front-end' cost of $200 million. It is very difficult for one firm independently to cover the risks of such a financial burden. This provides another reason for the increased emphasis on collaboration within industry. Firms increasingly are looking for complementary funds from within industry and from government. Technology strategy is important, therefore, to see firms through periods of technological turbulence and uncertainty, and to deal with the high complexity and cost of technology.

2.2 Globalisation

Developing and marketing contemporary technology are essentially international activities. The new pervasive or 'generic' technologies — IT, new materials and biotechnology — are worldwide phenomena. There are numerous examples of public policies and private corporations' strategies reflecting recognition of comparative technological advantages on a global scale. The Japanese 'Fifth Generation Computer Project' catalysed IT policies worldwide (Arnold and Guy, 1986); ICI's new materials research centre, and Siemens' ISDN telecommunications research, are based in the US; Monsanto invests heavily in biotechnology research at Oxford

University. The evidence presented in this book reflects the international nature both of corporate technological development and of governmental policy responses to technological challenges. There are very real differences in the strategic competences of, for example, UK and Japanese corporations, and within the same countries marked differences in the ability of Ministries to foster and direct technology strategies. Nonetheless, there are more similarities than differences in the manifestly worldwide pressures influencing private and public strategies for technological development. For this reason the empirical research presented in the book is multinational; from the US, Japan, UK and the rest of Europe. Evidence may be presented referring to a particular nation, but the problems facing corporations and governments are essentially common to most industrial economies. While corporations in particular countries may enjoy certain advantages, there are few industrialised nations that cannot boast a world leading corporation.

International intercorporate collaboration extends beyond sharing the heavy financial (and intellectual) burden of R&D in systems such as aircraft and automobiles, and includes manufacturing and marketing. For Japanese corporations, the concept of globalisation of markets is paramount (Porter, 1987a). Baba and Hobday show this to be so in Chapters 3 and 5, and they argue that direct foreign investment in manufacturing plant is a similarly crucial component of strategy. Jones, in Chapter 2, describes the development of global activities in the automobile industry, and argues that the international auto trade will come to resemble the classic pattern of intra-industry trade. There are, as yet, few studies of the global nature of markets, and certainly much more research is required into this area.

2.3 Complementarities

Technology strategy is important as it needs to complement overall company strategy: encompassing business, marketing, manufacturing, personnel, investment and financial strategy. Project SAPPHO in the early 1970s showed that successful innovative firms matched their technological developments with complementary marketing, advertising and manufacturing efforts (Rothwell et al, 1974). SAPPHO also showed that successful innovators made use of external technology and scientific advice. Teece (1987a) similarly refers to the importance of 'complementary assets' (marketing expertise, distribution networks etc) in realising full returns from technological innovation. He also highlights the importance of accessing external technological expertise.

For a company to have an effective strategy for innovation, all the aspects of the innovation process have to be considered, and strategies for change merged into a coherent whole. Belussi's chapter on the Benetton company provides a convincing testament to the efficacy of a 'total innovation strategy'. It charts the very rapid growth of the company, and relates this to a holistic and complementary strategy of product, process and organisational innovation. Both Baba and Hobday also emphasise the need for a successful technology strategy to encompass both product and process innovations. Jones describes the success Japanese firms have had in integrating their R&D and manufacturing efforts.

Too little empirical research has been undertaken into the complementary relationship between strategies for technology and manpower. But Senker and Brady, in Chapter 10, using case study material argue how important it is for firms to complement their processes of technological development with appropriate human resource development strategies. They conclude that it is only those firms which provide adequate and relevant training for their workforces that will change technological threats into opportunities.

External complementarities are also required. In the R&D process '...the growth of world competition in technology-related areas makes (the) strategy of sole reliance on internally financed and internally conducted R&D insufficient and perhaps suicidal' (Link and Tassey, 1987, p10).

An example of this point is the biotechnology industry in the US, where Hamilton (1986) found a widespread use of external links between firms, and that these links were a significant part of the firms' technology strategy. Dodgson and Rothwell's chapter describes the importance of external linkages for the technological development of their sample of highly successful small and medium-sized firms.

Firms increasingly collaborate in their technological efforts. Guy, in Chapter 12, describes some of the advantages and disadvantages of collaboration. Joint ventures and 'strategic alliances' designed to merge firms' specific technological competences are now a feature in a number of industries. Sharp and Hobday, in Chapters 13 and 5, highlight the use of these partnerships in consumer electronics and semiconductors. They are also a feature in the automobile, pharmaceutical and aircraft industries (Hladik, 1985; Mowery, 1987).

Thomas and Miles, in Chapter 6, emphasise the problems associated with the convergence of different technologies and skills in the generation of NIS. The ability creatively to integrate in-house expertise, and access external expertise, into rapidly deployed R&D or new product teams or corporate venture is described by much recent management literature as an essential element of successful strategic management (Burgelman and Sayles, 1986).

Like Thomas and Miles, Gardiner and Rothwell, in Chapter 11, describe how important it is to link well with users of new products and services. Dodgson and Rothwell, in Chapter 9, emphasise the need for high technology small and medium-sized firms to gain technical feedback from customers. Jones describes how Japanese auto firms successfully build long-term links with their suppliers. Belussi shows the importance for Benetton's development of having good contacts with agents and retailers and with a wide range of upstream and downstream activities.

Our contention is that contemporary technology extends the boundaries of the firm. It becomes essential to relate to the behaviour of firms in complementary horizontal and vertical activities, as the new technologies provide wider opportunities for those firms to affect competitiveness. To overcome the problems of complexity, high cost and high risk, activities previously proprietorial to individual firms such as R&D and manufacturing may become shared between a number of firms. The necessary sacrifice of autonomy in the generation and diffusion of technology involves a strategy of sharing control in order to retain it. Without participation in multilateral technological arrangements, even the most advanced companies may lose their leadership positions.

There exists a diverse and growing literature on the changing nature of the firm. There are calls to limit research into the behaviour of firms as distinct units. Pfeffer (1987) argues the need to study the social context of business strategy, in particular the concept of interorganisational power. He calls for 'relationships, quasi-firms, trade associations, and interfirm organisations of all types and other manifestations of networks, resource dependencies and relations' to be understood as an important determinant of industrial dynamics. This book adds further evidence of the extension of the boundaries of firms by concentrating on the prevalence and necessity of technological partnerships (*see*, in particular, the chapters by Hobday, Guy and Sharp).

2.4 Failure of existing strategies

Recent turbulence in world markets and extensive currency fluctuations compound and accentuate corporate uncertainty in existing strategies for growth and profitability. This, added to the growing evidence putting into question the strategic efficacy of the US and UK acquisition boom necessarily focusses attention on the importance and potential of key elements of corporations' assets, most particularly on technology and innovation. The reasons why technology demands greater strategic consideration are compounded by the failure of past corporate strategies. Two of the major factors which have in the past discriminated against the formulation of coherent technology strategies in the UK (and US) are: corporate obsession with acquisition as the method for achieving growth, and short-termism in corporate investment. These will briefly be examined.

Acquisition as a strategy for growth

As Chandler argued in the 1960s, there is a tendency for large corporations to diversify (Chandler, 1962). In 1950 the majority of the UK's largest 200 companies were undiversified, and operated in single or dominant business areas. By 1980, however, nearly two-thirds of the largest 200 firms were diversified, and one-fifth were conglomerates (Channon, 1982). This change has largely been achieved via acquisitions and mergers and not through internal creation of new activities (Constable, 1986). The 1980s have seen a massive boom in acquisition activity in the UK. Expenditure increased from £1 billion in 1981 to £5 billion in 1984 to £15 billion in 1987. UK companies have acquired many US companies; in 1986 $8.8 billion was spent for this purpose, and this figure was estimated to have doubled in 1987. The 1985/86 annual reports of 50 of the UK's largest companies showed 22 to have acquired substantial US interests in the previous year.

Research in the US by Porter (1987b) shows the dangers of acquisitions made without strategic direction. He reports that over 50 per cent of all acquisitions made by 33 large US companies between 1950 and 1960 were subsequently divested; and for those acquisitions made in unrelated fields, three-quarters were divested. Doubts about the consequences of this considerable reliance by corporations on acquired growth are also raised by many UK observers, including the director of the British Institute of Management (Constable, 1986). It is often pointed out that the US high-tech successes of the past few decades — IBM, DEC, Hewlett Packard — were achieved by internal rather than acquired growth. In stark contrast to strategies for growth based on acquisition, Japanese corporations concentrate rather on organic growth. Baba's chapter highlights the long-term nature of Japanese strategies. Indeed, it is perhaps the ability to plan for long-term technology-based growth through high levels of R&D and direct foreign investments that is the primary characteristic differentiating UK and US companies from the Japanese.

Short-termism
One important explanation for the difference in time horizons for Japanese and UK and US corporations lies within the financial systems. The short-termism of the City of London and Wall Street is all too often evident.[1] The Japanese Keiretsu Group structure, by contrast, facilitates long-term investment (Freeman, 1987).

The inability of financiers in the UK to comprehend the long-term nature of technological development and accumulation is often matched by the boards of directors of large industrial companies. Over 25 years ago, Tibor Barna highlighted the poor quality and short-termism of management as one of the major constraints on British firms' investment and growth policies, and urged that this issue be given priority (Barna, 1962). Certainly, the most successful industrialists and managers appreciate the need to take the long-term view, particularly for R&D and technology (Harvey Jones, 1987). Yet, for many, technology is not perceived to be of major concern. One-half of 50 of the UK's top manufacturing companies think R&D to be of such marginal interest to their shareholders that their expenditure on it is not included in their annual reports. It is still rare to find information on R&D spend in investment analysts' company reports.

The long-term nature of technology strategies is apparent. Corporate ventures and new business developments can take up to ten years to become profitable (Littler and Sweeting, 1974; Bigadikke, 1979). Industrial clubs take many years to fuse cohesively (Sharp and Shearman, 1987). Building the entrepreneurial ethos into large organisations, and providing the management structures and reward systems to stimulate product champions and project leaders is a lengthy process (Burgelman and Sayles, 1986). Doz and Prahalad (1987), in their study of sixteen large multinational companies, found that a change in strategy, once formulated, takes between three and ten years to implement.

2.5 Public technology policy
Heightened international industrial competition has focussed attention on the sources of comparative industrial advantage, in particular technological

development. As the recent work by Patel and Pavitt (1987) shows, the behaviour of a limited number of key companies can determine the technological trajectory and economic competitiveness of industrial sectors in a country. Sharp, in Chapter 13, stresses the importance of three key companies for the future of the European electronics industry. Intra-firm spending on R&D is a critical component of sectoral and national R&D expenditure, and one that economists have tended to overlook (Cohen and Mowery, 1984).

There is little or no data available on changes in the amount of collaborative research undertaken in the UK. The Department of Trade and Industry (DTI), however, is currently involved in over 100 industrial collaborative 'clubs', and it is a major part of Government policy to increase collaboration in Europe.

This book describes the role public technology policy can play in influencing and encouraging the extended boundaries of firms. Porter has argued for the very important influence of governments' use of political pressures on global strategies...'The political imperative is to concentrate activities in some industries where governments provide strong export incentives and locational subsidies' (1987a, p43). Also, as the chapters by Guy and Sharp argue, public policies have directly influenced the collaborative behaviour of companies. There are nowadays few industrialised economies which do not have policies designed to encourage and support the growth of high technology small firms.

Guy argues that the UK's Alvey programme has catalysed, accelerated and expanded research activity in key technical areas for the future. Although Alvey funds usually contributed only a small proportion of firms' total R&D, they had a disproportionate effect. Guy found that Alvey has influenced the way in which firms conduct R&D, their interaction with government and universities and the way they interpret their role within the community. It has also had a marked effect in educating firms on the benefits of collaboration. Similarly, Sharp shows how ESPRIT has played a seminal role within Europe in changing attitudes and strategies amongst Europe's top electronics firms. She argues that it has acted as a catalyst for the process of rationalisation now underway. ESPRIT has also had an important psychological effect in three important aspects. It has created a channel for cooperation, a mechanism for creating convergent expectations, and a constituency pressing for the completion of the internal European Community (EC) market planned for 1992 and the harmonisation of standards. It also, like Alvey, has provided an important learning process in collaboration.

Hobday shows in his chapter on semiconductor manufacturers how government initiatives, in particular those instigated by MITI in Japan, have altered company strategies. He also describes the increased activity on the part of US and European governments to ensure the existence of internationally competitive domestic companies. On another level, Jacqueline Senker argues that changes in food legislation altered the technology strategies of some food retailers. And Thomas and Miles describe how recent legislative changes have encouraged new entrants into

NIS. Jones analyses the way pollution control legislation has in the past and will in the future influence auto engine technology.

It is important also to understand the role played by firms in framing public policies. Both Alvey and ESPRIT were formulated on the basis of representations by firms. It is essential for firms to present a coherent argument on the need for public support. A strategic view of the necessity and nature of government intervention in technology development improves industry's case for support.

Public research institutes are, of course, important sources of technology and technological support for industry. Some argue a convergence of technology with the science base (Narin and Noma, 1985; Dosi, 1988). It becomes essential for companies not only to access scientific information and technologies from new sources, but also to learn how to transfer and integrate knowledge from these previously separate sources. There are now a plethora of public programmes and intermediary organisations worldwide designed to improve the technology transfer process between infrastructural organisations and industrial firms (Rothwell, Dodgson and Lowe, 1988). The widespread growth of the science park movement, for example, highlights the increased emphasis placed by universities and similar institutions on attracting industrial collaboration. Whether this emphasis is reciprocated depends on the strategies for technological receptivity within firms.

3. Concluding remarks

This introduction has highlighted many of the reasons why technology should be viewed strategically within companies. The next twelve chapters provide substantial empirical evidence as to why this is so. They will examine the content and efficacy of some of these strategies in a wide range of industries, and some lessons will be drawn on the factors which stimulate and constrain strategy in particular sectors. Many of the chapters address key theoretical perspectives in the growing literature on technology strategy, and these are examined in the light of the empirical evidence presented. Some key management issues, such as managing novel technologies in highly uncertain markets, are also considered.

The concluding chapter draws together some of the themes developed throughout the book. It will attempt to evaluate the contribution of the book in an area which is notoriously difficult to research, and where there is a paucity of empirical work and sound theoretical insight.

Notes

1 Let one example suffice; Glaxo, the UK pharmaceutical company, more than quadrupled its sales between 1976 and 1987, at the same time its commitment to R&D, measured as a percentage of turnover, increased annually from 3.4 per cent to 8.5 per cent. It developed a reputation for rapidly producing highly innovative and profitable drugs. Yet when in 1987 it reported pretax profits up 22 per cent to £746 million, analysts were disappointed; their expectations were of £800 million profit. This 'disappointing' result was in part a result of Glaxo's high R&D spend, and as a result of City fears £1.4 billion was wiped off Glaxo's market capitalisation overnight.

Chapter 2

Corporate strategy and technology in the world automobile industry[1]

Daniel T Jones

1 Introduction

Like many other industries in the 1980s, new technologies and competitive challenges from the Far East are reshaping the world automobile industry. Traditionally this industry was characterised as mature, with a stable incrementally evolving technology and a well known organisational structure, supplying increasingly saturated markets. It was widely expected in the 1970s that the next two decades would see a gradual shift of production to low wage countries and a rationalisation of the number of producers on a global scale. The remaining production in the advanced countries would then be carried out in unmanned factories operating around the clock. In the event, none of these dramatic predictions was fulfilled.

This chapter starts by reviewing the nature and direction of technological change in the industry in recent decades, and the factors influencing the extent to which innovative activity features in corporate strategy. In particular it analyses the potential impact of electronic and materials technologies. This has to be set against other profound changes that have shaped the industry in the last decade, namely the development of a new form of social organisation by the Japanese and globalisation. However, as the consequences of these developments diffuse throughout the world, technology may again become significant for the strategies of the major players. To assess how well placed these corporations are in this respect we present some evidence of their technological strengths and weaknesses before concluding with a review of different strategies being pursued.

2 Technological change in the motor industry

It could be argued that once General Motors (GM) had displaced Ford as the leading auto manufacturer in the 1930s the major changes in automobile technology were over. What remained was a process of refinement and detailed embellishment. The development of the internal combustion engine powered vehicle a century ago settled the source of motive power and the combination of product and process technologies brought together by Ford for the Model T ushered in the mass production era. Certainly the automobile continued to evolve, as did the equipment used to produce it. Wooden bodies were replaced by steel, which in turn were replaced by monocoque bodies without the need for a separate chassis and later the configuration changed again to transversely mounted engines driving the front wheels. However, as Abernathy (1978) has shown in his classic study of the US auto industry, the pace of technological change slowed down in the postwar period and the focus shifted from product to process technologies. Competition became increasingly a function of price, derived from economies of scale, of styling and the size of the distribution network. Corporate strategies became constrained by what he called the productivity dilemma, ie the trade-off between production efficiency embodied in dedicated machines and the ability to innovate. As a result technology was no longer a major competitive factor.

However, if we for the moment accept this caricature of technological change in the auto industry, the question arises whether recent advances in both electronics and materials technologies herald a new period of radical change as they diffuse throughout the industry? There is no doubt that robotics and flexible manufacturing systems have changed the process of building cars and electronic control systems and plastic bodies are amongst the host of new technologies that may transform the vehicle. Even if we are in for a period of radical technological change the next question is what impact will this have on corporate strategies and on the structure of the industry? Before considering these questions it is useful to ask what causes technological change to occur in the auto industry and how these factors might change in the next decade. On the supply side it must be remembered that many of the significant technological developments in the industry come from elsewhere, either from related industries like the capital goods, component and material suppliers or from other industries such as aerospace, chemicals and electronics.[2] Therefore, new technological opportunities opened up elsewhere may, if the economics are right, diffuse also to the auto industry.

On the demand side a number of factors can induce manufacturers to search for new technological solutions, or to look back at the shelf of currently unused technologies developed previously. The first factor is regulatory pressure concerning such things as safety, emissions and fuel economy. The second is a major change in the price of oil, such as occurred in 1973 and 1979. The third is when the pattern and nature of demand changes with increasing affluence.

The fourth factor is when competitive conditions change in the relevant market. This can result from the opening up of markets leading to the entry of foreign producers offering alternative products to those available domestically. The impact is of course greater when a foreign producer not only offers alternative products but can do so with a significant price and quality advantage, as the Japanese have done. Another example is where a new producer enters the market against the established players or seeks to move into a new segment of the market. A reduction in industrial concentration, particularly when the market power of the dominant producer is weakened can be a powerful stimulus to technological dynamism. Whether this technological dynamism can be sustained depends on the degree of rivalry that exists between the leading players, frustrating the ability of one firm to establish a dominant design (Klein, 1977).

On the supply side, to what extent are we seeing a switch from one set of technologies to another? The diffusion of electronics and materials technologies into the auto industry began in the early 1980s. However, despite many predictions, the impact of technological change has not so far been dramatic. It has, as we shall see below, been overshadowed in the West by the productivity gains and employment losses associated with closing the productivity gap with the Japanese.

After decades of slow, incremental technical change the US auto producers began to pay more attention to product development in the early 1970s. Initially this was to meet tougher government regulations on safety, pollution and fuel economy. The first oil shock also started the move to reduce the size of US cars. In Europe, Japan and the US great strides were made in the 1970s to reduce the weight of the car, improve aerodynamics and stretch the performance of the internal combustion engine. Alternative engine options, such as the Wankel engine, the Sterling engine, gas turbines and various forms of electric power were explored, though none of them was successful in displacing the internal combustion engine. Mazda nearly went bankrupt as a result of its commitment to the Wankel engine in 1973.

In the late 1970s, and particularly once the shock of the second oil price rise in 1979 was over, the considerable improvements in engine efficiency were translated into much greater performance. A new generation of small performance cars, such as the Golf GTi quickly displaced the sports cars of the 1970s. In the 1980s further significant strides were made in engine technology using electronic design, measuring and testing equipment, more accurate electronically controlled casting, forging and machining techniques and the installation of electronic fuel injection and engine management systems to control engine performance. Turbocharging and multi-valve engines further extended the performance of internal combustion and diesel engines.

A detailed analysis of automotive patenting, described below, reveals that engine technologies were some of the most active areas of technological activity, growing as fast as computers. The Japanese auto industry was largely responsible for this growth, taking out twice as many patents in the US by 1985 as either the Americans or Europeans. The results of this research fed through very rapidly into a plethora of mass produced multi-valve engines that caught the rest of the world by surprise. After misjudging the pace of engine technology in Japan it is reported that Ford, for instance, has decided to scrap a new generation of European engines that are only just entering production.

Further improvements in internal combustion engine technology are likely as the Europeans and Americans redouble their efforts to catch up. The next step forward may result from the use of ceramics and other composites in the hot parts of the engine. Research is still continuing into alternative power plants such as gas turbines and two-stroke engines and on alternative fuels. Whether these alternatives ever come into their own may depend on the degree to which pollution laws are tightened in the 1990s.

A similar series of developments has also taken place in steering, suspension, braking and other subsystems of the vehicle. Electronic design, development and manufacturing technologies initially contributed to the refinement of existing systems. At the same time some producers turned to more complex systems, such as four-wheel drive, four-wheel steering and anti-lock brakes to cope with increased engine performance. In some cases this involved the refinement of mechanical systems previously used only in specialised and racing cars. In other cases they were developed around more sophisticated electronic control systems. At present both types of system co-exist in the market. Lucas, for instance, developed a much simpler mechanical anti-lock braking system than the electronic systems supplied by Bosch and others. Honda, having explored, researched and patented various electronic four-wheel steering systems opted instead for a mechanical system, whereas Mazda simultaneously introduced an electronic system. Lotus has gone further and has developed a completely electronic active suspension system that eliminates most of the conventional springs, dampers etc. If the manufacturing cost and reliability problems can be overcome, active suspension may offer significant improvements in handling, steering and suspension.

Although plastics have become the main material for interior trim parts and bumpers, the struggle to replace steel for exterior body panels has only just begun. While a number of cars, such as the Citroen BX and the Fiat Tipo, have single panels of plastic and composite materials, the Pontiac Fiero was one of the first cars to have a complete set of plastic panels mounted on a steel frame. Even though the success of the Fiero was short-lived, several forthcoming products are expected to follow this route.

Firms such as Dupont, General Electric, ICI, Hoechst and Montedison, searching for new markets for higher value products, have been ploughing large sums into R&D to solve the technical and manufacturing problems involved in the mass production of plastics and composites (Amendola, 1988). Likewise Alcan and other aluminium firms are looking to get away from declining markets for their traditional products by exploring the potential for aluminium bodied vehicles (Graves, 1988). The steel firms have also responded by improving the quality of steel supplied, which together with improved galvanising and painting offers better rust resistance. The auto firms on the other hand are torn between the sunk costs, accumulated knowledge and experience with steel and the expense and risks involved in switching to plastics in a big way. The Japanese firms in particular are active in improving the efficiency of the die making and stamping process, convinced that there is still a great deal of mileage in steel for car bodies.

The stage is set for a competitive race between plastics of different kinds, steel and aluminium as the material for car bodies in the 1990s. It is too early to predict the likely outcome, for many years yet each of these routes will be pursued and improved. However, if there is large scale substitution in the 1990s this could have a profound impact on the ways in which cars are designed and built in the future. Plastics will probably only come into their own when the car is totally redesigned to exploit the potential for fewer and more complex parts that can be glued together at the end of the assembly process rather than at the beginning. The French, Italian and US producers are actively looking towards plastics for a competitive breakthrough to challenge the Japanese. The Japanese on the other hand are adopting a more incremental approach, using plastics initially in low volume specialist niche and fashion vehicles.

The most important change of direction in process technology was the move from dedicated automation to more flexible equipment. This move began in the early 1980s and took two routes, the first from numerically controlled machine tools to ever more complicated flexible manufacturing systems and the second involving a range of handling, welding, painting and assembly equipment based on robotics. This equipment began in the stamping, welding, painting and machining areas and is now spreading to assembly, as more sensory capabilities are added. Alongside the automation of manufacturing the advent of computer aided design and scheduling opens up the prospect of better design for manufacture, simultaneous tooling design and linking design and manufacturing. At one point it was thought that not only would flexible automation directly substitute for labour but it would also prove to be an alternative to Japanese style production organisation. In the event, as outlined below, the greatest productivity gains today are being made from the reorganisation of production and not from automation. However, as this new best practice organisation diffuses and diminishing returns set in, it is likely that the gains from flexible automation will grow. So far the main benefits are in terms of better quality, consistency and accuracy as heavy, dirty and boring jobs are eliminated and from better coordination of the production process.

On the demand side the era of oil price and regulatory pressure is over for now. In fact the industry turned the gains in engine performance into increased power and better power to weight ratios with aerodynamics and lighter bodies. In the future regulatory pressures may return with pressure from organisations concerned about the environment, from moves to tighten up emissions legislation in California and possibly from tighter particulate emissions standards for diesel engines. There is also no doubt that increased affluence among car buyers in the West, and particularly in the US, has made consumers more receptive to paying for new technology. The search for differentiation which accompanies affluence and the growth of multi-car households means the market is fragmenting in smaller niches. Many first cars, and increasingly also second cars, in the US are bought loaded with extra features.

The main changes in the competitive environment have to do with the gap opened up by the Japanese and the internationalisation of the industry, and it is to these we now turn.

3 A new system of social organisation

The most significant change in the 1980s was the diffusion of a completely new model of production organisation that evolved over a 30 year period in Toyota in Japan. Faced with a different set of constraints and objectives, and without licence agreements with foreign manufacturers, Toyota developed a system that overturned most of the fundamental assumptions that had held good since Ford and Sloan in the early years of the industry. The individual responsible was Tiichi Ono, its production chief (Cusumano, 1985). Many books have described the essential features of this Ono/Toyota system, focussing on the Kanban system and Just in Time, and the other Japanese producers have developed versions of it (Schonberger, 1982, 1986). However what has become apparent with the benefit of hindsight is that the underlying philosophy of the production system pervades the whole set of activities involved in producing an automobile, from R&D through design, production and component supply to distribution and product strategy.

The Ono/Toyota system is based on the shortest possible production run not the longest, and it seeks to minimise the effort required by doing it right first time. The discipline of the system derives from the tight, uninterrupted flow of parts through the system with no duplication of fallback. The knowledge and cumulative experience required to constantly improve the system originates on the shop floor, not the higher echelons of management. Rigid functional divisions are avoided and activities are fully integrated with one another. In other words, it is a bottom-up system focussed on the experience of the people in the system and not the capabilities of the machinery. Exactly the same characteristics underlie the multi-functional team based, simultaneously engineering approach to product development.

The results of the system can be summarised as follows:

— Productivity and quality are dramatically improved. At the time of writing the Japanese take less than 20 hours to assemble a car that used to take over 30 hours in America and 40 hours in Europe, with one third of the delivered defects. This gap has nothing to do with automation (Krafcik, 1988).
— The Japanese product development process takes four years rather than five elsewhere, using 1.7 rather than 3 million man hours to accomplish the same tasks (Clark, 1988).
— The Japanese producers are able to offer many more models and variants than the Americans and Europeans, because these are renewed every four years rather than every eight to ten years. Average production volume over the lifetime of the model is therefore 500,000 rather than 2 million units as in Europe and America, ie their competitiveness is not based on scale (Sheriff, 1988).
— With a constant design team in being for each model, the cumulative experience of design for manufacture is retained and the feedback from the market place to the next generation of the technology shortened (Graves, 1988).
— The close integration of design with production ensures the smooth introduction of new models into production. New process equipment is introduced incrementally into the system rather than all in one go, once a decade with a new model introduction. New equipment thus augments the capabilities of the production worker rather than substituting for them.
— Suppliers with long term contracts are more closely involved in developing components and systems for the vehicle.
— The Japanese production system is far more flexible than in the West, able to cope with a greater mix complexity and to deliver customer-specified vehicles within a matter of days rather than months.

The initial western reaction to Japanese success was one of disbelief and a conviction that it was based on unique cultural features. The response was to redouble efforts to substitute technology for labour through ambitious and costly plant automation experiments in the use of these technologies, and these have so far failed to deliver productivity gains sufficient to close the gap with the Japanese (Krafcik, 1988). Indeed, after a massive investment in plant automation, GM is pulling back in this area and concentrating on improving the organisation of their plants. Other manufacturers have made much greater progress in closing the productivity gap without extensive new automation, in plants producing both new and existing models. The important lesson from this is that relatively inexpensive reorganisation of the production process and the mobilisation of the knowledge and experience on the shop floor yields greater dividends than major leaps in production automation. The development of a lean, bottom-up production system may be a necessary precondition for the full exploitation of these technologies in the future.

What finally brought about a realisation that the Japanese system was not only transferable but had to be matched was the opening of the Nissan, Honda and Toyota-GM joint venture assembly plants in the US, which replicated the performance of equivalent plants back in Japan. Until then the social resistance from middle management in particular blocked any progress in this direction. Now all the excuses have gone and there is no option but to match the performance of these new plants being opened up down the road. An enormous learning process is underway in the US industry as management and labour struggle to reorganise their operations along Japanese lines. As the Japanese move swiftly to open local design operations in the US, the US manufacturers are also reviewing the way in which their design process is organised. The Europeans, with so far only a limited exposure to local Japanese plants, are some years behind the Americans in this learning process.

The outcome of these developments is that the productivity gap between the western and Japanese producers will probably be closed during the 1990s. In the meantime, the Japanese will have established not only a significant market share in the US and Europe, but will also have built a strong design and manufacturing presence in both regions. New best practice plants will have forced the closure of the least efficient plants in the West and the level of concentration will fall. This has already happened in the US, where the Japanese have built over 2 million units of capacity and the Herfindal index of concentration has already risen from 3.1 in 1967 to 5.0 in 1987.[3]

As we shall see below, the Japanese, observing this process, are looking towards technology as their next competitive weapon. They are adding elements of flexible automation and are investing heavily in most areas of product technology, some of which are already showing up in the marketplace. Although the full systemic nature of the Ono/Toyota system is now apparent, the potential of this system to deliver a vast array of different products produced in limited volumes has yet to be fully appreciated.

On reflection, the productivity dilemma outlined by Abernathy turned out to be as much the result of a particular philosophy and organisational model as the constraints of the process technologies used. One wonders whether a greater degree of rivalry between a greater number of producers would have stimulated rather than eliminated the incentives to develop new product technologies in the US in the postwar period, and changed the orientation away from scale associated with ever more dedicated equipment?

4 The internationalisation of the industry

In a sense this industry has been international ever since its earliest days, when Ford and later GM established production operations across the world. However, because of political reasons and, in the case of Europe, differences in the size of cars demanded, these foreign operations were never truly integrated with the parent company. In Europe the US manufacturers established what became fully self-standing companies designing and building their own cars.

The projects to co-design world cars in the US and Europe in the late 1970s were the first major attempts to integrate operations on the two continents. They failed because of the 'not invented here' syndrome and different engineering traditions that clashed when two previously quite separate divisions tried to work together. Both the Escort and the Cavalier were substantially redesigned on both sides of the Atlantic and ultimately shared almost no common parts. Subsequent models did not follow this example, despite the fact that US consumers were buying cars of an increasingly similar size to the Europeans. Ford has recently tried to revive the idea with its centres of excellence concept, whereby Europe would design one size of car, Detroit another and Mazda in Japan another, each for worldwide production and sale.

Although the opening up of European markets began twenty years ago, Europe is still characterised by a series of national producers, each dominating their domestic market. While the few remaining internal barriers to trade should be removed by 1992, it will take considerably longer for the national producers in Europe to become truly European, in the way Ford of Europe has. In the face of Japanese competition, the leading European producers have reversed their attempts to follow the US producers in globalising their operations, Renault and Volkswagen having ceased manufacturing in the US and Fiat having withdrawn from the market.

The Japanese established a significant presence in all world markets during the 1970s before running into all kinds of import restrictions in the early 1980s. They then began an ambitious investment programme to build well over two million units of production capacity in North America, and to follow this by similar moves in Europe. The initial reaction of the local producers was to accuse the Japanese of keeping high value production and design in Japan while only assembling abroad to surmount these restrictions. However, the Japanese have perceived that demand in each of the main regional markets is subtly but significantly different, reflecting different patterns of urbanisation, road conditions and tastes. In the last few years companies like Honda, Toyota, Nissan and Mazda have begun to establish sizeable design facilities, both in North America and Europe and possibly later in South East Asia and Latin America.

Although the Japanese will obviously be trying to retain their export volumes for as long as possible, during the next decade many of these exports will be replaced by locally manufactured vehicles and the trade flow will become two way. Already Honda, Toyota and Mazda have begun exporting from the US back to Japan and will shortly do so also to Europe. While the one way flow of car exports from Japan dominated intra-area car trade in the 1970s and 1980s, exchange rate changes and local manufacturing will transform the pattern of auto trade in the 1990s.

The completion of the European market in 1992 and the moves to create an integrated North American market, including the US, Canada and Mexico, may be followed by the greater integration of the growing industry in South East Asia and possibly in Latin America. Krafcik's research into productivity and the transferability of new Japanese best production systems indicates that the significant competitive advantages opened up by the Japanese, that resulted in this large export flow from Japan, will be closed by the mid 1990s (Krafcik, 1988). The American producers, followed by the Europeans, have begun to make significant progress already in matching the productivity of local Japanese plants in their own facilities. It has also become quite clear that huge one way trade flows in automobiles are economically unsustainable in the medium term and are ultimately corrected by exchange rate adjustments.

Womack has argued that the world of the 1990s is likely to be characterised by a series of large integrated regional markets more or less in competitive equilibrium with each other (Womack, 1988). The bulk of auto demand will be satisfied by local production in each region. Trade between regions will be based on the differences in types of cars produced in each region, with each exchanging marginal volumes of those vehicles to each other to fill particular market niches in the recipient market. In other words auto trade will come to more closely resemble the classic pattern of intra-industry trade.

What then about the role of the leading newly industrialised countries (NICs) like South Korea and Mexico, who have had some success in recent years? Does not the product cycle theory predict that they will ultimately become major car exporters to the West in the way the Japanese did? (Vernon, 1966). The South Koreans were fortunate in that their success in the US market came just as the Japanese producers were quota constrained and as they vacated the bottom of the US market to seek a higher value added per vehicle sold. Faced with an inability to build small cars at home to compete with Japanese imports, the US manufacturers sought their own low cost sites and began to import cars and trucks from South Korea, Taiwan, Mexico, Brazil and later Thailand.

The very significant jump in productivity achieved by the Japanese and now emulated by the Americans and Europeans has blunted the labour costs advantage of the NICs. Also the much higher levels of component and build quality established by the Japanese present considerable problems for such countries with as yet inadequately developed local component industries. In the 1990s the expansion of the industry in the NICs will undoubtedly take place, but driven by the large anticipated growth in local demand and not so much based on export led strategies to the West. Krafcik has shown that it is quite possible to transfer Japanese best practice to the NICs and indeed, for them to compete in world markets, it will be imperative to do so (Krafcik, 1988). However, in so doing, the labour content of a finished vehicle is significantly reduced, eroding the low labour cost advantage still further.

In this emerging world of regions, some of which have great growth potential, auto companies without a presence in each of these regions may be at a disadvantage. They will be constrained in their growth prospects, will not be able to cope with cyclical demand fluctuations by exporting to other regions and will be vulnerable to exchange rate changes in a way that a company cross-trading between each region will not. The major challenge for those companies that do have multi-regional operations will be how best to combine and exploit the particular engineering and market characteristics of each region by transferring the knowledge, technology and people from one region to another. To do so requires not only managers with multi-regional experience, but engineers moving from one country to another. A corporate form that avoids the dominance of either Detroit, Tokyo, Nagoya, Turin or Wolfsburg with the attendant 'not invented here' mentality, will be required in the 1990s.

5 Investment in technology

Having considered the nature and direction of technological change in the auto industry we now consider indicators of the rate of technological change and the relative strengths and weaknesses of the leading participants. Expenditure on R&D in the motor industry has increased rapidly during the last decade, by 78 per cent in real terms between 1973 and 1985, during which time global vehicle output in unit terms rose by 9 per cent (Jones, 1988). Figure 2.1 shows that it is the Japanese who have increased their R&D spending fastest, to the extent that they are now spending more on R&D

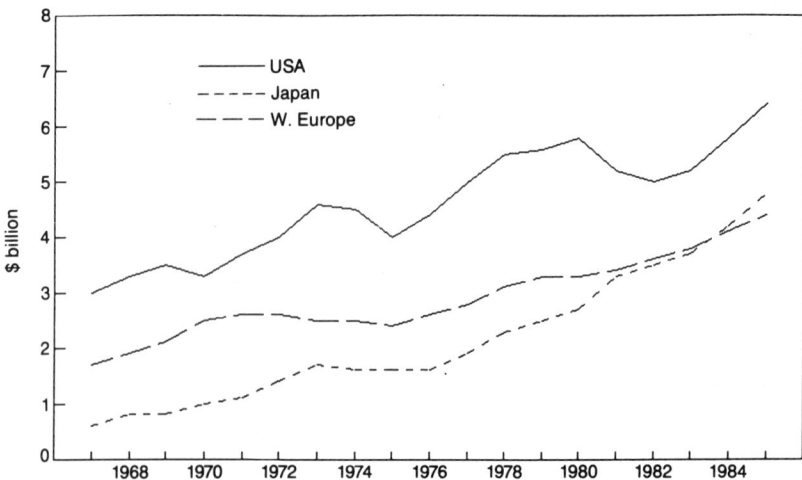

Source: OECD and National Statistics

Fig. 2.1 Motor vehicle R&D expenditure (at 1986 prices and exchange rates)

than the whole of Western Europe. It is also likely that on current trends they will overtake the US in the next cyclical downturn at the end of the 1980s. At first glance it seems puzzling that the Europeans, who have for years dominated world markets for the most technologically sophisticated cars, appear to spend less than the Americans on R&D. However, looking more closely, the German motor industry spent about $540 on R&D per car in 1985, compared with $450 in the US, $370 in Japan and about $300 in the rest of Europe. Even this probably overstates the American position as the definition of what precisely constitutes R&D in this industry is interpreted more liberally in the US than elsewhere.

In North America and Japan motor vehicle R&D expenditure is dominated by the largest companies, GM, Ford, Toyota and Nissan. In Europe the picture is more fragmented, the largest companies Volkswagen and Daimler-Benz only spend as much on R&D as the third ranking Japanese firm, Mazda. However, the combined R&D resources of Daimler Benz, VW and Bosch equal those of the Toyota group. The most striking performer of all is Honda, which spends over $700 per car, even after adjusting for its motorcycle output. This reflects Honda's strategy of relying on technology, multiple product lines and a move up market in the next few years.

Another partial indicator of technological activity is patenting which, despite obvious qualifications (Pavitt, 1988) reveals some significant trends. Figure 2.2 shows that the leading Japanese firms are now taking out more patents than the US firms in their home market. It would appear that there is significantly more appropriable technology in each car produced by Toyota, Nissan and Honda than by any of their competitors, and that the US firms are particularly poor at translating R&D into finished products.

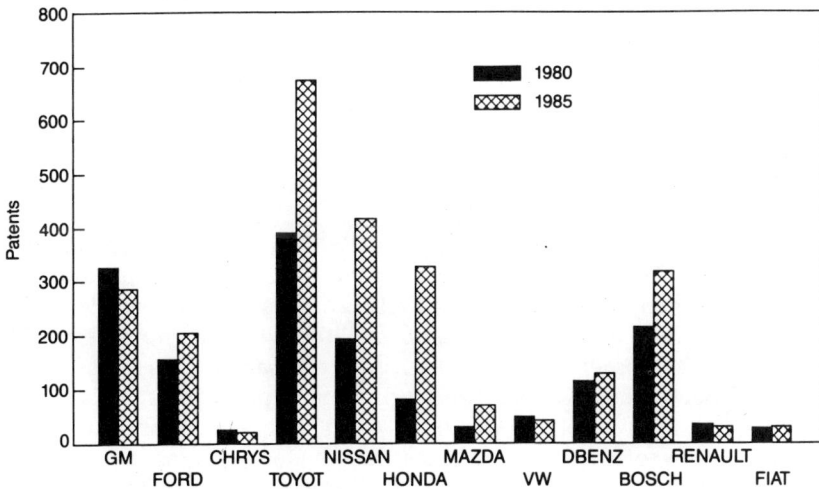

Source: SPRU OTAF Patent Database

Fig 2.2 Corporate patenting in the USA

As described earlier, a significant part of the growth of Japanese patenting is in engine technologies, see Figure 2.3. However, although the performance of the internal combustion and diesel engines has been stretched, the fundamentals of engine technology have not changed in recent years. A good deal of this upswing in patenting is associated with the addition of pollution control devices, electronic engine management systems and other incremental improvements. A similar picture emerges also with other technologies. This confirms the incremental nature of technological development in this industry, that builds on the cumulative experience of the firm and the constant review of the store of technological alternatives. Through this burst of technological activity the Japanese have brought themselves to the technological frontier in many key areas of automotive technology. The motor industry is one of the few industries in which the Japanese now run a surplus in their technological balance of payments. The ability of the Japanese to bring incremental improvements to the market quickly and thereby enhance the image of their products may be of greater competitive significance than the introduction of new technologies, such as four wheel steering, which can quickly be copied by others. The Japanese have also increased their patenting in process technologies, which are largely developed in-house in contrast to the US tradition of relying on independent equipment suppliers.

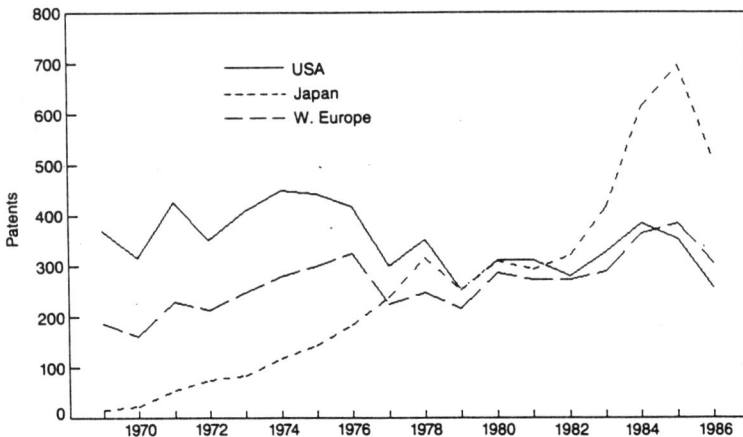

Source: SPRU OTAF Patent Database

Fig 2.3 Engine Patenting (Corporate patents only in the USA)

Graves has shown that the apparent inability of the US industry to translate high R&D spending into either patents or leading edge products is due to differences in the way in which R&D is organised (Graves, 1988). In the US R&D is conducted in large separate facilities which are not integrated with product development or manufacturing. In Japan R&D is team-based rather than functionally organised, and forms an integral part of the product development system, involving engineers from all the important functions in the firm. Many of the characteristics that make the Japanese product development system so efficient can also be found in their R&D system.

The other interesting factor that emerges from Figure 2.2 is the importance of Bosch as the technological powerhouse of the European motor industry. A more detailed analysis of patenting in the US by component suppliers indicates that they play a very important part in automotive technology. In both Germany and Japan component suppliers account for twice as many patents as the assemblers. Automotive technology is probably in the hands of 300 firms worldwide, with the top 30 firms (assemblers and component suppliers) accounting for 60 per cent of auto patents and the top 100 firms for 90 per cent.

6 Technology strategies

To a degree all firms have sought in the recent past to exploit technology as part of their corporate strategies, though more in terms of process technology than product technology. European and American firms in particular have been preoccupied with economies of scale, product rationalisation and globalisation. Process technologies were thought of as the next step in cost reduction, allowing a steady substitution of computer aided design and computer integrated manufacturing for human effort. The flexibility inherent in process equipment in this decade was, however, not fully exploited, being used more to balance production of different models with changes in demand. The impressive cost reductions sought have not in the main materialised. The Japanese, on the other hand, have shown that to fully exploit this flexibility entails different priorities, including a prior, bottom up reorganisation of the production process, incremental in-house development of process equipment and a product strategy based on model proliferation and shorter production volume per model. It is too early to say whether there will be a convergence between the western and Japanese approaches to flexibility in the 1990s or which will prove to be more productive.

On the product side the explicit use of technology in corporate strategy has been confined to either the luxury and exotic end of the market or to new entrants seeking to differentiate their products. The technological rivalry between Daimler-Benz and BMW has been particularly dynamic, and has set the standard for car design throughout Europe. Porsche has relied heavily on technology to preserve its lead in sports car design against Ferrari, Jaguar and others. Audi explicitly used four wheel drive to try to move up into the executive car market alongside BMW and Daimler-Benz. Interestingly, Audi has not completely succeeded in this and now its lead in four wheel drive has gone, it is apparent that technology alone is not enough to sustain such a strategy. The three smaller Japanese producers present another interesting case. Each has in different ways sought to establish its own position against Toyota and Nissan using technology. We have referred to Mazda's financial problems produced by its involvement with the Wankel engine. Mitsubishi has loaded its cars with technology but has failed to translate this into a strong image in the market place. The only company really successful in doing so is the latest entrant into the car business in Japan, Honda. Honda has has skilfully combined technology and design to create a very strong image that has to a degree set the trend even for Toyota. Indeed it is doubtful whether Toyota itself would have been so dynamic without the competitive rivalry from Honda. The same is also true for overseas investment, where Honda led the way in locating operations abroad.

In the history of this industry the largest firms, Ford, Toyota and General Motors, became so by developing new organisational innovations, thus confirming the importance of organisation skills in this industry. Small firms, however, seem more ready to introduce technological innovations. However, unfortunately for them, bigger firms appear to have the resources and ability to catch up again. They may be caught flat footed but under pressure the sheer scale of the technological resources available to the largest firms enables them to match the technological advances of others. As we have seen with four wheel steering the lead time in the market for any particular technology is short. Apart from scale, the larger firms, such as General Motors, have sought to compensate for internal rigidities by contracting out design and engineering, by buying high tech firms such as Lotus and by relying more on suppliers to innovate. However, in the longer term, the decision which technologies ought to be developed in house and out of house may change yet again. General Motors and others have also tried to diversify out of automobiles through the acquisition of aerospace and electronics companies, such as Hughes and EDS. The logic that a broader technological base is stronger in the long run and that technologies will thereby be transferred back to automobiles has yet to be proven.

There seems little doubt that technological change will become a more important factor in competitiveness in the 1990s, particularly if there is a major switch from steel to plastics. Automobile producers will have to reorganise their R&D operations, integrating them with design and production and with the R&D activities of their key suppliers. They will also have to reach beyond the traditional boundaries of the industry in recruiting engineers and managers in a conscious effort to bring new skills and technologies into the organisation. New working relationships will be required with electronics and new materials firms, both of which have quite different expertise to that required in the car business. Perhaps most important of all, the management culture of this industry will have to be prepared for more fundamental and rapid changes than at any time in the last 50 years.

Notes

1 This chapter reports on research being carried out at SPRU as part of the International Motor Vehicle Programme, of which the author is the European Research Director, and of the Research Programme of the Economic and Social Research Council's Designated Research Centre on Science, Technology and Energy Policy at SPRU. It draws on papers presented by IMVP researchers to the International Policy Forums in Niagara on the Lake, Canada in May 1987 and Cernobbio, Italy in June 1988, and to Research Affiliates meetings in Cambridge, USA in September/October 1986, 1987 and 1988. While I have been privileged to learn a great deal from my colleagues, particularly James Womack and Andrew Graves, they bear no responsibility for this interpretation.

2 Scherer in his input-output analysis of R&D in the US in 1974 shows that only 52 per cent of the R&D directed towards motor vehicles is carried out in the motor vehicle and engine sector, the lowest share of all the other main industries (Scherer, 1986).

3 We have used the same methodology as Abernathy, who showed that concentration in the USA has remained constant since 1923 (1978 pp29-30). See also Jones (1987).

Chapter 3

Characteristics of innovating Japanese firms - reverse product cycles

Yasunori Baba

1 Introduction

In an attempt to explain the growing competitiveness of Japanese firms, this chapter argues for the importance of technology in the strategies of the major Japanese corporations. Certainly in industries where their competitiveness has been acknowledged (automobiles and consumer electronics) Japanese firms have consistently attached importance to technical change. At the same time they have been expanding local production in developed countries. Put differently, the behavioural pattern of the Japanese firms deviates from the 'Product Cycle' tradition (Vernon, 1966) in that:

— in contrast to what Vernon (1966, 1979) argues as a natural course of events, Japanese firms seem not to have standardised their products in Vernon's sense, but have always concentrated on technical change; and
— again contrary to Vernon's prescription, the Japanese firms, having initially channelled their direct foreign investment to less developed countries, subsequently moved production to developed countries with high wages.

As we shall demonstrate throughout this chapter, these deviations are very closely associated with the record of the firms' overturning their US counterparts' competitiveness.

Bearing this in mind, we shall then ask the major questions: according to what economic rationale have Japanese firms made these unconventional decisions of managerial innovations, and what are the technological factors behind their strategies that have made their progressive internationalisation possible? In working towards the answers, our analysis will clarify some of the characteristics that have distinguished innovating Japanese firms' strategy from that of others. To explore and illustrate this question, Japanese colour television (CTV) firms have been chosen since the oligopolistic behaviour exhibited by these firms has been, and will continue to be, representative of a central stream of corporate behaviour in the dawning microelectronics era (Baba, 1985; Peck and Wilson, 1982; Sciberras, 1982). An attempt is made to answer the question of how the firms have managed to marry the two strategies of technical change (Section 2) and direct foreign investment (DFI) (Section 3). In doing so, the Japanese firms' corporate strategy is compared with that of their US counterparts, questioning the universality of the 'Product Cycle Approach' which attempts an explanation of the experience of some US firms (Section 4). In the final section, we shall briefly consider some lessons from our discussion.

2 The firms' technological strategy and the transformation of the industry

In this section, Japanese CTV firms' decision-making on corporate strategy will be historically reviewed focussing on the effects of technological strategy on the transformation of the industry. For this purpose, it is necessary to bring in the factor of 'strategic groups' (Porter, 1979; Caves and Porter, 1977) since, like other Japanese industries, the CTV industry has been composed of 'strategic groups' of firms, the groups differing from one another in their competitive managerial strategies. First, there was a group comprising Sony and Matsushita, led by their founding Presidents or their families. Having 'Schumpeterian' entrepreneurs as their top executives, the firms promoted managerial innovations in the CTV business by their top-down management. In other words, having held shared growth-oriented managerial principles, the firms invested heavily in their business resources. In concrete terms, aiming at exploiting benefits from oligopolistic competition with well-differentiated products, Sony, originally a technology-based venture business, put a disproportionate emphasis on R&D, especially in the field of product miniaturisation, and Matsushita, traditionally an imitator, developed the new marketing strategy of a systematised distribution network. These firms' preference for long-term profitability is again demonstrated by the fact that only Sony and Matsushita (including JVC as an affiliated firm) successfully continued the development of household-use videocassette recorders (VCR) where huge long-standing development costs prevented short-term profits.

Second, was the group comprising Hitachi, Toshiba and Mitsubishi. This was led by a technostructure providing 'group-centred decision-making'. Without the strong leadership of a 'Schumpeterian' entrepreneur, the firms generally lagged behind the first group in introducing managerial innovations. (In these cases, the firms' heavy investment in heavy electric and industrial electronics aggravated their stock turnover ratio, debt/equity ratio and so on, which slowed down their pace of investment in consumer electronics.) In addition, this group of firms adopted more or less a factory profit centre system, where strict accountancy control was imposed on the CTV division so as to secure short-term profits. Not surprisingly, such a system tended to prevent the firms from making swift and bold investments in the hope of uncertain long-term profits. Accordingly, these firms' decision-makers, adopting a rather risk-averting posture, tended to be 'defensive' innovators who 'do not wish to be the first in the world, but neither do they wish to be left behind' (Freeman, 1982, p176). (As is discussed in a following section, in recent years these firms have deliberately attempted to outgrow their previous strategy.)

Sanyo and Sharp made up a marginal group between the other two, in that while their will to introduce management innovations was weaker than in the first group, their entrepreneurs showed creative decision-making in some fields. Sanyo has been a pioneer in internationalisation strategy. Sharp, on the other hand, has been a remarkable figure in the introduction of microelectronics (eg electronic calculators). Thus there originally existed several strategic groups within the Japanese CTV industry, and their history of technical change and industrial transformation will now be described.

The Japanese CTV firms entered the field in the early 1960s and worked at improving their position throughout the decade, transcending their original status of imitators. Basically founded on imported technology, the firms on the one hand endeavoured to master the theoretical background to the imported technology, and on the other hand attempted to catch up with the original innovating firms by making carbon-copies of the original product, through straightforward imitation of the original production process. Up to this point, the firms could best be described as good imitators. A step forward from this stage was made by concentrating all their energies on remoulding inherited products and production process, regarding products as archetypes and factories as laboratories. Nelson and Winter (1982) describe the R&D strategy of innovating firms in the following way:

> A sensible R&D strategy might involve first testing the economic attributes of a mix somewhat richer than the prevailing one, and, if the results are favourable, trying out an even richer mix, and so on - in effect, hunting for the top of the hill. In general, a good strategy will stop the R&D project somewhere short of the top of the hill because the gains from varying the mix in one way or another are not expected to be worth the cost of performing another test (p256).

Japanese firms have naturally had opportunities to get further up the hill (if not to the top), opportunities which have derived in large measure from their own additional innovative activity (eg the 'Quality Control Movement').

Also important were the strategies of the offensive innovators, especially Sony, which brought about a change in the situation described above. The success of the transistor radio and the ensuing transistor boom were the first indications that the industry was tapping the new potential for incorporating microelectronics; the success of the Trinitron CTV again persuaded the other firms that even the Japanese could develop a new original product. Spurred by these factors and by the oligopolistic mode of competition, even the defensive innovators deviated from their usual stance, ie '… incorporating some technical advances which differentiate their products, but at a lower cost' (Freeman, 1982, p176) and headed into new technologies, shouldering higher costs and risks in the process. As a general result, the firms started incorporating microelectronics into their CTVs in the late 1960s. As for the development of microelectronics-related automation (process innovation), it was Matsushita, another offensive strategy firm, that cut a figure in the first half of the 1970s. This technical progress after a trial and error period resulted in remarkable cost reductions.

Each technical change has shifted cost curves downwards continually, along with external economies - (a phenomenon particularly seen in components industries). Active learning effects, combined with organisational innovations and various types of economies of scale, have resulted in no U-shaped long-run cost curve appearing among the Japanese CTV firms. Armed with the assumption of an ever-decreasing long-run average cost, we can explain some of the characteristic behaviour of the Japanese firms after the 1970s.

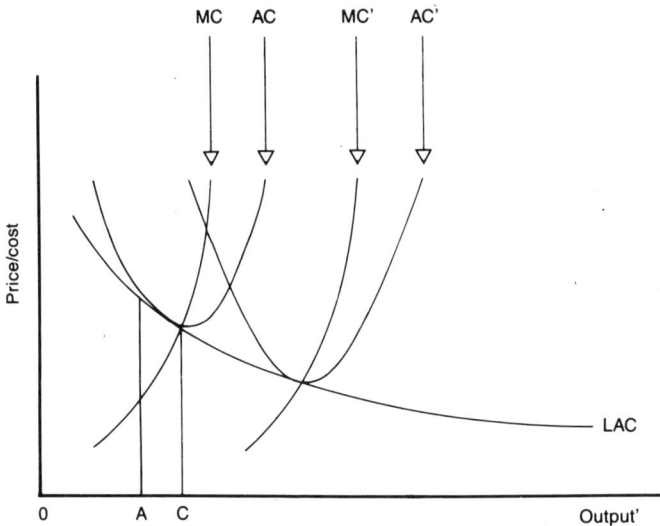

Fig 3.1. Assumed long-run cost curve for the firms

First, given the cost curve in Figure 3.1, the active investment pattern of the firms can be explained in the following way: when a firm decides to produce a certain quantity of output (eg A), it will be more profitable for it to set its fixed input (investment) so as to minimise its short-run average cost at a level of output slightly larger than A (eg C). Based on calculations like this, the firms tended to make larger investments to meet the demand they had acquired. Next, we should point to the tendency for this opting for excess capacity to imply by its very nature a situation where firms operate in the downward-sloping part of the short-run average cost curve (eg left of the point C). Given that, we must also take into account one special feature of the Japanese CTV market, ie the demand saturation which first appeared in the first half of the 1970s: sluggish demand had a definite effect on the firms' operation in the diminishing part of the short-run average cost curve (eg left of point A) and a resulting rise in production costs. It was to escape from this situation that the firms placed top priority on the attainment of higher operation rates. This realised uncalculated increases in production figures, as a corollary to the firms' efforts at cost reduction. It is also considered that the firms resorted to heightened price competition in the domestic market and an explosion of exports (eg the exports to the US in the mid-1970s) so as to find outlets for their increased production.

Alongside the firms' cost behaviour, we will now summarise another aspect of their technological strategy, ie the stimulation of product development and innovation. Guided mainly by the product differentiation policy previously adopted by the offensive strategy Sony and Matsushita, the firms began to take a greater interest in product differentiation. Particularly in the early 1970s, with the full-scale introduction of microelectronics, the firms carried out a host of product differentiations and developments in parallel with improving product quality. In doing so, they first constructed product line-ups and then assured new profit margins by upgrading the line-ups (in terms of their price ranges) by adding new-version CTVs. Also, in recent years, while the traditionally offensive strategy firms have still been in the forefront of the movement (eg in the cases of VCRs and digital CTVs), the others have moved towards the 'offensive' innovation strategy (Freeman, 1982) and towards branching out into product innovation.

Summing up the above discussions; the direct introduction of microelectronics has brought about remarkable cost reductions and, simultaneously, excursions into product development have fully transformed the industry in the process. As we have shown, the impetus for this transformation, ie active investment for long-term profits, was initially supplied by the 'offensive' firms. The other firms have gradually borrowed their behavioural patterns, so that there were few differences among the firms as to their business resources, and a 'watch and learn' effect (Dosi, 1984) must have worked within the industry, teaching the firms which way would lead them to business success.

From this stylised process can be extracted the formula that resultant product developments (innovations) and process innovations (together with organisational innovations) have brought about a coupling of continuing cost reductions with upgrades in product line-ups, and hence have contributed to profits. Applying this formula to the present CTV firms, it has emerged that the behaviour patterns of the 'offensive' and 'defensive' firms have now converged. Clearly this results from such economic reasonings as: first, that under the assumptions of a diminishing average cost, even the results of 'growth maximisation' and of short-term 'profit maximisation' become minimal since growth in output, in this case, serves to increase profits to the extent that the set price remains above the average cost-cum-required minimum profit; and, second, a risk-taking posture in a stabilised technological regime tends to be combined with outbreaks of product development or innovations where generation of new profit margins or innovator's profits are very confidently expected. As a corollary of all this, it is believed among the business fraternity that only a risk-taking posture investing in both product and process innovations will enable the firms to hold on to technological leadership, which alone will guarantee them profits in the long run.

The causal relationship between the CTV firms' technological strategy and the transformation of the industry has now been summarised. We will now proceed to another problem: how their performance in internationalisation can be explained in the light of their overall managerial principles. Let us start by referring briefly to the case of their US counterparts, which will enable us to consider our main subject in comparative terms.

3 The explanation of the firms' internationalisation strategy

US firms had established CTV as a marketable product by the late 1960s, and then, fully convinced of their technological superiority over international competitors, the firms set about benefiting from their advances. According to Baranson (1981) the firms chose to squeeze the maximum profit out of their existing product lines, together with 'concentrating their production efforts on high mark-up items, such as the larger TV consoles ...', and narrowed their attention towards the maintenance or improvement of existing product lines. On the other side of the equation, they cut R&D expenditure 'in particular, on the research necessary to develop new-product generations and to retain competitive production methods in the high-wage US economy'. Furthermore, faced with falls in profits stemming from competitive price practices, '[the firms] have uniformly reduced their R&D expenditure as one of the first steps towards cost reduction'. Accordingly, while the Japanese firms' average annual R&D amounted to 4.25 per cent of sales, the US firms spent approximately 2.6 per cent of sales on R&D (from 1975 to 1982) (Baranson, 1981, pp113-15).

What, then, emerges from all this? There seems to have been a standardisation process dominant in the US CTV industry: the firms' preference for increased productivity within existing product and production lines and the acquisition of short-term profits in consequence, accelerated by the firms' strategic neglect of R&D, seems to have shaped the process.

On the other side of the coin (turning to another side of the firms' oligopolistic behaviour, direct foreign investments), the US CTV firms, regarding CTV as a maturing product, shifted the labour-intensive production process, ie chassis production, to the countries of the South. The firms diverted their state-of-the-art technology to offshore plants, exploited the low labour costs in the South and then saved investments in the US through their dependence on the South for the key parts, such as the chassis. Thanks to this strategy, Ergas reports, the firms have ostensibly succeeded in improving their productivity in terms of paper profits, with levelling-off shipments and declining employment (Ergas, 1983). At the same time they have continually neglected innovations within the CTV industry by opting for legal action as their main counterattacking measure against their competitors, the Japanese. All in all, the dilemma between productivity and innovation which Abernathy (1978) initially observed in the US automobile industry, has been given much more drastic expression in the CTV industry due to its active internationalisation strategy. US firms have seen their main strategy as one of reaping short-term profits from their

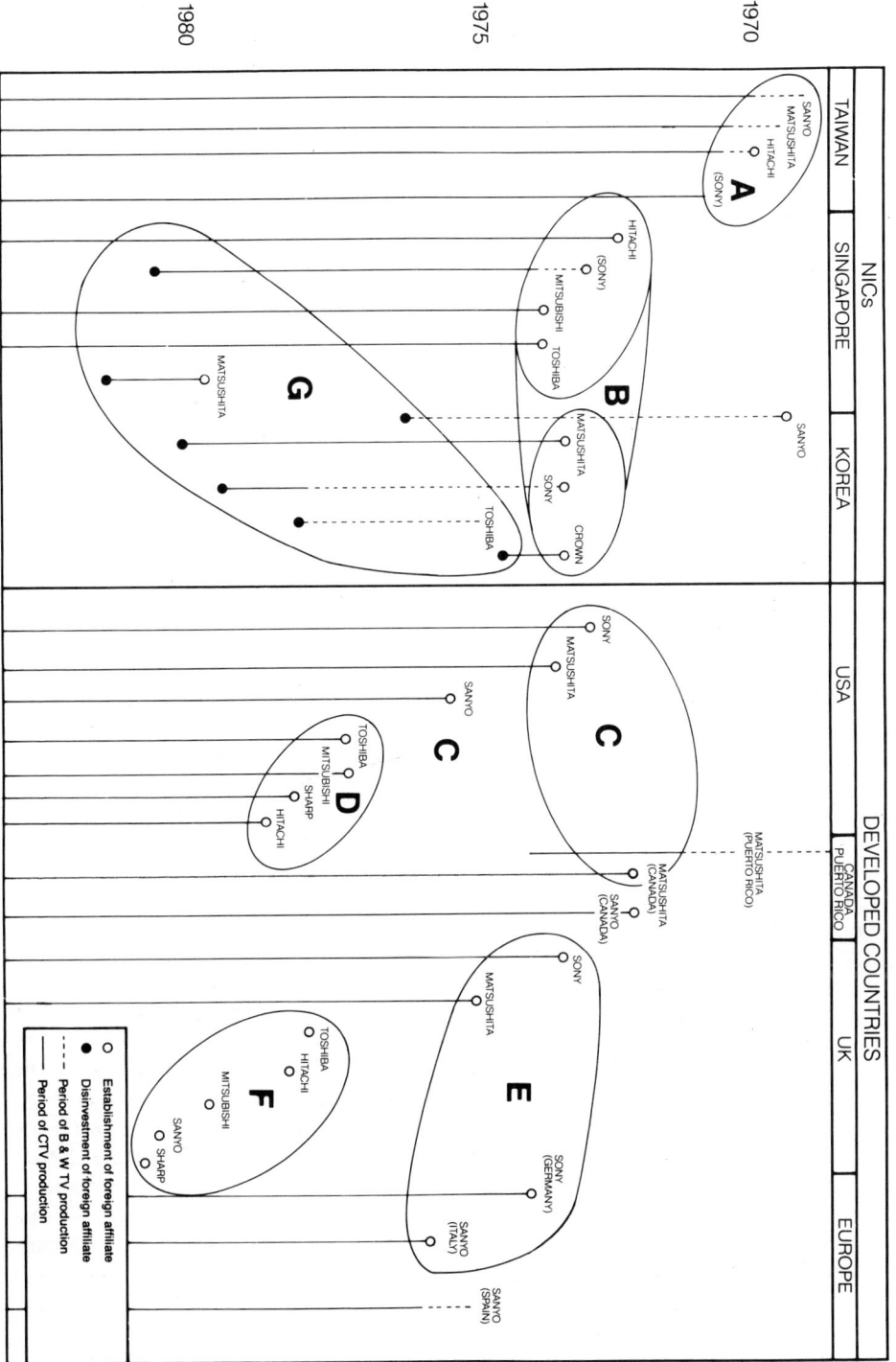

Fig 3.2 Chronological and geographical distribution of direct foreign investment by Japanese firms

direct foreign investments (DFIs), rather than investing in the upgrading of product and production technology aimed at long-term profits. How, then, can we explain the Japanese case as compared with the American?

To begin with, let us examine DFIs into the newly industrialised countries (NICs) (corresponding to DFIs type A and B in Fig 3.2). The settlement of these production bases as export bases to the US market was primarily the product of the Japanese firms' oligopolistic reaction to US firms' advances into those locations. Regarding DFIs of this kind, it should be stressed that the firms' decision-making did not deviate from orthodoxy (ie the traditional decision-making pattern of DFIs by US and European firms) since the Japanese firms too, would have benefited from lower wage rates at the production locations. Not surprisingly, the 'defensive' firms particularly (who tended to put priority on guaranteeing short-term profits) concentrated on this line of DFIs, as did the US firms.

In contrast, DFIs in developed countries as early as the first half of the 1970s (corresponding to DFIs type C and E) have to be strictly distinguished from the last type since it is hard to justify these business activities from the 'orthodox' point of view. The firms in this case shifted their production bases not to locations with lower wage rates, but to ones with a higher rate where a traditional cost-performance analysis would have prohibited this kind of DFI. Obviously, there is a definite managerial principle (and risk posture) to explain this particular pattern of internationalisation; as Dosi puts it, firms 'thinking ahead' and 'growth-maximisers' in particular might resort to DFIs, 'even if the present rate of profit (and for that matter, the *present* total profits) are lower with foreign manufacturing facilities than without them' (Dosi, 1984, p237), and, not surprisingly, it was the so-called 'offensive' firms, Sony and Matsushita, that actually undertook these DFIs. Our conjecture is again supported by the facts, viz: after their advance into the US, Sony stressed the long-term perspective in which this had to be justified; and Matsushita admitted the price it had had to pay for its progress. As shown in Fig 3.2, while Matsushita followed Sony's pioneering DFIs, *no bandwagon effect* (in the sense used by Knickerbocker, 1983) occurred among the other firms.

When we consider the other firms' internationalisation in the second half of the 1970s (corresponding to types D, F and G), we should first take account of the transformation of the CTV industry. As has been discussed before, the industry transformed itself by the mid-1970s into a structure where excess capacity and hence high pressure to ensure product outlets became absolutely inevitable. Under this structure, the frantic exports of the mid-1970s (especially to the US) were simply a natural consequence, and the sharp rise in export totals also triggered 'new protectionism' in the industry in due course. It was exactly this resultant market closure (eg the imposition of the Orderly Marketing Agreement (OMA)) that clinched the firms' final decision on DFIs. In other words, we can say first that the 'defensive' firms had brought their guiding managerial principle into full play in the field of internationalisation, as compared with what happened in technical change, and second the CTV firms' decision-making on technical change determined the decision-making pattern on internationalisation endogenously in the light of the progressing transformation. Because of the similarity of managerial principle among the firms, in this case *a bandwagon effect clearly occurred*. Concerning type G (ie disinvestments from Korea), decisions were also directly dictated by the transformation of the industry and its outcome, ie the firms' direct advance into developed countries.

In the second half of the 1970s, when market closure and local production in developed countries became a business norm in industry, the CTV firms seem to have laid the ground for the next step in their internationalisation. Partly supported by the fact that the new forms of protectionism in the US, ie voluntary export restraints (VERs) rather than tariffs, increased the profits of the Japanese firms and hence provided them with the financial resources to sustain R&D, the firms established offensive technological strategies, as is clearly evident today. As for the firms' response to export restrictions, in addition to the evidence that 'Japanese (electronics) firms responded to the OMA by pushing forward into a higher-technology and higher-value product line — the video recorder' (Yoffie, 1983, p219), we can point to the fact that the Japanese CTV firms (divisions) have taken the same line with their products, on the basis of the results of the process above. Starting with upgrades to larger CTVs (eg 26 inch), they are in the forefront of the move to introduce worldwide such products as new-version CTVs (eg pocketable CTVs, audio-multiplex CTVs, digital CTVs, etc). With their experience of this series of managerial advances, the Japanese CTV firms have evolved a dynamic combination of two strategies, ie technical change and the utilisation of international production location, and crystallised this into a corporate strategy for the microelectronics era. Evidently, under the current trend towards market closure, the firms, first of all, have been eager to diversify their markets by resorting to worldwide DFIs, which have been used over a wide range of their technical ability.

4 Reverse 'Product Cycles'

The 'Product Cycle Approach' proposes that, along the life of a product, the importance of technology, marketing and production costs as sources of competitiveness (or quasi-rent) progressively changes. Oligopolistic firms are keen on appropriating these sources throughout the cycle; as long as technological quasi-rent remains at a product, the firms stick to their oligopolistic positions, and when they lose technological advantage, they attempt to compensate for the loss by means of their abundant business resources. In addition to marketing efforts, the utilisation of untapped competitive resources, that is, differing factor endowments among countries, is thought to be the firms' next quest. In the following part of this section, the point at issue with this approach will briefly be exposed in the light of the newly-emerged Japanese corporate strategies.

Although Vernon himself admits the necessity for modifying his original approach (Vernon, 1979), one shortcoming seems to stem chiefly from the fact that it is originally derived from work in the field of international commerce, and hence from a business management viewpoint. As Abernathy et al (1983) point out, the model argues too little about 'the relation between industry maturity, on the one hand, and technology, markets, and competition, on the other' (1983, p17). Whereas marketing, too, exerts its influence on industry maturity in the prolongation of maturity or recuperation from maturity, we cannot ignore this interrelationship between industrial maturity and technology. As for Vernon's approach, it is not technology but market forces that play the role of prime mover in his scenario of the changing nature of a product. At the invention stage, provided that entrepreneurs are broadly equal in 'their access to scientific knowledge and their capacity to comprehend scientific principles' (Vernon, 1966, p191), their branching out into new products depends on their 'consciousness of and responsiveness to [the entrepreneurial] opportunity [in a market]' which, in turn, rely on 'ease of communication...[and] geographical proximity [to the market]' (Vernon, 1966, p192). In terms of this demand-pull view of technical change, the reactiveness of technology can only be passive and mechanical *vis-à-vis* market conditions. And, when a product enters the mature stage, market forces dictate and shape its standardisation. It can be said that this view permeates every stage of Vernon's approach.

In contrast to the demand-pull view above, there exists a school of thought which attaches great importance to the role of technology (Freeman, 1982; Pavitt and Soete, 1980). On technical change, it adopts an approach which allows us to observe the mature stage from a different angle: in terms of Freeman's observations, for instance, in the phase of the product cycle where 'technical factors will become less important, and other factors — such as material costs — will matter much more', there will certainly be opportunities for producers to 'introduce new and improved qualities in the old [products] and in this way open up new markets and retain old ones', and for the old producers 'to some extent to offset other cost disadvantages by continuing technical progress in processing and sometimes also by economies of scale' (Freeman, Young and Fuller, 1963, p44).

Once we acknowledge this potential in technology, which is exploitable even in the 'mature' stage of the product cycle, we cannot but question the universality of the 'Product Cycle Approach'. While it gives an explanation of the experience of some US firms which actually opted for standardisation in a particular period of time (from the mid-1950s to the mid-1970s), can it be applicable to those firms continuing technical change? Abernathy et al (1983) clearly deny this universality and suggest the alternative theoretical paths that the firms can opt for by way of presenting the possibility that 'de-maturity' could be brought about. And, while industrial 'de-maturity' still remains only as a possibility in the US, we know that Japanese firms have actually brought about industrial de-maturity (in the case of the CTV industry, we can recognise both the significant shift in market demands for new version CTVs and microelectronics-related technologies as new technologies). Obviously, the existence of the process contradicts the 'Product Cycle Approach' both theoretically and empirically.

In addition to the above, we have to question another assumption which stemmed from the fact that the approach was developed in an era of near-full employment, when the market was reasonably open in every production location. Under this open-market assumption, the US firms through their economic calculations could certainly afford to establish production bases. However, in tandem with turnovers of international competitiveness, the threat to employment posed by imports was becoming evident in the innovating economies, and hence a trend towards market closure has become the norm in these economies. As a result, in order to enter the markets of innovating economies, the Japanese firms are often obliged to run counter to the normal cycle of shifting production locations, by way of taking the wage rate as only one of many determinants in decision-making on DFIs. In contrast to the old paradigm, the firms make sure of having an alternative option, ie the full utilisation of technical change.

5 Conclusions

As has been suggested, the corporate strategy which provides a continuous flow of technical change and progressive internationalisation can be said to be one of the ideal models in the age of microelectronics. When we consider that the strategy is likely to be opted for regardless of the managerial principle (and risk posture) of the firm in question the significance of the lesson learned from the Japanese CTV firms will be greater. (Its applicability to the automobile industry seems clear, and still others may follow.)

Of course, how to put a firm into a virtuous circle guaranteeing its long-term growth is the point for learning. In this case, what is most important is to reconsider traditional oligopolistic corporate strategy which aims to promote profit maximisation by holding that any one product will become a maturing product in a mechanical way in accordance with the rotation of the product cycle. As illustrated, the profit potential of a maturing product must be fully exploited by coupling two factors: ie the technical seeds for generating new-version products, and consumer need for those products. The quick-return, low-risk management mentality will inevitably be detrimental to the course of action described above. In consideration of Schumpeter's remark that: '... someone is an entrepreneur only when he actually carries out new combinations, and loses that character as soon as he has built up his business, when he settles down to running it as other people run their businesses' (1983, p78). The industrialist must become a 'Schumpeterian' entrepreneur again when a product has reached the maturing stage and remain so.

Finally, we shall touch on the new trend in Japanese business and attempt to reinforce the relevance of our conclusions drawn from recent experience. Turning away from the traditional line of causal relationship (ie considering internationalisation at a *given* stage of technical ability), the firms now set the direction of their technical change in the context of their internationalisation strategy. As far as CTV production goes, where local production systems have already been established in the market countries, the firms have shown the new tendency above in the following way: instead of merely switching to local production of the product which was previously exported there, the firms now undertake R&D in some recipient countries. For instance, Sony has a local research institute in New York and another in California, and yet another in the UK.[1] In the case of Matsushita, which purchased the CTV plants of Motorola, the R&D centre for large-sized TVs is located in the US, while that for smaller TVs is situated in Japan. In the CTV case, as Morita suggests:

> ... sophistication in its use is under way consequent upon the introduction of new broadcasting systems (eg audio multiplex broadcasting, teletex, etc) and Sony is presently developing various CTV receivers in response to this new trend. As there is always a possibility that the US, Europe and Japan may not come up with the same broadcasting system, a uniform R&D activity may not be sufficient to cope with the situation. If this be the case, each one of the three research institutes must undertake its share of R&D independently of the others. Of course, this does not in the least mean an exclusion of the benefit of cooperation between the institutes, and an integration of their technology for more advanced application, and such division and integration of work are also applicable to actual production.[2]

There are therefore new possibilities for promoting commercialisation of products and the setting of a market orientation geared to the local markets.

Widening our perspective over CTV production, we can illustrate how the Japanese electronics firm has now tried to benefit from the same coupling of strategies. Naturally enough, the fundamental tendency derived from CTV production (ie positive technical change and progressive internationalisation) is also observable in electronics firms. However, another aspect has to be added in this case: to the extent that the firms borrow technology from abroad (eg the case of CTV), their business endeavour is likely to result in a series of trade frictions, and the loss of domestic employment is often brought about by resulting shifts of their production bases overseas. In contrast, if the firms use original technology (eg the case of VCR), less trade friction is likely and the firms can afford to benefit from the continuation of exports. As may be inferred from the above, with a trend towards market closure, technical change has become indispensable from the viewpoint of the firms' internationalisation strategy, in that only upgrades in product lines enable them both to secure exports with, most of all, 'trading-up' (ie improving the quality of these exports) and also to make up for the loss of employment resulting from DFIs (eg had it not been for VCR, the firms would have run up against the problem of labour surplus). As T Yamashita , the previous President of Matsushita, remarks: 'Matsushita is going to develop new products one after another, initially using the Japanese market as a testing market for new products such as VCR'[3]. Technical change lays a foundation nowadays for the firms' internationalisation strategy. In parallel with the advance of 'Action 86', a plan designed to transform Matsushita from a consumer electronics firm to one concerned with the information society (dealing with robots, office and home automation), they decided in 1986 to launch into US local production, not even including VCR, a decision obviously rationalized by the sharp revaluation of the Yen.

Summing up all the above, it is evident that the coporate principle of combining two oligopolistic strategies in innovative ways so as to generate maximum profits has now pervaded all Japanese electronics firms; its further applicability to the automobile industry also seems clear, and still others may follow.

Notes

1 Comment by A. Morita, The Chairman of Sony. *Will*, Nov 1982, p29.
2 Ibid.
3 Comment by T. Yamashita of Matsushita. Yamachi Research Institute (ed), *Matsushita Denki no Kernkyu* (A Study on Matsushita Electrics) (Tokyo, Tokyo Keizai Shinposha, 1981), p9.

Chapter 4

Accumulation, diversification and organisation of technological activities in UK companies, 1945-83[1]

Keith Pavitt, Mike Robson, Joe Townsend

1 Introduction

In this chapter we analyse the nature and organisation of technological activities in UK firms, as a function of their size and their core business (ie their 'principal activity'). There are at least two reasons why we think this is a useful thing to do.

The first pertains to the characteristics of the innovating firm. We show considerable variation, amongst firms of different sizes and different principal activities, in the nature, the dynamics and the organisation of their technological activities. These variations need to be incorporated into analysis of both the theory of the innovating firm, and of the practice of mobilising technology to the purposes of corporate strategy. At one level, we shall be stating the obvious. It makes little sense to expect an innovative firm with fewer than 50 employees to have a technology strategy spanning a broad technological front, or to ask a firm principally making wool textile products to begin making personal computers. We nonetheless think it useful to map out, more systematically than has been done hitherto, the technological opportunities and constraints, and the organisational forms, typical of firms of different sizes and principal activities.

The second reason concerns national policies for science and technology. As Nelson and Winter (1982) amongst others have shown, what a firm does in an uncertain and ever-changing world cannot be reduced to an automatic and unique response to ambient market signals, but to some extent reflects its accumulated experience from the past, and its judgement about the future - in other words, its strategy. In large oligopolistic firms, these strategies are both more likely to have an existence of their own, and to have a significant effect on national patterns and trends in technological activities. Observers have for a long time accepted the national technological influence of (say) Philips in the Netherlands, or Volvo in Sweden. In a recent analysis of British company-based patenting in the USA, Pari Patel and one of us have shown that UK technology depends heavily on (among others) ICI in chemicals, GEC in electronics, and Rolls-Royce in aerospace (Patel and Pavitt, 1987). Table 4.1 shows that, precisely in chemicals, electronics and aerospace, technological activities are heavily concentrated in a few large firms: and even in sectors of mechanical engineering and instrumentation, where technological activities are much more dispersed, significant technological contributions are made by large and technically aware users of equipment (eg British Coal in coal-mining machinery).

Table 4.1. Sectoral patenting in the USA by the top five British institutions

% of US patenting by top five	Number of technological sectors				
	Mechanical	Electrical/Electronic	Chemical	Aerospace	Total
0-20	6	0	1	0	7
20-40	2	5	4	0	11
40-60	1	2	6	1	10
>60	0	1	2	1	4
Total	9	8	13	2	32

Source: Patel and Pavitt (1987)

We shall use a large database on UK innovations and innovating firms to help identify some of the critical parameters for technological and strategic decision-making in firms, to help explain and predict how technological opportunities develop and emerge, and to contribute to the development of a much-needed theory of technology-based entrepreneurship.

We begin in the next section by reviewing the contributions made by the various literatures, and by describing the essential characteristics of the data collected through the SPRU Innovation Survey. In Section 3, we contrast the technological threats and opportunities facing firms in different sectors. In Section 4, we examine in more detail the technological opportunities - or 'trajectories' - open to firms in different sectors, and the degree to which these are transformed into products and output. In Section 5, we explore how the characteristics of innovating firms vary with their size, and in Sections 6 and 7 we draw conclusions for analysis and policy.

2 The theoretical and empirical basis

Four analytical traditions have made major contributions to our understanding of the role of technology in firm behaviour: corporate strategy, industrial economics, business history, and innovation studies.

2.1 Corporate strategy

Perhaps the most influential of recent writings on the subject have been by Porter (1980, 1985b). His prescriptions turn out to be similar to those put forward in the 1960s by Ansoff and Stewart (1967): a firm's technology should serve its overall strategy in developing and exploiting firm-specific advantage. This requires choices about relative emphasis on cost or quality, on broad or narrow product-market focus, and on being a technological leader or a follower.

Perhaps reflecting the origins of Porter's analysis in mainstream industrial economics, its main strength is in the discussion of the sustainability and the exploitation of technological advantages already achieved in the past, rather than the cumulative processes through which technological advantages are created for the future, or the organisational forms through which such advantages are exploited. (A similar point has recently been made by Rosenbloom and Cusumano (1987) in their comparison of firms' strategies in the emergence of the videocassette recorder: '....the benefits that a firm can realize from alternative strategies for innovation — the consequences of choices about timing, positioning, and implementation — are shaped substantially by steps taken years earlier during the development of the technology. For an emerging technology, a firm's success...depends on its prior conduct as a technological pioneer.')

More specifically:

— Although Porter recognises that the range of technological threats and opportunities varies amongst sectors, he does not explore what the differences are. In Section 3, we shall describe and classify some of the key differences that emerge from our database.

— He gives little attention to the cumulative nature of firm-specific technological competence, which strongly constrains the range of technological paths that a firm can follow (*see* Chapter 8). In Section 4, we shall describe the characteristics of these paths and constraints, and the degree to which they are reflected in firms' production profiles.

— He does not analyse the organisational problems and requirements for implementation, ie for transforming firm-specific technological competence into competitive products, processes and services. Furthermore, most of his policy prescriptions about technology have been at the level of the business unit rather than of the firm as a whole. In his more recent writing (1985), he does stress the importance of a 'horizontal strategy' which exploits interrelationships amongst business units, and argues that technical change — especially in computing and communications — is increasing them. As we shall see, many technologies other than computing and communications did not fit tidily into discrete business units.

2.2 Industrial economics

The relationship between technology and firm behaviour has also been analysed within the tradition of industrial economics. Of particular relevance to this paper has been research to measure and explain the level and pattern of diversification, especially amongst large firms. Measures of diversification have been based on the proportion of output produced outside firms' principal activity. However, the theoretically postulated positive relationship between technological opportunity (measured in terms of R&D intensity) and diversification has not been confirmed in statistical analysis. The relationship generally turns out to be negative at the 2-digit level, or indeterminate at the 3-digit level (*see* Scherer, 1980, for a review of findings; *see also* Doi, 1985, for a recent confirmation for Japan). Furthermore, Hughes (1987) has recently shown for the UK a significantly negative relationship across industry between R&D intensity and technological diversification, measured as the proportion of R&D undertaken outside the firms' (mainly 2-digit) sector of principal activity.

These somewhat unsatisfactory results reflect both inadequate theoretical specification, and inadequate measurement. The theory is based purely on risk: since R&D are risky activities, it is argued, their results are more likely to find some application in large and diversified firms. When, however, one admits to technology that is firm-specific, cumulative and differentiated, the key question changes to the following: to what extent does greater, lesser or a different type of technological opportunity reflect itself in no diversification, narrow diversification (at the 3- or 4-digit level), or broad diversification (at the 2-digit level)? As we shall see in Section 4, there are very different patterns across sectors, including a major proportion of technologically related activities that go beyond the measure normally used by industrial economists (ie proximity in the 3- and 4-digit categories of the Standard Industrial Classification).

A number of studies have also explored the relationship between the 'proximity' or 'relatedness' of firms' diversification, and their performance in terms of growth or profitability (*see*, for example, Berry, 1971, and Rumelt, 1974, for the USA; Grant et al, 1986a and 1986b for the UK). We shall not undertake such an analysis in this paper. Instead, we shall concentrate on the directions and the degree to which firms in different 2-digit activities translate their accumulated technology into output.

2.3 Business history

Historical studies of the development of large firms have demonstrated the importance of technology as a source of opportunities for firms to diversify into new and related product markets (Chandler, 1962 and 1977; Rumelt, 1974; Bigadikke, 1979; Didrichsen, 1982). This is reflected in a variety of traditions of theorising about the large firm (Penrose, 1959; Ansoff, 1968; Nelson and Winter, 1982; Teece, 1982; Kay, 1982). Central to these traditions is firm-specific knowledge, that is often tacit (ie uncodified, and acquired and transmitted through experience and example), embodied in individuals and their organisation, and developed cumulatively over time. As a consequence, Cohen and Mowery (1984) have argued that R&D investment behaviour is a function of firm-specific variables such as internal resources (firm-specific human and material assets), cash flow, internal structure and corporate strategy.

An understanding of the nature, determinants and impact of firm-specific technological assets is a central objective of this chapter, as is another key characteristic emerging from empirical studies: namely, the considerable variance amongst firms in the nature and the munificence of the technology-based opportunities for growth and diversification that are open to them. Following the theoretical work of Rosenberg (1976), Nelson and Winter (1982) and Dosi (1982) on the concept of 'technological trajectories' (at the level of a country or of a technology, as well as a firm), increasing attention is now being devoted to their measurement. In section 4, we shall therefore compare the characteristics of our trajectories — measured according to the principal activities of innovating firms, and already outlined by one of us in an earlier paper (Pavitt, 1984) — with those recently described by Archibugi (1986), Kodama (1986a, 1986b), de Bresson (1986), and Jaffe (1989).

Given variance amongst sectors, studies of business history do not lend themselves easily to generalisation, but they offer important insights into the nature of technological accumulation within firms. For example, Didrichsen (1982) describes the differing patterns in such firms as Du Pont (based on chemical technology), International Harvester (based on mechanical engineering), and 3M (based on abrasives and adhesives). We shall try to systematise such patterns in Section 4. In addition, Bigadikke (1979) and Teubal (1982) have shown that successful diversification into related product markets involves extensive and lengthy entry costs associated with technological and market learning. These have implications for methods of evaluating programmes and projects associated with such diversification. Unfortunately, our data do not enable us to pursue them in empirical detail.

2.4 Innovation Studies

Another tradition of analysis has focussed on the management of innovation. It has been problem- rather than discipline-oriented, and has attempted to identify systematically the characteristics differentiating successful from unsuccessful implementation of innovation (see, for example, Rothwell et al, 1974; Rothwell, 1977; Freeman, 1982; for more recent results, see Cooper, 1983; Maidique and Zirger, 1984).

A number of robust empirical conclusions have been reached on the basis of this research. In particular, successful implementation depends on three factors: effective horizontal links, internally amongst R&D, production and marketing, and externally with customers and other sources of relevant scientific and technical competence; the characteristics of the so-called 'business innovator' responsible for the innovation's outcome, and whose effectiveness is positively related to the degree of authority, and to the range of experience in the various functions; and finally, flexibility and speed in decision-making.

Given these requirements, implementation is likely to be facilitated by decentralisation of decision-making down to the business innovator, and by relatively small innovating units that facilitate both horizontal communications and commitment (for a recent analysis of the economic implications, see Aoki, 1986). As Section 5 shows, there has in fact been a continuing reduction in divisionalised firms since 1945 in the size of the divisions implementing innovations.

It is perhaps for this reason that the focus of analytical attention is shifting from implementation to strategy. One current of analysis stresses 'technological discontinuities'. It derives in part from product cycle analysis, emphasising the role of new small firms in exploiting radical new technologies (Utterback and Abernathy, 1975). However, it now argues that new entrants can also be either large firms diversifying into related product markets, or user firms (Utterback and Kim, 1986). As we shall see in section 3, these are precisely the major sources of potential new entrants into the product groups with the most munificent technological opportunities.

The concept of 'technological discontinuity' also derives in part from analyses of organisational discontinuity associated with corporate crisis and executive succession. Tushman and Anderson (1987) make the distinction between competence-enhancing and competence-destroying innovations, and argue that technological discontinuities are associated with the latter, and result in the emergence and establishment of new firms. However, one of us has argued that competence-destroying innovations are now rare, given the systematic, varied and continuous accumulation of technological competence in large firms, typified by R&D laboratories (Pavitt, 1987).

The organisational challenge lies in the effective exploitation of synergies within large, divisionalised firms (Kay, 1982; Pavitt, 1986). Successful innovation depends heavily on the firm's prior familiarity with the technology and its market (Maidique and Zirger, 1984; Cooper, 1983). Successful entry into a relatively novel field not only requires appropriate methods of evaluation but also the ability to learn from mistakes (what Maidique and Zirger have called 'learning by failing', 1985), together with the ability to mobilise the required complementary assets (*see* Teece, 1986). This does not happen automatically in the large, divisionalised firm. As Kay (1982) has pointed out, complete divisionalisation is fully efficient only when functional activities (including technology) are fully decomposable: in other words, without cross-divisional synergies. We shall see in Section 5 that this is far from being the case. A large proportion of innovations continue to be made outside the principal activity of innovating divisions.

2.5 The SPRU Innovation Survey

As with all the above traditions of analysis, our focus will be the ability of firms to create and sustain new business opportunities based on accumulated, firm-specific technology, and our analysis will be guided by the important problems emerging from the above discussion. It will build on a unique database describing more comprehensively than has been done previously the characteristics of innovations and innovating firms in the UK. This has emerged from a survey of more than 4000 innovations, compiled at SPRU over a period of fifteen years and completed in 1984 (*see* Townsend et al, 1981; Robson and Townsend, 1984). The procedure was to write to experts in each sector of commerce and industry, asking them to identify significant technical innovations that had been successfully commercialised in the UK since 1945, and to name the firm responsible. Questionnaires were then sent to these innovating firms, requesting information on a range of variables, including: the employment (World and UK) of the innovating firm, and — where appropriate — the innovating unit, at the date of the innovation's commercialisation; and the firm's and the unit's principal product line, together with those of the innovation and its first user.

Nearly 400 experts were consulted in the survey. They were drawn from research and trade associations, government departments, academic institutions, trade and technical journals, individuals and consultants, as well as from firms. The distribution of the innovations over the time period turns out to be relatively even (*see* Table 4.2). The smaller numbers before 1960 probably reflect the difficulty of finding, in the 1970s, experts who had been active in the earliest period. The consequent variation in coverage over time is therefore likely to be uniform across sector.

The distribution of the sample of innovations according to the principal activities of the innovating firms is shown in column 1 of Table 4.3. Innovations made by government departments and quasi-public R&D laboratories have been excluded, reducing the sample by 240 innovations (ie 5.5 per cent of the total). Of the remainder, 91.7 per cent were made by firms principally in manufacturing, within which the sectoral distribution is closer to that of patenting activity ($r^2 = 0.69$, significant at the 99.9 per cent level), than to either industry-financed or total industrial R&D ($r^2 = 0.12$ and 0.10 respectively, non-significant). When compared to R&D activities, the shares of innovations and patenting in mechanical engineering and instruments are relatively high, and that of aerospace relatively low.

In spite of information on more than 4000 innovations, the SPRU Innovation Survey is still not sufficiently rich to enable the detailed tracking

Table 4.2. Distribution of identified innovations by years of first commercialisation

Years	1945-9	1950-4	1955-9	1960-4	1965-9	1970-4	1975-9	1980-3	1945-83
Number	226	359	514	684	720	656	823	396*	4378

* Equivalent to 660 over a five year period.

Source: SPRU Innovation Survey (1984)

Table 4.3. Technological opportunities and threats for firms in 19 sectors

Firms' Principal Activity	1968 SICH categories	1 Number of innovations	2 Percentage product innovations	3 Ratio of innovations purchased to those produced	4 Percentage of innovations made by firms from other 3-digits	5 Average size of innovating firm (employment)
Agriculture (AG)	001-003	12	16.7	9.2	46.7	7.7
Mining (MI)	101-104	126	47.6	1.7	15.4	230.0
Food (FO)	211-240	112	50.9	0.4	23.2	48.9
Chemicals (CH)	261-279	421	80.8	0.2	66.6	69.5
Metals (MT)	311-323	186	43.0	0.5	43.4	118.5
Mechanical Engineering (ME)	331-339, 341-349	1126	77.0	0.1	48.8	14.7
Instruments (IN)	351-354.2	332	80.2	0.2	55.0	23.7
Electrical-Electronic (EE)	361-369	774	60.2	0.1	71.6	90.7
Shipbuilding/Offshore (SH)	370	67	49.3	1.2	71.7	9.3
Vehicles (VE)	380-382, 384, 385	212	40.6	0.6	40.7	62.6
Aerospace (AE)	383	85	37.6	1.4	56.7	38.7
Textiles, Leather, Clothing (TE)	411-450	144	16.7	2.5	43.8	30.2
Materials (MA)	461-469	157	59.2	0.3	26.4	16.8
Paper (PA)	481-484	54	53.7	0.7	37.5	17.7
Printing (PR)	485-489	29	20.7	2.8	33.3	4.1
Rubber and Plastics (RP)	471-479, 491-499	96	63.5	0.3	64.8	45.5
Construction (CO)	500	39	46.2	4.2	65.1	8.4
Utilities (UT)	601-603, 701-709	82	41.5	2.4	8.3	108.1
Services (SE)	810-866, 871, 879-899	84	59.5	1.7	57.1	24.0
Average		217.8	49.7	1.61	46.1	50.7
Standard deviation		283.4	19.1	2.15	18.7	55.0

Source: SPRU Innovation Survey (1984)

of the technological activities of individual firms over time. Our analysis will therefore be for aggregates of firms, according to their principal 2-digit or 3-digit SIC activity.

3 Technological opportunities and threats

The SPRU Innovation Survey shows that technological opportunities and threats vary considerably amongst sectors, and the picture is a complicated one. Based on an earlier and incomplete version of the Survey, one of us proposed a classification of the major technological paths, or 'trajectories', followed by firms as a function of their principal activity (Pavitt, 1984, Table 5). The main technological opportunities and threats of the proposed categories of firms are the following:

— supplier-dominated: most new technology comes from suppliers of equipment, materials, software and other inputs. As a consequence, the opportunities for firm-specific technological advantage are few, and generally relate to process technology, rather than products. And the main threat of technology-based entry comes from the suppliers who control most of the technology.

— scale-intensive: most technology is developed, applied and improved in and around investment and production activities, and related to complex, interdependent and often large-scale production systems. The main sources of new technology are production engineering departments, design offices and suppliers of specialised inputs, all drawing upon a wide range of advances in knowledge and techniques. Threats of technology based entry are small, given the relatively small size of technologically strong suppliers, and the widely different nature of processes, products and their markets.

— specialised suppliers: firm-specific technological advantage is based on the capacity to improve the performance of specialised inputs (machines, instrumentation, materials, software) into complex and interdependent production systems. The main focus is product innovation, and the main sources of technology are the firm's design office, and the production engineering and systems activities of customers. The main threat of entry is from technologically dynamic firms in these user sectors.

— science-based: in-house R&D activities are the basis for the exploitation of munificent core technologies — emerging from scientific advances in physics, chemistry and (increasingly) biology — and enabling horizontal diversification into new product markets. The main threats of entry are from other science-based firms diversifying horizontally into related product markets.

Based on these and related characteristics, we would expect the pattern of technological opportunities and threats facing a firm to vary according to its principal activity, as shown in Table 4.4.

1 Technological opportunities, measured by the number of significant
   innovations, are highest in science-based firms (given munificence in

Table 4.4. Patterns of technological opportunities and threats

CATEGORY OF FIRM	OPPORTUNITIES		THREATS		APPROPRIABILITY	PRINCIPAL ACTIVITY OF FIRMS FITTING THESE CHARACTERISTICS (see table 4.3)
	1 *Number of innovations*	*2* *Percentage product innovations*	*3* *Ratio of innovations purchased to those produced*	*4* *Percentage of innovation made by firms from other 3-digits*	*5* *Average size of innovating firm (employment)*	
Science based	High	High	Low	High	High	Chemicals Electrical-Electronic
Specialised suppliers	High to Medium	High	Low	Medium to High	Low to Medium	Mechanical Engineering Instruments Rubber & Plastic Products
Scale intensive	Medium	Medium	Medium	Low	High to Medium	Mining Food Vehicles Metals Utilities Textiles
Supplier dominated	Low	Low	High	Medium	Low to Medium	Paper Agriculture Printing Construction

technologies), and in specialised suppliers (given continuous pressures to improve productive efficiency), and are lowest in supplier-dominated firms (given lack of in-house technological expertise).

2 For similar reasons, the relative emphasis on product technology (ie embodied in products sold to other sectors), compared to process technology (ie embodied in own production systems), and measured as the proportion of innovations made that are used in other 2-digit sectors, is highest in science-based and specialised supplier firms, and lowest in supplier-dominated firms.

3 The threat of technology-based entry by suppliers, measured as the ratio of the number of innovations embodied in purchases from suppliers outside the sector, to the number of innovations produced by firms within the sector, are greatest to supplier-dominated firms, and least to science-based and specialised supplier firms.

4 From elsewhere, the greatest threats of technology-based entry are to science-based firms (horizontally, from other science-based firms), reflected in a relatively high proportion of innovations made in their core 3-digit activities by firms with their principal activities elsewhere.

5 Innovating firms will be relatively large when they are science-based (given the appropriation of munificent technological opportunities) and scale-intensive (given the technological requirements of efficient production), but small amongst specialised suppliers (given low technological barriers to entry by numerous users) and in supplier-dominated sectors (given low technological opportunities and requirements).

Table 4.4 summarises the predicted characteristics of each type of firm, and categorises them according to principal 2-digit activity, in the light of the empirical data presented in Table 4.3. As we can see, most sectors fit into the categories pretty well:

— firms principally in chemicals and electrical-electronics have characteristics that are clearly science-based;
— firms principally in mechanical engineering, instruments, and rubber and plastic products have the characteristics of specialised suppliers;
— firms principally in mining, food, vehicles, metals and utilities have scale-intensive characteristics;
— firms principally in agriculture, printing and construction are supplier-dominated;
— firms principally in textiles and paper have characteristics between supplier-dominated and scale-intensive, suggesting that at least some of the (probably larger) firms have developed in-house technological capabilities. At the same time, firms principally in four of the sectors do not fit the pattern:

— shipbuilding, which comprises both conventional ships and offshore equipment, each with very different external sources of technology (upstream for the former, and downstream for the latter);

— aerospace, where a (no doubt large) number of significant military innovations have not been identified in the SPRU sample, and where a major source of innovation has been firms, classed as principally in mechanical engineering, that have developed and produced jet engines;

— non-metallic materials, where firms have some of the key characteristics of specialised suppliers (strong stream of product innovations from small firms), but without a relatively high technological contribution from firms outside the sector;

— services, with a quite high priority given to product innovation, coupled with a strong technological contribution made by both suppliers and other outside firms. This pattern is consistent with the 'reverse product cycle' model proposed by Barras (1986) to explain patterns of innovation in services, and suggesting that the assimilation of electronics (initially from suppliers) into firms' process technologies has been the basis for the subsequent development of new products (see Baba, Chapter 3, and Thomas and Miles, Chapter 6, for further discussion of this model).

To sum up, these data show that the technological opportunities and threats facing a firm are strongly conditioned by its principal activity, reflecting the nature and extent of its accumulated technology. Thus, a firm in electronics cannot neglect product technologies or entry threats from

Table 4.5. Types of innovating firm in product groups of greatest technological opportunity

Product Groups	PRINCIPAL ACTIVITY OF INNOVATING FIRM (%)				Total (%)
	Same 3-digit	Different 3-digit, same 2-digit	Different 2-digit, user firm	Different 2-digit, non-user firm	
Chemicals	33.4	36.8	4.4	25.4	100
Electrical-Electronic	28.4	40.6	8.8	22.2	100
Mechanical Engineering	51.2	17.7	11.5	19.5	100
Instruments	45.0	0.9	16.8	37.3	100

Source: SPRU Innovation Survey (1984)

other electronics firms in related markets, steelmakers cannot ignore process technologies, firms producing agricultural products cannot neglect the technological activities of their suppliers, whilst those producing instruments must be ever mindful of those of their customers. Of particular interest is a comparison of columns 1 and 4 in Tables 4.3 and 4.4, which shows that firms principally in sectors of greatest technological opportunity also face the greatest threats of technological entry from outside, which may explain the widespead assertion that radical innovations are often made by newcomers to a sector. Table 4.5 shows that such patterns of entry are not random, but are consistent with those proposed by Utterback and Kim (1986): namely, firms moving horizontally into related product markets, or user firms moving upstream. The former are relatively more important for science-based firms (chemicals and electrical-electronic), and the latter for specialised suppliers (mechanical engineering and instruments). Amongst the non-user firms in the 'different 2-digit' category, those principally in electrical-electronics are particularly important sources of technological entry into mechanical engineering and instruments, as are those in mining (petrochemicals) and food into chemicals.

This leads naturally to the next stage of our analysis, where we shall explore the pattern and the path of technological activities of firms producing in the different sectors, and the degree to which these activities are transformed into output and sales.

4 Technological trajectories

4.1 Differentiation amongst sectors

Table 4.6 identifies the main loci of technological activities of firms principally in different sectors. The concentration in most sectors of firms' technological activities in their principal sectors of production reflects the differentiated nature of technological knowledge. Outside their core products, the main patterns that emerge are as follows.

In scale-intensive and supplier-dominated firms, the main directions of movement are upstream into related production technologies, mainly in mechanical, instruments and electrical-electronic engineering, but sometimes in other sectors: for example, into offshore (shipbuilding) for firms in mining (ie petroleum products) and utilities (ie gas production).

In science-based and specialised supplier firms, there are also technological movements upstream, but they are relatively less important than horizontal (ie in related product markets) or downstream (ie in user sectors) movements. In chemical firms, the main loci are horizontal in other synthetic products, and downstream in user sectors. In mechanical, instrument and electrical-electronic firms, they are horizontal, into related product markets, or into one of the other three, thereby reflecting the complementarities amongst mechanical, electrical and electronic technologies, in the design and development of machinery and control systems; they are also downstream in user sectors in transport.

c

Table 4.6. Directions of technological activity outside core products

Firms' principal activity	Percentage of innovations in principal 2-digit activity	Main directions of technological activity		
		Upstream	Horizontal	Downstream
Mining (MI)	8.7	ME, SH	CH	
Food (FO)	58.0	ME	CH	
Chemicals (CH)	68.9	ME, IN	CH	VE, TE, PR, RP, CO
Metals (MT)	63.4	ME, IN		
Mechanical Engineering (ME)	76.0	MT	ME, IN, EE	SH, VE, AE
Instruments (IN)	75.6		ME, IN, EE	
Electrical-Electronic (EE)	70.7	MT, MA	ME, IN, EE	VE, AE
Shipbuilding/Offshore (SH)	58.2	MT, ME, IN		
Vehicles (VE)	71.2	ME, RP		
Aerospace (AE)	71.8	ME, IN		
Textiles, Leather, Clothing (TE)	61.8	ME, CH, IN		
Materials (MA)	70.0	IN		EE
Paper (PA)	50.0	ME, IN		
Printing (PR)	34.5	ME, EE		
Rubber and Plastics (RP)	55.2	CH, ME		VE, AE
Construction (CO)	38.5	ME, MA		SH
Utilities (UT)	26.8	ME, EE, SH, VE		
Services (SE)	19.0	ME, IN, EE		

Source: SPRU Innovation Survey (1984)

A correlation matrix of the sectoral distribution of technological activities of firms principally in the different sectors in Table 4.7, reveals hardly any significant similarities, reflecting the concentration in most sectors of firms' technological activities in their principal 2-digit activity. This is consistent with the conclusions of Jaffe (1988), based on patent statistics, who found significant correlations between firms in the same sector (eg computers), but no relation between firms in very different sectors (eg computers and pharmaceuticals). However, rank correlations of our firms' technological priorities, according to their principal activity, confirm closer links amongst firms principally in mechanical, electrical/electronic and instrument engineering; all of whom are at a considerable technological distance from firms in chemicals, whom in turn are closer to those in metals, and in rubber and plastics.

4.2 Cumulativeness and diversification over time

We have too few data points to make a rigorous statistical analysis of trends over time in the sectoral pattern of firms' technological activities, according to their principal sectors of production. However, Table 4.7 shows that sectoral priorities are relatively stable over a nearly 40 year period, reflecting the cumulative nature of firm-specific technological activities. At the same

Table 4.7. Trends in technological priorities of firms principally in different sectors

Firms' principal activity	1945-54	1955-64	1965-74	1975-83	1945-83 Activity
Mining (MI)	CH(40), ME(20), IN(10)	CH(42), ME(18), IN(12)	CH(31), SH(27), ME(18)	SH(38), CH(24), ME(10)	CH(35), SH(21), ME(16)
Food (FO)	FO(14), CH(29), IN(7)	FO(84), ME(8)	FO(47), ME(22)	FO(35), ME(18)	FO(58), ME(18), CH(11)
Chemicals (CH)	CH(85), ME(8), TE(5)	CH(78), ME(9), TE(6)	CH(60), ME(14), IN(8)	CH(57), IN(13), ME(9)	CH(69), ME(11), TE(6)
Metals (MT)	MT(85), ME(9)	MT(70), IN(16), ME(13)	MT(63), ME(10), IN(10)	MT(37), ME(29),	MT(63), ME(15), IN(17) IN(12)
Mechanical Engineering (ME)	ME(78), MT(8), AE(8)	ME(79), MT(5)	ME(78), IN(5), AE(4)	ME(69), IN(10), EE(5)	ME(76), IN(5), AE(4)
Instruments (IN)	IN(84), ME(10)	IN(77), EE(19)	IN(73), EE(14), ME(7)	IN(75), EE(11), ME(5)	IN(76), EE(13) ME(5)
Electrical-Electronics (EE)	EE(74), AE(9), IN(6)	EE(79), IE(5), VE(5)	EE(65), IN(14), ME(10)	EE(69), IN(15), ME(8)	EE(71), IN(11), ME(7)
Vehicles (VE)	VE(73), ME(8)	VE(74), ME(13), RP(5)	VE(75), ME(11), MT(5)	VE(64), ME(22)	VE(71), ME(14), RP(4)
Textiles, Leather, Clothing (TE)	TE(77), ME(23)	TE(68), ME(15), CH(9)	TE(63), ME(30), IN(4)	TE(43), ME(43), EE(7)	TE(12), ME(27) CH(3.5)

Note: Only for sectors with more than 100 innovations. ( ) = Percentage of all innovations made by firms in the sector
Source: SPRU Innovation Survey (1984)

time, there has been increasing technological diversification at the 2-digit level, the directions of which can be anticipated from our earlier analysis: upstream into production technologies for scale-intensive and supplier-dominated firms; upstream, horizontal and downstream for chemical firms; and horizontal for mechanical, instrument and electrical-electronic engineering firms.

4.3 Technological opportunity and output diversification

The first four columns of Table 4.8 translate the sectoral patterns of firms' technological activities so far described into categories familiar in the economic analysis of firms' output diversification: 'specialised' (innovation in same 3-digit as principal 3-digit sector of production), 'narrow' (same 2-digit, different 3-digit), and 'broad' (different 2-digit). It emerges that technological 'relatedness' is not confined to close proximity in the 3- or 4-digit categories of the Standard Industrial Classification, but extends upstream (into producers' goods), horizontally (amongst mechanical, instrument and electrical-electronic machinery) and downstream (into user sectors), all of which are measured as 'broad' diversification in other 2-digit sectors. Only about 10 per cent of the total SPRU sample of innovations are outside the sectoral patterns of technological activities identified in Table 4.6.

It also emerges that the prevalence of 'broad' technological diversification by firms in a sector is not a symptom of high technological opportunity, but of upstream activity in related producers' goods, and is typical of scale-intensive and supplier-dominated firms. In firms with high technological opportunity — typically in chemicals and engineering — technological diversification is more typically 'narrow'.

To what extent do these sectoral patterns of technological activity correspond to their patterns of output? Since the SPRU Innovation Survey did not collect information on the sectoral patterns of output of innovating firms, we cannot answer this question solely on the basis of our own data. However, we can compare patterns of technology with those of output, in all manufacturing firms in 1963 and 1968 (Hassid, 1975), and for the top 200 manufacturing firms in 1972 (Utton, 1979). Given problems of matching sectors, and occasionally of small numbers in our survey, the restricted number of sectors of principal activity of innovating firms precludes rigorous statistical tests[2]. Nonetheless, the comparisons are suggestive.

Thus, in Table 4.8 we list, for each of the principal 2-digit activities of innovating and producing firms, the principal sectors of broad, 2-digit diversification in technology (according to the SPRU Innovation Survey, 1945-1983), and in output (according to Hassid for 1963 and 1968, and to Utton for 1972). It shows similarities in the directions of diversification of technology and of output. Of particular significance, we find mechanical and electrical-electronic (including instruments) engineering prominent in both columns.

However, Figure 4.1, based on SPRU and Hassid's data, shows that —

Table 4.8. Sectoral distribution of innovations and output according to firms' principal activity

Firms' principal activity	Distribution of innovations (%)			Main sectors of broad diversification in innovations to Hassid (1975) and Utton (1979)	Main sectors of broad diversification in output, according
	Specialised	Narrow diversification	Broad diversification		
Agriculture (AG)	66.7	0	33.3	SH, ME	*
Mining (MI)	8.7	0	91.3	ME, CH, SH	*
Food (FO)		58.0	42.0	ME, CH	CH, PPP**, ME
Chemicals (CH)	32.8	36.1	31.1	ME, TE, IN, PA, VE, PR, RP	TE, MT, ME, FO
Metals (MT)	57.5	5.9	36.6	ME, IN	VEH/AE, MT, EE
Mechanical Engineering (ME)	56.5	19.5	24.0	IN, AE, EE, MT, SH, VE	VE/AE, MT, EE
Instruments (IN)	74.1	1.5	24.4	EE, ME	ME, EE
Electrical-Electronic (EE)	29.1	41.6	29.3	IN, ME, VE, AE, MT, MA	ME, VE/AE, IN
Shipbuilding/Offshore (SH)	58.2	0	41.8	ME, IN, MT	MT, ME
Vehicles (VE)	63.2	8.0	28.8	ME, RP	MT, ME
Aerospace (AE)	71.8	0	28.2		ME, IN
Textiles, Leather, Clothing (TE)		61.8	38.2	ME, CH, IN	ME, CH, MT
Materials (MA)	69.4	0.6	30.0	EE, IN	PPP**, ME, TE, MT
Paper (PA)	46.3	3.7	50.0	ME, IN	ME, IN
Printing (PR)	34.5	0	65.5	ME, EE	ME, EE
Rubber and Plastics (RP)	46.9	8.3	44.8	CH, ME, VE, AE	*
Construction (CO)	38.5	0	61.5	ME, MA	*
Utilities (UT)	26.8	0	73.2	EE, VE, SH, ME	*
Services (SE)	10.7	8.3	81.0	EE, ME, IN	*
Total	46.1	20.0	33.8	ME, IN, EE	ME, VE, MT, EE

* Not available   ** PPP = Pulp, Paper and Printing
Specialised: Innovation 3-digit SIC = Firm 3-digit SIC   Narrow Diversification: Innovation 3-digit SIC = Elsewhere in Firm 2-digit SIC
Broad Diversification: Innovation 2-digit SIC ≠ Firm 2-digit SIC

Source: SPRU Innovation Survey (1984)

when classified according to their principal sectors of output - the extent of firms' 'broad' output diversification is not correlated with that of their 'broad' technological diversification. Perhaps of equal or even greater interest is the location of all sectors in Figure 4.1 above the unit-slope diagonal line, showing that firms in them are in aggregate more diversified in technology than in output. Similar comparisons using Utton's data confirm these findings. In other words, only a proportion of firms' technological activities upstream (into related producers' goods), horizontally (amongst mechanical, instrument, and electrical-electronic engineering) and downstream (into user sectors) are transformed into corresponding output.

4.4 Why more diversity in technology than output?

How can this greater diversity in firms' technology than in their output be explained. As suggested by de Bresson (1986), both transaction costs and technical interdependencies may be partial explanations. On the former, writers like Mowery (1983) might argue that, given that technological knowledge is specific and idiosyncratic, the possibilities of opportunistic behaviour by suppliers, customers or partners are considerable, and the future (in terms of competitors' response and of size of market) is uncertain. For all these reasons, firms may decide to maintain a technological capacity without corresponding output as a hedge against opportunistic behaviour and an otherwise uncertain future.

Alternatively, technological diversity may reflect technical interdependencies with suppliers, customers and partners. Thus, a firm with a complex and interdependent process technology may require modification or even novelty in the equipment, materials and components that it integrates (eg machine tools, CAD/CAM), and must therefore have the upstream technological capacity to meet such requirements. The same may be true horizontally in product development (eg the interaction between the mechanical and the electronic in machine design), or downstream in user applications (eg fibre technology in textiles).

4.5 Technological 'fusion'

Such technological interdependencies involve reciprocal relationships between sectors, with firms principally in 2-digit sector A making innovations in 2-digit sector B, and firms principally in sector B making innovations in sector A. Our analysis shows that this is in fact the case for about 1000 innovations (ie about 24 per cent of the sample, and 71 per cent of all broad technological diversification). The three-way interactions amongst machinery, instruments and electrical-electronics are particularly intense. Together with chemicals, these three sectors account for about two-thirds of the reciprocal relationships. Other important nodes of activity are around vehicles involving 10 per cent of the total and interaction with firms in seven other sectors, and aerospace with 7 per cent and interaction with firms in two other sectors.

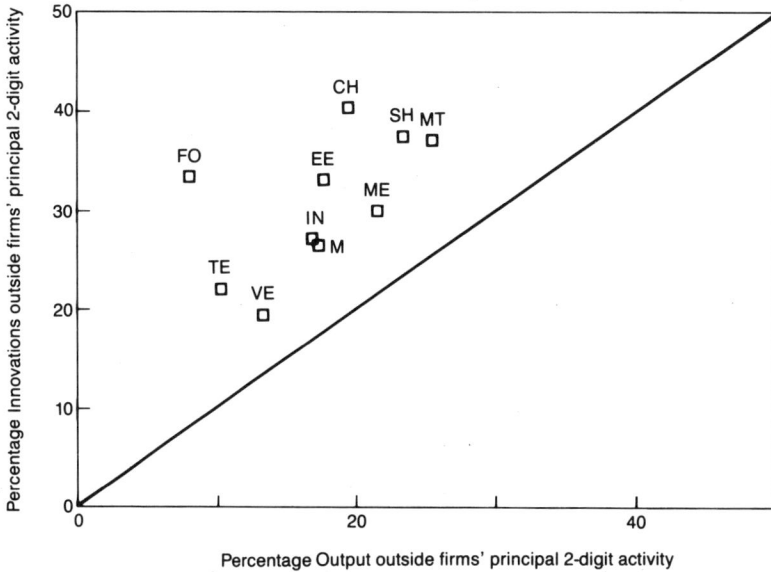

Fig 4.1 Broad technological diversification (compared to output diversification)
Sources: SPRU Innovation Survey (1984); Hassid (1975)

This pattern of technological activity and interaction is consistent with those described by Archibugi (1986) and Jaffe (1989). It is almost identical to that described by Kodama (1986a) for Japan. He argues that there are two types of innovation: technological breakthrough and technological 'fusion':

> Breakthrough-type innovation is associated with strong leadership of a particular industry, and fusion-type research becomes possible by a concerted effort of the several different industries involved...Fusion-type innovation contributes not to the radical growth of certain companies, but to the gradual growth of all companies of the relevant industries...The essence of technological fusion is its reciprocity: it is only realised when there is two-way investment thus becoming reciprocal between two industries.....technological fusions are clustered around three major industries - ordinary machinery, electrical machinery, and industrial chemicals.

Kodama stresses the importance of such linkages in 'mechatronics' (ie the fusion of electronics and mechanics). His analysis and our data suggest that science-based breakthrough technologies, like electronics, offer opportunities - not only to firms where they are core activities - but also to specialised suppliers, and to scale-intensive and supplier-dominated firms, that are able to integrate aspects of breakthrough technology into their machines, their production, and (increasingly) office and distribution systems. In this context, it is relevant to note that about a quarter of the electronics innovations (including electronics instruments) in our sample were made by firms with other core businesses, of which about 8 per cent were from firms in mechanical engineering, and 2 per cent each from chemicals, metals, other materials, utilities and services.

5 Technological trajectories according to firm size

5.1 The importance of small firms

Patterns and trends in firms' technological activities vary as a function of their size, as well as their principal sector of output, and smaller firms cannot be neglected as important sources of technology. Based on one of our earlier analyses of the SPRU innovation data base, Table 4.9 shows that R&D statistics greatly underestimate the volume of technological activities in firms with fewer than 1000 employees. It also shows that innovating firms in mechanical engineering and instruments are prevalent amongst those with fewer than 1000 employees, and firms in electrical-electronics and chemicals amongst those with more than 10,000 employees. Over the period from 1945 to 1983, the shares of innovating firms with fewer than 200 and more than 50,000 employees increased significantly, whilst that of firms with between 1000 and 9999 decreased.

Table 4.9 Comparison of level and composition of technological activities in innovating firms of different sizes

	Firm size (number of employees)			
	1-999	1000-9,999	10,000+	Total
Percentage distribution of business enterprise R and D expenditure (1975)	3.3	16.4	80.3	100.0
Percentage distribution of significant innovations (1970-79)	34.9	18.1	47.1	100.0
Top three sectors of principal production of innovating firms (% of total)	ME (40.1) IN (11.7) EE (10.7)	ME (28.9) CH (15.0) EE (13.7)	EE (29.9) CH (14.1) ME (11.8)	ME (27.2) EE (18.7 CH (10.2)

Source: Pavitt, Robson and Townsend (1987); SPRU Innovation Survey (1984)

5.2 Technological diversity and firm size

Table 4.10 shows that, as might be expected, a firm's size is a major determinant of the diversity of its technological activities, with the latter increasing as a function of the former. More than 60 per cent of the innovations made by firms with fewer than 1000 employees are in their principal 3-digit activity of production, compared to only about a quarter for firms with more than 10,000 employees. Over time, the general trend is towards more broad diversification, resulting in large part from the growing interaction in the small innovating firms amongst mechanical, instrument and electrical-electronic technologies.

5.3 Divisionalisation and size

Table 4.11 shows that size of the innovating firm is also a major determinant of its organisational form, as reflected in the existence of divisions: hardly any innovations in firms with less than 100 employees are made by divisionalised firms, whilst very few made by firms with more than 1000 employees are not.

Table 4.12 shows that, over the period from 1945 to 1983, both the average size of innovating firms and the proportion of innovations made by divisionalised firms has been increasing. However, whilst the average size of divisionalised innovating firms has not been getting any bigger - that of its divisions has been declining steadily: from just under a third of the former from 1945-54 to less than a tenth from 1975-83. Whatever the reasons for this latter trend, it has probably created more favourable conditions for the implementation of innovations.

5.4 Goodness of fit between divisions and technologies?

Table 4.13 compares the broad sectoral pattern of innovative activities in undivisionalised firms, with those in divisionalised ones and their units, and in the sample as a whole. Rows 1 and 2 confirm that undivisionalised firms are far less diversified in their technological activities than divisionalised ones. Row 3 shows that divisionalisation considerably increases the goodness of fit between divisions principal sectors of production, and the sectors of technological activity, since the proportion where both are in the same 3-digit category doubles to just over 60 per cent. Nonetheless, this remains 10 per cent less than the fit achieved in undivisionalised firms (row 1), and nearly 40 per cent of the innovations continue to be made outside units' principal activities. The time trends also show that the share of innovations made outside the principal 3-digit activities of divisions hardly changed at all between 1945-49 and 1980-83. In other words, there appears to be a large and irreducible proportion of innovations that do not fit tidily into divisional organisations. What are their characteristics?

Technology strategy and the firm

Table 4.10. Trends in technological diversity according to firm size (%)

	Total			1-999 employees			1000-9,999 employees			More than 10,000H employees		
	S	ND	BD	S	ND	BD	S	ND	BD	S	ND	BD
1945-54	51.3	20.9	27.8	71.4	14.1	14.5	40.2	27.6	32.2	23.7	28.8	47.5
1955-64	51.2	20.9	27.9	69.6	12.9	17.5	56.9	18.8	24.3	25.4	32.0	42.6
1965-74	44.7	19.4	35.8	62.6	13.2	29.2	48.2	21.7	30.1	24.2	25.1	50.7
1975-83	39.8	19.6	40.6	59.3	11.0	29.7	36.9	26.1	36.9	22.0	25.7	52.3
1945-83	46.1	20.1	33.8	65.2	12.7	22.1	47.2	22.6	30.2	23.8	27.5	48.7

Note: S = Specialised
ND = Narrow diversification
BD = Broad diversification
S + ND + BD = 100%

Source: SPRU Innovation Survey (1984)

Table 4.11. Relative importance of divisionalised innovating firms according to their size

Size of innovating firm (employment)	Proportion of innovations made by divisionalised firms (%)
1–99	4.8
100–199	14.8
200–499	17.1
500–999	45.8
1000–9,999	85.5
10,000–49,999	91.1
50,000 +	91.1

Source: SPRU Innovation Survey (1984)

In order to try to answer this question, we identified — for firms in each principal 2-digit activity — the frequency with which innovations in each product group are different (at the 3-digit level) from the principal activity of the innovating division: in other words, the types of firms and product groups where technology is not neatly decomposable into divisionalised activities, but badly behaved. Altogether, there are 1011 such innovations, amounting to 24 per cent of the total sample. The sectoral distribution of 'badly behaved' innovations is very similar to that of the sample of innovations as a whole, in terms of both product groups, and principal activities of firms. (The coefficients of determination between the two sets of distributions are 0.9).

This diversity of potential synergies across divisions serves to explain the irreducibly high proportion of innovations made outside the principal sectors of production of divisions. Under such circumstances, rigid policies to make divisions adhere to their previously defined 'business' will result in missed technological opportunities. The successfully innovative large firm will not only have to tolerate disorganisation and untidiness, but also to question divisional arrangements when they get in the way of technological opportunities and synergies.

6 Conclusions for analysis

In relation to the four traditions identified in Section 2, our analysis leads to the following conclusions:

— The nature of the technological opportunities and threats facing firms varies considerably as a function of their principal activity. Rich technological opportunities are associated with science-based firms and specialised suppliers, with relatively many opportunities for product

Table 4.12. Trends in the characteristics of divisionalised innovating firms

Period	Share of all innovations by divisionalised firms (%)	Average size of all innovating firms (thousands employment)	Average size of divisionalised firms (thousands employment)	Average size of divisions (thousands employment)
1945-54	51.1	45.3	79.7	24.7
1955-64	56.2	48.8	79.4	18.2
1965-74	64.7	56.7	78.0	13.1
1975-83	63.7	64.2	86.1	6.7
1945-83	60.0	55.3	80.9	13.9

Source: SPRU Innovation Survey (1984)

Table 4.13. Comparisons of sectoral patterns of innovative activities: independent and divisionalised firms

Type of firm	Sectoral distribution of innovations (%)		
	Specialised	Narrow diversification	Broad diversification
1) Undivisionalised firms (1945-83)	71.7	5.9	22.4
2) Divisionalised firms (1945-83)	31.7	16.0	52.3
3) Divisions (1945-83)	61.2	5.3	33.5
Divisions (by period)			
1945-49	59.7	7.3	33.0
1950-54	60.5	5.9	33.6
1955-59	67.6	5.7	26.7
1960-64	65.4	6.0	28.6
1965-69	63.0	5.7	31.3
1970-74	59.3	4.1	36.6
1975-79	58.9	4.7	36.4
1980-83	54.0	5.6	40.4

Specialised: Innovation 3-digit SIC = Firm/Division 3-digit SIC
Narrow diversification: Innovation 3-digit SIC = Elsewhere in firm/ division 2-digit SIC
Broad diversification: Innovation 2-digit SIC ≠ Firm/Division 2-digit SIC.

innovations, and high outside threats from others diversifying horizontally, and from technologically active users. Supplier-dominated firms have fewer technological opportunities, and are under threat of entry from suppliers. Scale-intensive firms focus on improving complex and interdependent production technologies. Together with specialised suppliers, they can exploit opportunities for 'fusion' with radical breakthrough technologies.

— Science-based firms and specialised suppliers spread their technological activities horizontally into related product markets, and downstream into user applications, whilst scale-intensive and supplier-dominated firms typically spread upstream into related production technologies. The sectoral composition of technological activities of firms with different core activities are very stable across time but highly variable across sector, reflecting the cumulative and differentiated nature of technological knowledge.

— These patterns of technological activity do not fit tidily into the Standard Industrial Classification. 'Related' technologies often exist in other 2-digit categories, but the sectors of greatest technological opportunity are typified by activity in proximate 3-digit categories. This is probably why economists have found poor statistical relations between sectoral technological intensities and output diversification.

— The sectoral patterns of firms' technological activities in core production sectors are similiar to those of output in direction, but are consistently greater in extent. This reflects technological interdependencies amongst sectors, with firms principally in engineering and chemicals at the centre of clusters of innovations spread over a wider number of sectors and firms. Effective fusion across sectors and technologies depends on technological capabilities on both sides that are beyond the strict requirements of production at any given time.

— Rich technological opportunities are not associated solely with large firms. Innovating small firms typically follow 'specialised' technological strategies in engineering. Innovating large firms typically follow 'broad front' strategies and are divisionalised. The size of innovating divisions has declined steadily and substantially, thereby facilitating the implementation of innovation.

— Divisionalisation also improves the goodness of fit between the principal activity of the business, and the sector of the innovation. However, about 40 per cent of the innovations by divisionalised firms remain outside the principal 3-digit activity of innovating divisions. Technology remains 'badly behaved'.

7. Conclusions for policy

Having summarised what we think we have added to earlier analyses of technology and firm behaviour, we shall now chance our arm and set out what we believe to be the normative implications of our own and related analyses. The reasons for doing so are the recognised importance of the subject amongst practioners (see, for example, Booz Allen, 1985), coupled with the belief that what we say may be useful: in particular, that firms' technological strategies are heavily constrained by their core activities, their size, and their forms of organisation. Discussion of policy implications can, we suggest, be grouped around four of its key characteristics: functional and technical specialisation in its production; uncertainty in its outcome; cumulativeness in its development; and differentiated and specific in its nature.

The implications of the first three of these characteristics are set out in Table 4.14 and of the fourth in Table 4.15. Many of these implications have already been discussed earlier in this paper. The following additional points must also be made:

Table 4.14. Characteristics of innovative activities and their implications for management

Characteristics of innovative activities	Implications for the firm	
	Objectives	Means
1 Functional and technical specialisation	Quality in, and balance amongst R&D, production and marketing	+ Business innovator with strong knowledge of all functional areas + Horizontal links
2 Uncertainty in outcomes	Flexibility and speed in decision Cover contingencies	+ Decentralisation of implementation + Portfolio investment + Avoid 'sophisticated' decision algorithms
3 Cumulative in development over time	Exploitation of learning: – by doing – by using – by failing	+ Feedback from marketing and and production to technical functions + Skilled work force in production and marketing + Creation of 'technological slack' in product and process design + 'Patient' money
4 Differentiated and and specific	Exploitation of technological trajectories	See Table 4.15

— The notion of cumulative and firm-specific technological trajectories has already entered management practice, especially in Japan, through the use of maps or graphs of technological improvement, including tree or 'bonzai' representations of the cumulative emergence of technological opportunities for specific firms (for an excellent summary, *see* Centre de Prospective et d'Evaluation, 1985, pp 34-5,39,50,84,102-4).

— Compared to the earlier work by one of us (Pavitt, 1984), we have added to Table 4.15 one new trajectory that we describe as 'information-intensive'. Recent empirical work (*see*, for example, Barras, 1986; Belussi, 1987) suggests that information and computing technologies are now creating opportunities for software-based technical change in processing information, with the same revolutionary potential as the development of steel and mechanical engineering in the nineteenth century for the processing of materials.

— We have also excluded a 'supplier dominated' trajectory since, as Porter (1985b) has rightly pointed out, it leaves accumulated technological skills and the strategic initiative with suppliers. Firms intending to move from this position try to adopt either scale-intensive strategies (eg certain textile firms), or information-intensive strategies (eg certain retailing firms).

— In 'science-based' trajectories, we stress the strategic importance, recently discussed by Teece (1986), of obtaining complementary assets to core technologies, when moving into new but related product markets: for example, a firm moving on its technological trajectory from pharmaceuticals to pesticides will need to understand and service a new market, as will a firm moving from office machinery into telecommunications.

— Similarly, in 'scale intensive' and 'information-intensive' trajectories, 'technological fusion' will benefit firms that can mobilise and integrate advances in rapidly changing technologies to form part of their firm-specific technological competence. This competence is often based on scale and complexity in design, in production, and (with the advent of information technology) in marketing and coordination. Fusion of this competence with advances in rapidly changing technologies can lead, not only to reduced costs and increased flexibility, but also to potential for new product development (for a major illustration in the automobile industry, *see* Altshuler et al, 1984).

— Finally, we now argue that specific firms can follow more than one technological trajectory. For example, a large computer firm can at the same time be science-based (electronics), scale-intensive and information intensive. At the same time, as we have seen in Section 3, it would find it hard to join the science-based (chemicals) trajectory.

Notes

1 This chapter has been prepared as part of the Programme of the ESRC funded Designated Research Centre on Innovation. It is based on a paper by K Pavitt, M Robson and J Towsend entitled 'Technological accumulation, diversification and organisation in UK companies, 1945-1983' *Management Science*, 1989, 35(1), pp1-19.

2 In Figure 4.1, the source of the data on broad diversification in output is Hassid (1975). In order to match it with the data from the SPRU Innovation Survey, the following adjustments were made.
   Output
   – coal and petroleum products excluded

Table 4.15. Basic technological trajectories of firms

Definition	Source of technology	Trajectory	Typical core product groups of firms	Strategic problems for management
Science-based	R and D laboratory	Synergetic new products applications engineering	– Electronics – Chemicals	– Complementary assets – Integration to exploit synergies – Patient money
Scale intensive	Design, production engineering and specialised suppliers	Efficient and complex production and related products	– Basic materials – Durable consumer goods	– Balance and choice in production technology among *appropriation* (secrecy and patents), *vertical disintegration* (cooperation with supplier), and *Profit Centre*
Information intensive	Software/ systems dept and specialised suppliers	Efficient (and complex) information processing, and related products	– Financial services – Retailing	– 'Fusion' with fast-moving technologies – Diffusion of production technology amongst divisions – Exploiting product opportunities – Patient money
Specialised suppliers	Small-firm design and large-scale users	Improved specialised producers goods (reliability and performance)	– Machinery – Instruments – Specialty chemicals – Software	– Matching technological opportunity with user needs – Absorbing user experience – Finding stable or new product 'niches'

– mechanical engineering and metal goods not elsewhere specified combined in an unweighted average.
– textiles, leather and clothing combined in an unweighted average.
– timber, furniture, paper, printing, rubber and plastic and other manufactured goods were combined in an unweighted average.
– unweighted average used to combine the 1963 and 1968 data.
Innovations
– grouped for analysis into the same combined categories created for the output data.
– innovations by firms taken from years 1961 to 1970 inclusive.

Chapter 5

Corporate strategies in the international semiconductor industry

Mike Hobday

1 Introduction

Within the complex of information technology industries, the semiconductor (SC) industry has become one of the main competitive 'battlegrounds' for the major US, Japanese and, more recently, European information technology (IT) Corporations. Most industrialised countries consider the SC industry and SC technology as strategic for several reasons. It is both a major world industry in its own right and, perhaps more importantly, a vital supply industry to the wide range of downstream IT industries. In fact, SC components can be seen as the physical 'building blocks', or material inputs, to the final IT goods industries such as telecommunications, computers, office equipment, informatics and electronic consumer goods. The rapid diffusion of leading-edge SC technology into many 'traditional' industries such as machine tools, the automotive industry, industrial processes, the military sector and so on has also accentuated the strategic importance of advanced SC technology.

The aim of this paper is two-fold: first, to analyse the contemporary strategies of the SC corporations of Japan, the US, and Europe in their efforts to maintain and improve their competitive positions in the SC industry; second, to use the case of the SC industry to explore three widely held assumptions regarding technology and competitive performance: that technology strategy is a crucial factor underpinning corporate performance in the electronics and IT industries; that technological leads provide the basis of competitive advantage; and that technological capability is, in general, firm-specific, cumulative and path dependent.[1]

An attempt to identify the factors which lie behind Japan's performance in coming to dominate major sectors of the SC industry during the 1980s (Section 2) is followed by an examination of the responses of US corporations to Japanese competition (Section 3). For the first time in the history of the SC industry, and in diametric opposition to their natural 'corporate culture', the major US corporations have proposed a large-scale programme of joint technology collaboration and requested large subsidies from the US Government. At the same time, the emergence of a new 'technological trajectory' in the industry, the shift to Application Specific Integrated Circuits (ASICs), has led several of the large European electronics manufacturers to announce their intention to become major players in the international SC industry. In Section 4 the prospects are considered for European industry to successfully leapfrog earlier generations of SC technology and enter the business at the same level as the Japanese and US competitors. Section 5 returns to Japanese corporate strategies and describes their counter-response to recent events in the US and Europe.

Most of the evidence presented is based on research into the activities of SC firms over the three year period, 1984 to 1987. This evidence is presented in 'current events' fashion. However, throughout the paper an effort is made to separate out the important determining factors which underpin longer-term structural change in the industry, from the complex web of conjunctural short-term events. Hopefully, this will provide greater analytical insight into the major driving forces for change, and throw some light on relationship between technological strategy and other important dimensions of competitive performance.

2 Japanese corporate strategies in semiconductors

The most striking event in the international SC industry in the first half of the 1980s was the replacement of the US by Japan as the major international supplier of SC components.

Table 5.1. Shares of world semiconductor sales by region (percentage)

	US	Japan	Europe
1980	61	26	13
1981	55	34	11
1982	54	34	11
1983	53	37	9
1984	51	39	9
1985	48	41	10
1986*	43	44	11

* Estimated

Source: Financial Times, quoted in Electronic Times (7 Aug 1986, p1)

Table 5.1 illustrates the rising share of Japan in world SC sales over the period 1980 to 1986. From the position of controlling approximately 80 per cent of world sales in the early 1970s, the US has steadily lost market share to Japan. In 1986, Japanese corporations succeeded in capturing a larger share of the world market than US producers. For the first time in the 30 year history of the SC industry the US fell to second place, holding only a 43 per cent share of the market compared with Japan's 44 per cent.

The historical change in ranking of the ten largest SC corporations is illustrated in Table 5.2. In 1985 Texas Instruments (TI) was toppled from its historical position of leader of the SC industry by NEC of Japan. By this year Japanese corporations occupied five of the top ten industrial positions with total sales of $6.9 billion. US corporations occupied only four of the top ten positions with sales of $5.3 billion. Within the global SC market European producers have consistently retained a comparatively low share of the market, with only one firm, Philips, in the major ten manufacturers.

Dataquest and Integrated Circuit Engineering, two leading consultancy agencies in the field, show a further deterioration in the ranking of US firms for 1986. The Japanese corporations NEC, Hitachi, and Toshiba moved into first, second and third places with sales of $2.6 billion, $2.3 billion and $2.26 billion[2]. At the same time the leading US firms, Motorola (with sales of $2.03 billion) and TI ($1.8 billion), slipped to positions four and five, while Intel with $0.99 billion fell to number ten. Mitsubishi entered the top ten at number nine, while National Semiconductors of the US fell out of the ranking.

Table 5.2. The ten major semiconductor manufacturers

Ranking 1980	1985	Firm	Sales ($m)
4	1	NEC	1950
1	2	TI	1815
5	3	Hitachi	1750
2	4	Motorola	1650
6	5	Toshiba	1370
11	6	Fujitsu	950
7	7	Intel	900
3	8	National	890
14	9	Matsushita	870
9	10	Philips	850

Source: Molina (1986)

Several factors may help explain the Japanese success in penetrating US and European markets in the volume SC business. To begin, as Table 5.3 shows, Japanese firms are far less dependent on semiconductor sales than their US counterparts.

Table 5.3. Dependence on semiconductor sales, US and Japanese firms - 1985

Japanese Firms	SC Sales as percentage of total sales	American Firms	SC Sales as percentage of total sales
NEC	17.8	AMD	89
Fujitsu	6.7	Fairchild	69
Toshiba	5.5	Intel	75
Hitachi	4.1	Mostek	93
Mitsubishi	3.8	Motorola	31
Matsushita	2.3	National	85
		TI	36

Source: Molina (1986)

In contrast to most of the US firms, Japanese firms are highly vertically integrated. Japanese companies manufacture not only chips, but also the final IT products and systems which incorporate the SC components. As Table 5.3 shows, apart from NEC whose dependence on chip sales is around 18 per cent of total sales, the other leading Japanese corporations' dependence on SC sales is on average well under 10 per cent. American companies on the other hand range from 31 per cent to 93 per cent dependence, with five of the leading seven companies depending on SC revenues for over 69 per cent of total corporate sales.

From the Japanese point of view, low dependence on SC revenues enables relatively long-term investment planning. If short-term losses are experienced in SCs, say as a result of cyclical business fluctuations, or competitive pressures, investment can be cross-financed from other equipment areas (Molina, 1986). Relatively low Japanese interest rates, and the close association of the large corporations with Japanese banks, have also played a part in permitting Japanese firms to invest during recessions and encouraged a relatively long-term perspective on technological investments.[3] In contrast, US corporations have tended to cut back capacity, reduce investment, minimise costs, and introduce redundancies in response to cyclical recession. As a result, during the cyclical upturns during the 1970s and early 1980s, Japanese companies have been better placed to meet rapid surges in demand and US corporations have steadily lost overall market shares.

Several other reasons also help explain the Japanese success in capturing the volume SC market (besides the accusations of 'dumping' components at lower-than-cost price). These include: first, the aggressive and planned 'targeting' of world markets; Wilmot (1985), for example, describes how successive waves of Japanese IT firms target US and European markets, each with the aim of achieving a given percentage of the world market. Once NEC, Fujitsu, Hitachi and Toshiba, had gained 5 per cent of the world market in their respective fields, a new wave of firms surfaced - Matsushita, Mitsubishi, Sharp and Oki - closely followed by a third wave of international IT competitors, Ricoh, Sony and NMB.

Second, Japanese companies, often with Government coordination and support through the Ministry of Trade and Industry (MITI), have invested heavily in advanced manufacturing technology, as well as in basic and applied R&D. The focus on Japanese investments in advanced fabrication technology in SCs often draws attention away from their heavy programmes of basic and applied R&D in new products and processes. IEEE *Spectrum* (June 1986), for example, reviews the Japanese position in advanced telecommunications technology. In this field, as in others, heavy investment in SC R&D is one of the most crucial factors in their market success, and their sustained technological 'catching-up' with the US.

Table 5.4 expresses the US Defence Science Board's perception of how Japanese technological capability matched up to the US's in 1986. In a selection of critical technologies, including silicon and non-silicon products and processes as well as materials, Japan had a clear lead in nine out of a listing of 13. Of the remaining four, the US is losing position in microprocessors and custom circuits and only maintaining its lead only in EPROMs and Linear devices.

Investment in fabrication technology proved especially important in the high volume memory markets (Dynamic Random Access Memories (RAMS) and Static RAMs) where the Japanese have excelled. With each successive US memory innovation (eg the 1K, 4K, 16K and later the 256K and 1 Megabit RAM) Japanese firms have succeeded in upstaging US innovators with less

Technology strategy and the firm

Table 5.4. Where Japan has a technological lead

Product or processes	Japanese lead	US/Japanese parity	US lead
Silicon products			
D-RAM's	●		
S-RAM's	●		
Eproms		■	
Microprocessors			●
Custom logic			●
Bipolar	●		
Non-silicon products			
Memory	●		
Logic	●		
Linear			■
Opto-electronics	●		
Hetero-electronics	●		
Materials			
Silicon	●		
Gallium arsenide	●		

Key ● US position declining ■ US position maintaining

Source: Defense Science Board (cited in *New York Times*, 6 Jan 1987)

expensive products of equally high quality. Koepp (1986) argues that Japanese success in the manufacturing-intensive general purpose integrated circuits, is partly to do with Japanese industrial 'culture', where equal prestige and status are accorded to manufacturing technology, as to design.

As already noted, this commitment to production excellence should not draw attention away from the serious effort devoted to basic R&D. In addition, as Porter (1985b) argues, Japanese corporations have demonstrated an understanding of the dynamics of competitive advantage, and a flexibility of response to market environment second to none on the world scene. Some of the factors noted by Porter include a strategic focus on product quality, inventory reduction and incremental technical improvement. Japanese firms have demonstrated their capacity to utilise overseas distribution channels and joint ventures effectively and to favourably influence institutional factors often taken for granted by US firms. What these activities amount to is organisational control over cost, innovation and quality and the capacity to translate technological innovation into market success.

3 The US response

In the face of successful Japanese competition US SC corporations have devised strategies to respond both to the current competitive environment and to longer-term technological change and opportunity. Recent signs indicate that the US Government will play an increasing role in defending the indigenous SC industry and that US corporations will collaborate in various ways to defend themselves against what is perceived to be unfair competition from Japan and, more recently, Korea and Taiwan.[4]

3.1 Offensive strategies

Led by Texas Instruments (TI) and National Semiconductor, US corporations have adopted both defensive and offensive strategies to protect existing market shares and to gain new markets. TI, for instance, has responded aggressively to Japanese competition announcing its intention to lead a counter-offensive against the Japanese chip producers. TI intends to regain market shares in memory products through heavy investment in the next generation of the 4 Megabit DRAMs.[5] This places TI in direct confrontation with NEC, Hitachi, Fujitsu, Mitsubishi, Toshiba and the Korean corporation Samsung, in a segment of the IC market currently dominated by Japanese suppliers.

TI and other US corporations are also concentrating effort in the rapidly growing ASIC market both within the US and in Europe. This is perceived to be an area of comparative market and technological strength for US manufacturers.[6] The shift away from general-purpose integrated circuits (such as TTL logic circuits) to ASICs presents a qualitatively different challenge to the Japanese corporations. In the field of ASICs, several US firms believe that design, rather than manufacture, is the main determinant of market success. Expertise in software and Computer Aided Design (CAD) is viewed as the crucial competitive factor in capturing market shares. Also, in order to meet the ASIC demands of system manufacturers the 'commodity' marketing strategies which served the Japanese in memory products may no longer be tenable.

Close market proximity and intimate relations between leading IT system manufacturers and chip producers are becoming increasingly important with the rapid diffusion of design-intensive SCs. US and European corporations hope that the perceived relative disadvantage of Japanese corporations in these areas will allow them to regain market ground, as Japanese firms struggle to cope with the exigencies of this new technological direction.

To gain ground in ASIC technology, TI has forged a major joint venture with Philips/Signetics to collaborate in setting up cell library design centres in close proximity to system houses (*Electronics and Power*, June 1986, p422). TI has set up fourteen such design centres (seven in North America, six in Europe and one in Japan), which provide customers with direct access to sophisticated CAD facilities and training in chip design. Texas Instruments has also decided to expand its SC manufacturing facility in Freising, West Germany and Nice in France, to 'attack the ASIC market in Europe' (*Electronics Times*, 19 Mar 1987, p48). The new manufacturing capacity is viewed as world class leading-edge technology in this area (one micron CMOS technology).

An additional strategy being pursued by TI is further diversification into IT systems.[7] In comparison with most other US chip manufacturers TI has traditionally had a low dependence on SC revenues in total sales (approximately 36 per cent in 1985, *see* Table 5.3 above). Further forward integration and diversification into IT systems and products is seen as insurance against the violent fluctuations of the SC market.

National Semiconductor is attempting radically to reorganise its technological and marketing strategies around similar principles to those adopted by TI: aggressive entry into customer specific (or ASIC) technology, increased diversification into systems production, and strategic business partnerships with IT system producers. During 1986 National formed technological partnerships with Thomson CSF to develop ISDN telecommunications devices; with Xerox to develop and supply ASICs; with Delco to supply one of National's proprietary packaging technologies; and with NMB/Minabea to form a joint, five year programme to develop SRAMs and other VLSI circuits (*Electronics Weekly*, 15 Apr 1987, p16).

National has traditionally based its SC operations on high volume, low profit margin, standard chips. The company is now making major efforts to reverse this image and to build up a flexible capability to supply a broad range of ASICs. National refers to their customer-specific ASICs as proprietary chips. Over the period 1985 to 1986 National introduced around 100 new products of which 75 per cent were proprietary devices - this compares with 20 per cent in 1982 (*Electronics Times*, 18 June 1987, p14). To support this shift into ASICs, National has increased its R&D expenditure from around 12 per cent of sales in 1982 to over 23 per cent of sales in 1986.

National still believes there are strategic advantages in remaining an independent, merchant SC producer. These advantages revolve around business dynamism, technological flexibility and the capacity to build up a range of strategic partnerships with a variety of final IT system manufacturers, rather than suffer the inflexibility of being an operating division of a large systems company.

One of the key elements of National's ASIC strategy and other US suppliers such as TI, Intel and AMD, is to introduce highly flexible, automated production systems which are capable of responding rapidly to changing market requirements. One aspect of this transition is the attempt to move away from the 'standard product scenario', characterised by large, inflexible, standard product lines, heavy (often under-used) fixed assets, high inventories, lack of design flexibility and ever-increasing capital requirements. Instead the larger US firms are moving towards smaller product lines, low inventories, design flexibility and as far as possible, automated fabrication lines.

As part of this strategy, over the period 1987 to 1992 National is planning to install relatively small scale, modular, automated wafer fabrication lines to meet the demand for ASIC products. Improvements carried out during 1987 include reducing the wafer fabrication cycle time of existing lines by 30 per cent, with a target of a further 30 per cent reduction by the end of 1987 (*Electronics Weekly*, 15 Apr 1987, p17). The modular approach is intended to allow the various product divisions to share the same basic, digital, wafer fabrication facilities, which can then be applied to various types of product designs including high speed circuits, mixed bipolar and CMOS products (bicmos), linear devices and many other forms of ASICs. Through this strategy National aims to meet the demand for ASIC products and to be in a position to supply highly integrated VLSI circuits based on the most advanced fabrication technology available. Overall, this new production philosophy can be described as a change of emphasis from economies of scale to economies of scope.

A further element of National's strategy is diversification into systems production. National reorganised into two core businesses, Semiconductors and Systems, in 1986. In the final quarter of 1986 the Systems division sales outstripped the SC division's. National hopes to gain the advantages of stability through vertical integration of in-house SC operations and in-house, IT systems divisions. At the same time the company is attempting to retain the dynamism and flexibility of remaining a merchant SC producer.

Other US firms have adopted similar offensive competitive strategies to respond to Japanese competition and new technological opportunities. Intel has installed a new ASIC design centre in the UK in Swindon to meet the demand for full custom circuits, gate arrays, programmable logic and standard cell devices.[8] To gain access to leading-edge fabrication technology Intel has linked the new UK design centre to its 1.5 micron manufacturing capability in Santa Clara in the US (*Electronics Weekly*, 18 Mar 1987, p6). Other new US start-up companies also see the European market as a major opportunity in ASICs. Sierra SC of California, for instance, is building a custom chip design centre in Holland with subsidiaries in the UK, Germany and Italy (*Electronics Weekly*, 28 Jan 1987, p3).

US IT systems companies, also facing stiff competition from Japanese and Far Eastern IT producers, are playing an important part in supporting domestic SC producers. The objective of systems companies is to ensure rapid access to leading-edge VLSI technology. US system corporations have looked towards acquisition and more recently, strategic alliances with SC producers to sustain their market positions. During the late 1970s several large US system companies acquired Silicon Valley SC corporations. Gould purchased AMI, Schlumberger acquired Fairchild and United Technology bought Mostek (*Electronics Weekly*, 14 Jan 1987).

More recently and possibly in view of the lack of success of some of these takeovers, direct acquisition has given way to strategic alliances between IT systems companies and VLSI technology producers. IBM has formed a strategic partnership with Intel to gain access to Intel's advanced chip capabilities. National Semiconductor has aligned vertically with Xerox Corporation, General Motors and others, while AMD has linked up with Sony to supply consumer integrated circuits. The advantage of these alliances is that the system companies avoid the difficult process of integrating and managing a major new business operation, while the SC supplier receives support from the system company yet retains operational independence.

3.2 Defensive strategies: legal, institutional and governmental reponses

In addition to 'conventional' competitive strategies based on technological investment and diversification, new forms of competition appear to be emerging in the US centred around legal protection of property rights, and legal defence against unfair competition. The use of legal mechanisms as a major competitive weapon in the IT industry began with IBM's successful lawsuit against Hitachi of Japan. IBM's success against Hitachi in patent infringement may have set a new precedent in the IT industry, introducing legal action and counteraction as a powerful new form of corporate industrial strategy.

In the SC industry US manufacturers have 'informed' Japanese chip producers that they will legally defend any infringement on patent copyrights, and take legal action against unfair trading practices. TI recently began legal action against eight Japanese companies as well as Samsung of Korea, for patent infringements, breaking a long tradition of fairly liberal cross-licensing and technology swapping.[9] As a result of this lawsuit TI succeeded in reaching a major settlement out of court. Toshiba, Sharp, Fujitsu, Oki, Mitsubishi and Matsushita will make 'significant fixed royalty payments' (*Financial Times*, 18 Feb 1987, p5) for every DRAM chip sold by the Japanese corporations. While the exact magnitude of the settlement is unknown, in the first quarter of 1987 TI was expected to announce a pre-tax gain of $108 million as a direct result of these settlements (this compares with a net loss of $23.4 million for the first quarter of 1986).

The importance of various kinds of intellectual property rights in the many areas of IT, including software, informatics and SC technology, suggests that these incidents are not isolated. Increasingly, national and international law will intervene as a significant weapon in the competitive process.

In conjunction with the legal activities of the SC corporations, one of the most significant developments in the US in this area is the growth and influence of pressure groups and associations of SC firms whose main function is to deliver US government support to the indigenous SC industry. The SIA (Semiconductor Industry Association), for instance, was formed for the purpose of organising and coordinating an industrial, government-backed, response to what for several years was considered unfair Japanese competition:

Japan has used the mechanics of industry and market targeting with a liberal interpretation and in some instances, the violation of the rules of the General Agreement on Tariffs and Trade, to overwhelm our markets. The process of market designation, the closing of Japanese domestic markets to imports, the marshalling of resources by cartelisation and subsidy of industry and the cooperative support of the attack on US markets, with the joint efforts of trading companies, financial institutions and product companies, is generally recognised as the framework for their success. We have seen many variations on this formula in the process of losing major fractions — and sometimes control of — our markets for automotives, steel, machine tools and consumer electronics. Our alarm today is related to their desgnation of semiconductors, computers and telecommunications which strikes at the core of our industrial capacity of the future. We have no reason to believe that the practices of the past, together with techniques not yet called upon, will not be successful in overwhelming these markets and crippling our economy if the US does not mount an effective response. (Presentation to the US Department of Commerce, International Trade Administration, April, 1983, p70.)

This, by no means exceptional, US view of Japanese competitive strategy, is partly responsible for US institutional counter-actions in SC technology.

The SIA, as well as coordinating the US response over dumping allegations against Japan, has produced detailed bilateral trade and price agreements with Japan, backed by the US's International Trade Commission. Through the SIA, US government pressure has achieved, in principle at least, Japanese government agreement to open up the large internal Japanese market to US competitors.

While the outcome of such bilateral agreements and collusive US/Japanese trade practices is uncertain, what is clear from recent events is that the free trade principles of the US are increasingly being suspended under the weight of successful Japanese competition, and that the boundaries of international competition are being overtly shaped by legal and institutional mechanisms.

Probably the most significant US institutional response to Japanese competition lies in the area of industrial strategy. The SIA, backed by the leading US chip producers, has begun to coordinate a very large scale, collaborative, research programme in advanced SC technology. Under this latest initiative 'the Semiconductor Manufacturing Technology Project' (Sematech), the US government will be asked to subsidise SC firms in establishing a jointly owned manufacturing facility for volume production of ultra large scale integrated circuits (ULSI) such as the 16 Megabit DRAM (*Financial Times*, 24 Oct 1986)[10]. Texas Instruments, Intel, National, Motorola, Hewlett Packard and Digital Equipment Corporation have given their full support to the project. IBM has publicly expressed its willingness to share its own 4 Megabit DRAM technology with Sematech in order to assist the US SC industry (*Electronics Weekly*, 4 Mar 1987, p40).

Industry is likely to request that half of the finance for the proposed project is provided by government, probably from the Department of Defense. At the time of writing most observers placed the total cost of Sematech at around $1 billion, although some have reported a figure as large as $2 billion (*Electronics Weekly*, 11 Mar 1987, p2) for the five year operation. Given the strategic role of advanced SCs in the military and industrial spheres, and the support from both the SC industry and the American computer industry, the US government is highly likely to agree to support the project.

These types of administrative government interventions are not entirely new in the US SC industry. Under the Department of Defense the government has already funded major defence initiatives in SC, most notably the $1 billion VHSIC (very high speed integrated circuit) programme. Under VHSIC the Pentagon funded US chip producers to support projects for military requirements. Corporate associations have also emerged to support R&D, in particular the MCC (the Microelectronics and Computer Corporation) and the SRC (the Semiconductor Research Co-operative). Under these associations joint R&D is funded both in industry and academia and agreements are reached on the sharing of research results.

Nevertheless, there can be little doubt that the scope and role of institutions backed by the US government is increasing. From pre-competitive research collaboration, industrial cooperation in development and manufacture is now being seriously proposed. Trade agreements with Japan have been reached and large subsidies for commercially oriented product lines are likely to be granted. Where previously government support has been justified on defence grounds, the new project, Sematech, is explicitly commercial; aimed at recapturing components sales for the computer and consumer end markets.

Curiously, these recent US initiatives of collaboration and subsidy resemble the aims and methods of European programmes such as ESPRIT, Eureka and the UK Alvey programme (see Guy, Chapter 12 and Sharp, Chapter 13). The rationalisation of research, the acceptance of the principle of government subsidy, the shift towards collaboration as a legitimate means of corporate competition — are all factors underpinning the UK and European IT initiatives. From a tradition of free market competition and laissez-faire, the US SC industry appears to be moving into an era of government subsidised industrial development, industrial collaboration and trade agreements. These new policy innovations may well prove to be the first in a series of attempts to move government support out of the research/military sphere, directly into the commercial arena of production and competition in the US.

3.3 Are US strategies sufficient?

The main question to be asked is whether US corporate responses adequately address the factors which underpin Japanese corporate success. If not, then US efforts will not change the underlying trend of increasing Japanese dominance in the SC industry. US corporations are pinning their hopes on acquisition of advanced manufacturing and design technology, strategic partnerships with IT producers and increased in-house diversification into IT products. On the defensive side, legal protection of property rights and trade restrictions have been introduced alongside subsidised, inter-corporate collaboration in R&D and possibly manufacture.

Although it is impossible to predict the outcome of these measures for several reasons, the US response may prove inadequate. First, the underlying financial/industrial structure of the US corporations has not changed. Japanese corporations still maintain the advantage of close links with the financial sector and a far greater degree of insulation from short-term cyclical recessions in the industry. In addition, the efforts towards integration and diversification by US firms fall far short of the current SC/IT integration achieved by Japanese firms. This factor too may allow Japanese firms to sustain heavy losses in SC production during recession, yet to maintain long-term investment in R&D and production capacity (*see* Section 4). Also as Teece (1986) points out, when *core* technologies become widely available to imitators, as they are in the SC industry, copyright and defensive protection cannot hope to sustain competitive advantage. At this stage of 'paradigmatic development' other complementary and business assets become of greater importance. It is in these areas, particularly finance, where the Japanese firms retain advantage.

As to inter-firm collaboration, this may well help to rationalise duplicated R&D efforts across US firms. Subsidies from the US government may also compensate to some extent for the financial disadvantages of the US firms. However, as yet, collaboration and subsidy are unproven mechanisms and may well 'backfire' as competitive weapons. Possible undesirable effects include: the subsidisation of inefficient practices as an alternative to genuine and necessary industrial restructuring; the undue influence of government (through the Department of Defense) on firms' strategic direction and in particular a possible drift toward protected military markets away from the competitive commercial arena. Subsidy, collaboration and extracorporate direction may have the effect of dampening the entrepreneurial, independent, market orientation of the US merchant SC producers, upon which they came to dominate the world SC industry and upon which they hope now to compete with the Japanese. Within three to four years the answers to many of these questions will have emerged.

4 Europe's resurgence in semiconductors

The extremely weak position of Europe in semiconductor technology is well documented and need not be dealt with in detail here.[11] In the list of top international SC manufacturers Philips, the Dutch consumer goods manufacturer, is the only European company (*see* Table 5.2). With an SC output of around $850 million in 1985, Philips was in tenth position. Roughly two-thirds of Philips SC output is from its US subsidiary, Signetics (*Financial Times*, 30 June 1986).

Table 5.5 provides estimated SC revenues for the leading 25 SC suppliers producing in Europe. Among the indigenous European producers Philips/Signetics is in first position, Siemens (West Germany) stands at number four, Thomson (France) at number five, and SGS (Italy) at number six. The only UK firms in the league are Plessey (17th) and Ferranti (19th). Throughout the past decade US manufacturers have supplied the bulk of Europe's SC requirements. More recently, Japanese corporations have been making headway into the European market and NEC, Hitachi and Toshiba were ranked 10, 13 and 14 respectively in 1986.

Over the period 1980 to 1984 Europe's share of the world market in SCs fell from 15.2 per cent to 11 per cent.[12] Part of the reason for Europe's traditional weakness in the SC industry is the vigorous technological and marketing lead displayed by US and, more recently, Japanese firms. In contrast, European companies' product and technology strategies have been relatively conservative, and to a large extent inward-looking and nationalistic. Most European manufacturers have remained outside the

Table 5.5. Leading semiconductor suppliers in Europe: estimated 1986 revenues in Europe ($m)

Company	Integrated circuits	Discrete	Opto-electronics	Total
Philips-Signetics	549	228	25	802
(Signetics	109	0	0	109)
Texas Instruments	448	27	13	488
Motorola	275	146	4	425
Siemens*	192	125	40	357
Thomson**	198	101	3	302
SGS Semiconductors	192	52	0	244
National Semiconductor	233	2	1	236
ITT	115	100	0	215
Intel	214	0	0	214
NEC	193	4	1	198
AMD	172	0	0	172
Telefunken Electronic	52	68	44	164
Hitachi	151	6	3	160
Toshiba	82	20	8	110
Fairchild	95	7	0	102
RCA	64	15	6	85
Plessey	67	0	11	78
Fujitsu	70	0	0	70
Ferranti	53	13	0	66
Analog Devices	65	0	0	65
Monolithic Memories	48	0	0	48
Hewlett-Packard	0	5	41	46
Semikron	0	43	0	43
Matra-Harris	40	0	0	40
Harris	38	0	0	38

* Includes Litronix (US) ** Includes Mostek (US)

Source: Dataquest (cited in *Financial Times*, 23 Feb 1987, p30)

mainstream SC market concentrating on low volume, high return, often domestic, niche markets. Also, a fairly large proportion of Europe's SC production is in mature, discrete, components rather than integrated circuits (*Financial Times*, 30 Mar 1986).

Despite Europe's historically poor performance in SCs, European firms are currently staging a major coordinated effort to enter the international SC industry. The present efforts deserve serious consideration for at least three main reasons. First, market growth in Europe is forecast to continue at an even faster rate than the world Compound Average Growth Rate (CAGR) of more than 18 per cent per annum, and total market size will rise from the present level of roughly $5.6 billion (1986) to $25 billion in 1996 (Dataquest, quoted in *Electronics Times*, 18 Sept 1986, p60). The European market is, therefore, very large and growing rapidly.

Second, (paradoxically) as a direct consequence of their lack of competitive presence in integrated circuit production, European chip producers have been insulated from the worst effects of the recent SC recession. Sales by European producers have fallen only marginally while, for example, over the 1984 to 1985 period US and Japanese sales fell by 23 per cent and 5 per cent, respectively (*Financial Times*, 30 June 1986). As a result, and in contrast to US companies, European SC manufacturers have not been forced into investment cutbacks and redundancy programmes as a result of the recession.

Third, and most importantly, several European companies with government support are forcefully attempting to regain lost ground in IT through entry into leading-edge SCs. Recognition of the key role of SC technology in the IT business, and new market opportunities in ASIC technology, have led to a major new European response to US and Japanese competition. A range of pan-European government initiatives such as ESPRIT 1 and 2, Eureka, RACE and FRAMEWORK, illustrate the determination of European governments to strengthen indigenous capabilities across the spectrum of IT industries. SC technology, coupled with advanced software design capabilities, is seen as the route to advanced, competitive IT systems. At the national level countries such as France, Italy, Spain, West Germany and the Netherlands are channelling resources directly to their leading electronics manufacturers.

In the very recent period, European firms have begun to form strategic partnerships with other European companies and have begun to pursue aggressive investment and marketing strategies to capture not only European but also wider international markets. Some examples of these activities serve to demonstrate the new aggressive investment behaviour of the leading SC companies in Europe.

One much publicised strategic partnership is the Siemens/Philips 'megaproject'. Siemens and Philips are together committed to an expenditure of $430 million on submicron (leading edge) SC technology. Each company is also expected to invest a further $500 million by 1989 (*Business Week*, June 1986, p22). The Dutch and West German Governments are financing approximately one-third of the total development cost. The project is a four year joint R&D venture in memory chip technology. The aim of the project is to acquire the production capability needed to produce submicron memory technology. Once world class fabrication facilities are acquired the process capabilities can then be used to manufacture ASICs for in-house IT systems and the merchant market.

The rationale for sharing the development costs and risk in this manner is that Philips will gain access to advanced ASICs for consumer electronics, while Siemens will concentrate on ASICs for telecommunications, automobiles and factory automation systems. This particular project is an example of a complementary strategic partnership where the two corporations are not engaged in direct competition in most of their final product ranges. In addition, the venture helps to overcome the problem of the segmented, nationalistic European market.

Thomson, the state-owned French electronics group has recently invested $71 million to acquire SC production capacity from Mostek, the US chip company. (Mostek was reported to be losing $1 million per day in its SC activities, *Financial Times*, 17 Dec 1986). By acquiring Mostek's advanced SRAM process technology and applying this to ASICs for in-house equipment production, Thomson intends to maintain and improve its international position in advanced military systems.

The leading Italian SC producer, SGS, has also undergone 'revitalisation' under a radically new management recruited from the US chip maker Motorola. During the early 1980s SGS was losing in the region of $2.3 million per month on SC operations. By 1984, as a result of SGS's new organisation, sales had expanded considerably and for the first time in more than a decade the firm was producing a profit.[13] SGS recently began semiconductor production in Singapore producing specialist chips for high volume automotive applications.

In 1986 SGS and Thomson jointly applied to the Eureka programme for £150 million funding to back a new investment project in 4 Megabit and 16 Megabit EPROMs (erasable programmable read only memories) (*Electronic Times*, 26 Mar 1987, *Financial Times*, 17 Dec 1986). In January 1987 the new project 'Megaproject 2' was approved by the Eureka Commission. The partnership is aiming to achieve an 0.8 micron process to produce 4 Megabit EPROMs and to progress to 0.5 microns to run 16 Megabit EPROMs (*Electronics Weekly*, 14 Jan 1987, p16). These levels of technology are equivalent to the leading-edge Japanese and US technologies. Each company is expected to invest $200 million in the project. One of the stated aims of the venture is to produce design intensive ASICs, as well as mainstream, volume SC components.

The speculation that more formal shareholding links would develop between the SGS and Thomson has also recently been confirmed. In April 1987 the two corporations formally launched a jointly-owned, pan European, microchip company which will place them second only to Philips in the European SC league with sales of around $800 million (*Guardian*, 30 Apr 1987, p19) and a world market share in SCs of roughly 3.2 per cent (*Electronics Weekly*, 25 Mar 1987). In important technology areas such as EPROMs, CMOS gate arrays, programmable logic devices and other ASIC technologies, the merger places the two companies in a prominent international marketing position. The headquarters of the new company is to be set up in Holland adding a further cross-European dimension to the enterprise and helping to overcome the segmentation of the European market.

If these ventures are successful Europe's leading SC companies will have established an indigenous leading-edge capacity across the broad range of mainstream SC technologies — memories, microprocessors and logic circuits. The strategic partnerships between the major corporations will help to overcome the national segmentation of the European market and provide a sufficiently large home base from which to launch internationally marketable components and systems.[14] With the world class fabrication capabilities in place, European companies will then be in a position to retain a competitive edge in advanced ASIC technologies and the IT systems which increasingly depend upon them.

4.1 New European start-ups

With the new ASIC 'trajectory' firmly established,[15] the traditional manufacturing-intensive corporations have come to face increasing competition from new, start-up companies exploiting the rapidly growing

Table 5.6. Examples of new European start-ups in ASIC technologies

Firm name	Start date	Technology activities*	Location	Investment capital	Strategic linkages
European Silicon Structures (ES2)	1985	ASICs, E-beam other design tools	Germany, France, UK	>$60m	Philips, Brit. Aerospace Olivetti, Saab–Scania (purchase of Lattice Logic)
Mietec	1983	Standard cells, Bomos, CMOS and NMOS processes	Belgium	>$40m	Univ. Leuven ITT
Integrated Power Semiconductors (IPS)	circa 1984	Power integrated circuits	Scotland	>$40m	not available
Advanced Silicon Corporation (ASIC)	circa 1984	Broad range of ASICs, design tools	Holland	—	Ricoh (Japan) AMI (Austria)
Lassaray	1985	E-beam, design tools, ASICs	Switzerland	Substantial**	Swiss financial

* For simple explanations of these technologies, *see* Hobday (1987) ** Heavy financial backing reported from Swiss financial sector
Sources: Electronics Weekly, 25 Feb 1987, 4 Jan 1987, 7 Jan 1987
Electronics Times, 30 Apr 1987
Electronics and Power, Nov/Dec 1985

design-intensive segment of the SC market. Several new small and medium-sized European firms have recognised these new technological opportunities and have rapidly set up manufacturing and design facilities to serve, mainly, the European market. Table 5.6 provides a listing of some of the main new entrants.

The most publicised new venture is ES2 (European Silicon Structures). ES2, the largest international SC start-up company in 1985, is a pan-European corporation with headquarters in Munich, production capacity in France and R&D facilities in the UK. The company has received backing from the European technology initiative, Eureka, as well as Philips, Olivetti, British Aerospace and Saab-Scania of Sweden. Initial venture capital for ES2 is reported to exceed $60 million.

The technology strategy of ES2 is to exploit new silicon design tools, such as electron-beam equipment to provide users with fast turnaround, inexpensive and highly integrated ASIC products. In addition the company will allow IT systems companies to try out new innovations with less investment in time and finance. In order to strengthen its ability to develop sophisticated design tools, ES2 in April 1987 purchased Lattice Logic, a medium-sized UK software company which specialised in design tools.

In its marketing strategy ES2 is attempting to overcome the segmentation of the European SC market by setting up a genuine pan-European corporation, with financial and other links with several major European corporate backers. By these means the company hopes to capture the necessary economies of scale to sustain long-term growth in the industry.

Lassaray, a new Swiss corporation was launched in 1985 with substantial backing from Swiss financiers. Like ES2, Lassaray is exploiting the developments in ASIC technology to provide IT equipment manufacturers with the capability of designing and producing semi-custom gate arrays in-house, at low cost with fast turnaround. Lassaray is also a pan-European operation with designer centres in several European locations.

In general, the new start-up companies are responding to the need for customer-specific components in small quantities and also ASIC training facilities (CAD, Computer Aided Engineering (CAE), etc) for system designers in IT systems companies across Europe. By linking closely with system designers these design-intensive firms promise to help alleviate the widespread shortage of integrated circuit designers, by transferring the ability to design chips to IT systems engineers. In addition to ES2 and Lassaray, Mietec of Belgium and Scotland's Integrated Power Semiconductors, have both raised more than $40 million in start-up venture capital in the recent period. In 1987 Mietec opened a customer design centre in Brussels and claimed to have mastered all the technologies of BIMOS (combined bipolar and MOS devices), CMOS and NMOS. Mietec's sales were around $20 million in 1986. A new Dutch SC start-up, Advanced Silicon Corporation is aiming to gain a 30 per cent share of the European custom chip market by 1992. This company, like many new Californian start-ups, will design and test ASICs locally, and have the circuits manufactured by outside SC suppliers under licence (in this case Ricoh of Japan and AMI of Austria).

The growth of the design-intensive ASIC market is also providing opportunities for software companies to enter the silicon design market. Logica, the UK software and systems firm launched a new chip design service for IT system firms involved in data communications and medical electronics in 1987 (*Electronics Weekly*, 28 Jan 1987, p1). Like the new start-up companies, Logica is exploiting the technological progress in CAD and CAE to provide design services relatively independent of the SC supplier and chip user.

Systems companies are also taking advantage of the growth in ASIC technology. Plessey Semiconductor of the UK, for example, is aiming to more than quadruple current sales to reach $450 million by 1991 (*Guardian*, 30 Apr 1987 p11) making Plessey a major international SC supplier. Plessey has set up a new SC plant at Roborough in Plymouth with an investment of around $50 million (*Guardian*, 1 May 1987 p29). Plessey's SC strategy is to supply a wide range of high profit, relatively small niche markets, mostly in the area of ASICs. By establishing itself as a major, broad based, ASIC supplier, and by forming strategic technological alliances in the UK and abroad, Plessey intends to make enough revenue and profit to be able to sustain the successive investments required in advanced fabrication technology. In 1987 Plessey acquired Ferranti, another major UK specialist component supplier, adding further weight to its ambitions.

4.2 The 'professionalisation' of European management

It is important to stress that these major European initiatives in the SC industry are not simply a 'response' to technological and market opportunity. Their initiation, and their probability of success, depend crucially on the marketing and technological capabilities embodied in the management teams leading these firms. In this respect it is interesting to note that many of the leading directors and senior managers of these activities were trained within US multinational corporations during their domination of the European market in the 1960s and 1970s.

The president of Thomson's SC components group, Jacques Noels, is a former Texas Instruments executive. Other prominent TI managers such as Carlo Zanni have also joined the Thomson management (*Business Week*, June 1986, p22). The Italian SC manufacturer, SGS, has also recruited US trained executives with considerable experience in the international SC industry. The new president, Pistorio, formerly of Motorola, is considered more or less personally responsible for the new fortunes of the company. In the case of ES2 the company's joint founder and president Rob Wilmot is also a former Texas Instruments manager. After leaving TI (UK) as managing director, Wilmot pioneered the successful restructuring of ICL, the ailing UK computer company, and then moved on to begin ES2. Within ES2 key management positions are now held by ex-TI employees such as Rod Attwooll, the company's UK managing director.

Plessey's 'target oriented' marketing approach is again driven by a new management team, recruited from the US corporation Motorola. The overall style and aggressiveness adopted by Plessey is viewed by the local electronics press as highly 'unusual' for a UK SC company — and more in keeping with the successful US start-up companies such as Intel (*Electronics Weekly*, 11 Mar 1987). If Plessey's corporate objectives are met, and the company is able to build up supply links with system producers and gain access to world-class fabrication technology, then for the first time the UK will be provided with a strong broad-based, world class SC component supplier.

4.3 Technological discontinuity and European market opportunity

The above examples of new start-ups and strategic partnerships suggest how technological discontinuity and change can provide market opportunities for firms, despite a lack of cumulative know-how, long-term experience and established technological strength. Then, given the wide availability of *core* SC technology rather than technological capacity, it is the 'other' complementary skills and assets which are brought to bear on the enterprise which will ultimately determine market success or failure. In Europe, one is witnessing an unprecedented entry attempt into the mainstream SC business, based on management and marketing abilities, access to investment capital, strategic partnerships between European firms (and between European and non-European firms).

The major challenge to Europe's attempt to revitalise its IT industry through the acquisition of advanced SC technology, lies in the fierce competition from both Japanese and US corporations who increasingly see Europe as the next 'battleground' in their struggle for domination of the world SC business. At present, however, Europe appears to be well placed to capture large shares of the rapidly growing European markets and to stage a major entry into the international SC business. Within Europe, European SC firms have a 'natural' competitive advantage over their Japanese and US competitors by virtue of the geographical and cultural proximity to their IT customers. In several of the cases described above, the SC producer is integrated into the IT system company, and this may well provide a base of demand to sustain large continuing investments in SC fabrication technology, and to insulate the SC divisions, to some extent, from the violent cyclical downswings and upswings in the industry. In this sense the large firms in Europe resemble their Japanese counterpart, rather than the US merchant SC producers.

The emergence of a number of small to medium-sized firms in the design-intensive segment of the market is also extremely important for Europe's growing base of independent technological capacity in the SC industry. Sustained, high rates of growth in this market segment suggest that the new design-intensive ASIC market will continue to provide market opportunities for relatively small-scale entrants for some time to come. These firms act not only to provide design expertise in an industry bedevilled by skill shortages, but may also act to support the large scale IT system corporations in their efforts to gain competitive advantage in world markets by introducing ever more sophisticated circuit designs for new systems.

For the relatively small European start-ups the major challenge in the medium-term is how to mature into larger volume ASIC producers. For this to occur it will probably be crucial for them to gain secure access to volume SC fabrication technology. An arms length dependence on US and Japanese SC manufacturers may well prove to be an insecure and erratic source of leading-edge technology, especially in periods of rapid market growth when capacity is limited. In fact, a *dynamic* indigenous European, leading-edge fabrication technology may well prove to be *the* critical factor in Europe's IT market fortunes over the next five to ten years. If the present attempts to acquire world class fabrication facilities prove to be a static one-off venture, then the resulting market inroads may well prove to be short lived given the speed of advance of the US and Japanese technology frontier. If, however, the large European companies internalise a dynamic technological capacity in this area, then they will be well positioned to exploit their 'natural' competitive advantages over US and Japanese corporations and reap the benefits of SC/IT business integration. In addition, the installation of a dynamic European volume SC base may well provide a more secure access to fabrication technology to enable the emerging start-up companies, to realise their ambitions of becoming major international merchant SC producers.

5 Japanese counter-strategies

Both in response to government backed actions of the major US corporations and in line with long-term industrial strategy, Japanese firms have recently embarked on a series of measures involving various forms of direct overseas investment, and strategic joint ventures. Rather than retrenching in the face of the recent recession and the heavy operating losses sustained over the 1985/86 period, Japanese companies have followed their traditional behaviour of vigorous technological and industrial investment through the downswing of the SC industry cycle.

5.1 Direct foreign investment

One set of measures taken by Japanese SC companies is to increase manufacturing and technological activities outside Japan. (As Baba shows in Chapter 3, this is common in other sectors of Japanese industry.) Virtually all major corporations including NEC, Toshiba, Fujitsu, Hitachi, Mitsubishi, Matsushita and Oki, have begun to step up their direct foreign investment in the US, and Europe, and to some extent the Pacific Basin.[16] Some recent examples help illustrate the scale and nature of Japanese direct foreign investment.

Toshiba has recently invested $33 million in 1 Megabit memory production in West Germany and currently has full scale production capability in 1 Megabit memory chips (1.8 million units per annum). With this facility Toshiba becomes the first producer in Europe of the 1 Megabit chip, which is currently the most advanced memory technology in production and is expected to form the basis of the next generation of many IT products and systems. Toshiba's aim is to improve its market position in Europe roughly to that of its international standing in terms of SC revenues (ie a move from fourteenth to third position, Table 5.5). Despite the broad final product base of the corporation, and the recent SC recession, Toshiba has continued to invest around one-half of its capital investments, and one-third of total R&D expenditures, in SC technology.

A second component of Toshiba's international strategy is substantially to increase its share of the European and US ASIC market. The company has already estabished design centres in the US, Sweden, West Germany and the UK and is shortly to set up a further centre in Braunschweig (West Germany) close to its new SC facility. Local design facilities and close geographical proximity to buyers are recognised as crucial factors in the competition for ASICs. The present Toshiba ASIC strategy focusses on gate array and standard cell technologies.

On the heels of Toshiba, NEC is set to be the next Japanese corporation to establish a major SC production plant in Europe. NEC also plans to locate gate array manufacturing facilities in the US. In 1987 NEC began volume production of 1 Megabit memory chips and ASIC components in Livingstone in Scotland. This particular facility involved an investment of £80 million and will employ a workforce of 550. The company is to locate its ASIC design facilities in Milton Keynes in the UK and has offered to make available the latest ASIC technology to UK users of custom chips (*Computer Weekly*, 30 Oct 1986, p14). NEC currently have seven ASIC design centres in the US, nine in Europe, two in Asia and 20 in Japan. Despite the recession in SCs NEC has also decided to expand its capacity to produce memory components in the US, from the present level of two million 256K RAMS, to 3.5 million units (*Electronics Times*, 6 Nov 1986).

The attempted purchase of the large US SC corporation, Fairchild, by Fujitsu in 1986 also illustrates the Japanese commitment to expanding production facilities in Europe and the US. By acquiring Fairchild, Fujitsu would have approximately doubled its SC revenues from $500 million to over $1 billion. Fujitsu had planned to convert Fairchild's US and European facilities into a wholly owned Fujitsu subsidiary in control of Fairchild's extensive distribution network (*Electronics Times*, 30 Oct 1986). As an alternative strategy, Fujitsu is now planning to build its own manufacturing facilities in the US. In October 1988, a wafer fabrication facility was to be opened in Oregon. In Europe, Fujitsu have established one ASIC design centre in Manchester and further centres are being planned.

Other new investments and acquisitions are currently taking place. Mitsubishi, for example, has taken over a major US supplier of silicon wafers, Siltec of Menlo Park, in a venture which involved roughly $29.5 million. By acquiring Siltec, Mitsubishi gain access to a large US based producer of the raw materials of microelectronic components, as well as the capital goods needed to manufacture the wafers. Mitsubishi has not yet achieved substantial market share in the US and Europe in ASICs. To remedy this, the company is training foreign engineers in Japan as a prelude to opening design facilities in the US, West Germany, the UK and Taiwan, in 1988.

Most large Japanese companies are also expanding investment in the Far East. NEC and Matsushita are both planning to build up memory capacity in their Singapore subsidiaries, while Oki Electric is assembling VLSI circuits in Taiwan in an effort further to reduce final SC prices. This is partly as a result of the rapid appreciation of the yen over the 1985 to 1987 period, but according to the companies, the more important reason is the longer-term globalisation strategies of the corporations, as well as the need to respond to customer requirements in ASIC technologies.

5.2 Japanese strategic partnerships in SC technology

Several Japanese IT corporations are following a strategy of forming technological joint ventures with US, European and other Japanese corporations. The reasons for these partnerships in SCs and most other areas of IT, appear to include the Japanese determination to: gain a competitive lead in the next generations of SC and computing technologies, reduce dependence on US licensing agreements for advanced information technology; and to gain more direct access to foreign markets through marketing and technological joint ventures. Strategic SC partnerships tend to occur within Japan at the level of R&D development and between Japanese and foreign companies at the levels of technology transfer, production and marketing.

Within Japan, Hitachi and Fujitsu have agreed to develop, together, the next generation of microprocessor chips - the 32-bit microprocessor unit (MPU). To date, Japan has had relatively little success in capturing large shares of the microprocessor market internationally. The 32-bit MPU is expected to play a leading role in the computer developments in the late 1980s and 1990s, but in spite of strenuous efforts Hitachi has been unable to license Motorola's recently developed 32 bit MPUs. (Previously Hitachi have second-sourced Motorola's earlier families of MPU designs).[17]

Hitachi have conducted an in-house development programme in 32-bit MPU technology for roughly two years, and recently decided to complement this activity with the Fujitsu joint venture. This project is conducted in collaboration with the Tron project on MPU architecture design at Tokyo University. In the longer term, the Tron project (also involving NEC, Mitsubishi Electric and Matsushita) hopes to provide Japan with an operating system specifically designed for the needs of Japanese typescripts and the more advanced MPU process capabilities of the 1990s. If successful, this strategy will provide autonomous technological capabilities in advanced MPUs for Japan, in order to supply the next generations of computers.

In parallel with Hitachi and Fujitsu's efforts to develop the 32-bit MPU, Toshiba have formed a major new joint venture with Motorola to gain access to 32-bit MPU technology. This represents a major coup in Toshiba's competition with Hitachi, the other Japanese licensee of Motorola's previous generations of MPUs. Toshiba aims to begin production in May 1988 with geometries of between 0.8 micron and 1.2 micron. In the new 50/50 jointly owned subsidiary, located in Japan, Toshiba will produce MPUs and in return, Toshiba will supply Motorola with its own advanced DRAM and SRAM technology. Motorola will also gain access to the large Japanese RAM market. It remains to be seen which of the two companies gains most from the endeavour, but the capability to manage strategic partnerships will certainly play an important part in the distribution of rewards.

Toshiba's long-term strategy is probably aimed at the next generation of final IT markets such as engineering work stations, factory automation and high performance personal computers, rather than the MPU market itself. One of the aims of the agreement is to develop ASICs using Motorola MPU cores which will then be used to produce extremely high performance, customised, final goods.

Matsushita, the world's largest consumer goods producer, is also reported to be in discussions with various major US chip manufacturers to try and reach a production sharing agreement in SCs. Strategic partnerships of this kind would help to ease the trade conflict between the US and Japan and at the same time facilitate further rapid growth in overseas markets (*Financial Times*, 25 Feb 1987, p48).

Other partnerships among Japanese and US IT companies include Hitachi-Sperry, RCA-Sharp, Mitsubishi-Chrysler, NTT-TI, LSI Logic-Kawasake, NTT-IBM, GCA-Sumitomo, Mazda-Ford, GMC-Hitachi. Strictly within the SC industry, in addition to the ones described above, recent joint ventures include GE-Toshiba (DRAMs), National-NMB (SC foundry), Sony-AMD (consumer SCs) (*Electronics Weekly*, 21 Jan 1987, p14).

SC joint ventures in Europe include a partnership between Siemens and Toshiba whereby the Japanese company will supply Siemens with 1 and possibly 4 Megabit chip technology. Philips is also rumoured to be conducting a similar joint venture to gain 1 Megabit memory technology from Toshiba. In the growing ASIC technology market Toshiba has forged a joint technology venture with General Electric of the US and Siemens of Germany. The aim of this venture is rapidly to develop Toshiba's capability in standard cell, ASIC, technology.

5.3 Japan's long-term globalisation objectives in SCs

It would be wrong to suggest that these recent strategic partnerships and direct investment activities are totally new phenomena, or primarily a reaction to US and European policy measures. Since the early 1970s the main Japanese IT corporations have gradually built up international links via acquisitions, joint ventures, sales and marketing agreements, R&D arrangements and so on (Gregory 1986). The current strategy, as repeated historically, is to continue to invest during periods of short-run recession. Indeed, despite very heavy losses sustained by the SC operations of Japanese corporations (in the order of $2 billion over the 1985-86 period - *Electronics Weekly*, 4 Mar 1987, p15), Japanese firms have continued with their heavy overseas investment programmes. In contrast, with similar losses, US corporations have retrenched and cut back on technological investments.

While these most recent Japanese ventures are not, therefore, an entirely new phenomenon, they do appear to mark a new, advanced phase in Japan's attempts to dominate the international SC industry, and to capture ever increasing shares of the final IT goods and systems which depend on leading-edge SC technology.

At least four main factors help explain the current globalisation strategies of the Japanese multinationals in SCs. First, in order to achieve larger shares of non-commodity ASIC markets, close geographical proximity between technology suppliers and buyers is required. In the areas of distribution and marketing especially, the commodity product strategies which have served Japanese firms in volume memory products are not appropriate or adequate for ASIC technologies.

A second important factor is the move towards protectionism, particularly in the US. By establishing joint ventures and direct investments, behind tariff barriers, Japanese firms can circumvent government protection to a large extent and meet the demands upon them to reduce their trade surplus in SCs. A third reason is Japanese firms' relatively poor performance in Europe and their desire to expand in this region. Here too, investment within national boundaries helps to overcome possible protectionism and to match their increasing supply capability with the demand for design-intensive ASIC products. A fourth, probably subsidiary reason, is the rapid appreciation of the yen over the 1985 to 1987 period. The dramatic increase in the value of the yen in relation to most other currencies has substantially reduced the initial cost of direct foreign investment abroad.

These explanatory factors, however, should not draw attention away from the overarching rationale for Japanese strategies in SCs. For the integrated Japanese SC/IT corporations successful SC developments are seen primarily as a route to success in the massive IT final product markets, including informatics, computers, office automation equipment, industrial machinery and electronic consumer goods. The recent vulnerability of several major SC and computing companies has provided Japan with an opportunity for large-scale investment, at low cost, in preparation for future assaults on these final IT product and systems markets in the US and Europe. Unless the US and European response to Japan activities is highly effective, the next 'boom' phase of the SC and IT industry cycles will witness a further restructuring of the information industries based upon Japan's current market activities.

6 Conclusions: implications for technology and competitive performance

Although one cannot generalise too much from case study evidence, the SC industry does provide certain insights into the relationship between technology strategy and competitive performance and, in particular, the three assumptions outlined in the introduction. Regarding the first assumption, it was clear from the activities of the SC corporations of Europe,

US and Japan, that an explicit technology strategy was indeed a fundamental element of competitive behaviour and revealed competitive advantage. For example, the possibility of European corporations successfully leapfrogging several generations of SC technology and moving directly to state-of-the art SCs, depends critically upon the ability of the firms to acquire leading-edge SC fabrication technology, through the management of strategic partnerships between European and non-European firms.

However, technology strategy, although an important and necessary element is an insufficient explanation of competitive performance and prospects. Japanese success in SCs was predicated upon the business *integration* of the large corporations. The strategic integration of Japanese SC firms took place at three important levels: first, through their close linkage with financial institutions through the structure of the Japanese corporate groups; second, their close relationship with government policy formation and execution through MITI (Ministry of Trade and Industry); and third, the integration of their SC objectives within the broader corporate aims towards information technology products and systems. These powerful linkages were crucial to Japan's successful targeting of international markets and the ability of the corporations to sustain long-term technology investments and strategies through periods of short-run recession. In contrast, US corporations suffered competitive disadvantage as a consequence of their greater exposure to short-run market recession. The 'lesson' from Japan, at least in this sector, is that technology strategy has to be integrated within a total business, financial and marketing strategy to be translated into competitive advantage.

Following on from this perspective, the second assumption that technological leads provide the basis of firms' competitive advantage also requires qualification. The idea that short-run technological leads may underpin Japanese corporate success is, on the whole, not supported by the evidence presented above.[18] If technology is interpreted in the broadest possible sense (for example, as suggested by Porter, 1985b) as determining product excellence and price, process quality and cost, factory and business organisation etc, then technology leads, almost by definition, will be reflected in competitive performance. But even in this widest possible sense, technological leads, cannot fully explain competitive advantage in the SC industry. With a fairly mature industrial technology such as SCs it is very much the complementary skills, know-how and capabilities, which are brought to bear on the core technology which appear to determine competitive success.[19] With the wide availability of core SC technology, competitive edge is increasingly being determined by business, financial and marketing skills and flexibility, as well as sheer industrial 'muscle'.[20]

Regarding the third proposition, it is certainly reasonable to expect that in some cases technology is cumulative, specific and path dependent at the firm level. This argument, for instance, is borne out by the international telecommunications industry where many of the leading corporations have sustained their competitive positions in spite of the destabilising effects of the rapid diffusion of microelectronic technology during the 1970s and 1980s

(Hobday, 1986a, Chapter 5). Also for firms which have matured along with a technological trajectory, it is reasonable to expect that their future direction will to some degree be determined by their past activities. Again, however, the case of the SC industry suggests that this general picture requires close scrutiny and qualification.

In the case of the development of a new technological direction (or trajectory) within an established paradigm, as exemplified by the emergence of design-intensive ASICs, the technological disruption and discontinuity brought about may be sufficient to allow waves of new entrants. This phenomenon has occurred recently in the European and US SC industries with many new start-up firms entering the market to exploit new technological opportunities in this rapidly growing design-intensive segment of the SC market.

Also, even in the case of a mainstream established technological trajectory such as volume, memory SC production, once the core technology is widely available, then other corporations of sufficient scale and financial resources have the opportunity to leapfrog several generations of technology, to enter the industry and to compete with the established market leaders. As described above, this is the strategy currently being adopted by the prospective European entrants to the mainstream SC industry. Similar leapfrogging strategies have already proved successful for new entrants from Korea and Taiwan in both the mainstream SC industry and in the related field of computing.[21] In the SC industry and in the range of IT-intensive industries based upon SC technology, rapid technological change is constantly occurring and new technological trajectories are constantly emerging. In addition, technological convergence between the final product technologies is progressively breaking down the industrial boundaries between the established industries in sectors such as computing telecommunications, office equipment, informatics, software and SCs. Under these conditions, there exist many entry opportunities for latecomers in the industrialising countries and laggers in the mature industrialised countries.

Notes

1 *See*, for example, Soete (1985) who presents a technological lead view of Japan's progress in SCs, and Pavitt (1986a) who argues that the nature of technological change is generally stable and cumulative.
2 Dataquest, cited in *Electronics Weekly*, 28 Jan 1987, p2.
3 This point is made by Arnold and Guy (1986). Molina (1986) records how the Japanese invested in memory products throughout the 1974-75 recession. In the 1978-79 market upturn the Japanese were in a prime position to supply the market with 16K RAM chips. Over this period they increased their market share from less than 5 per cent, to 40 per cent.
4 The implications of the emergence of Korean and Taiwanese producers of SCs cannot be discussed here; *see* Park (1987) for a thorough examination of Korea's entry as a major supplier of memory SCs.
5 For explanations of these and other technical terms, together with a simple technology map of the semiconductor industry, *see* Hobday (1986a) and (1987).

6 To some, this may be 'wishful thinking' (*see* Section 4).

7 Interviews: TI, Bedford, UK in 1986, TI, Japan in 1987.

8 *See* note 5 above.

9 Johnstone (1986), discusses the legal responses to allegations of patent infringement, and dumping.

10 At the time of writing there was some disagreement within Sematech as to whether the venture should be aimed at high volume manufacturing, or confined to R&D and pilot line production.

11 *See* Mackenzie (1985) for a comprehensive summary of Europe's historically weak position in SCs in terms of production, international trade, and deteriorating balance of payments performance.

12 Dataquest figures quoted in *Business Week*, 30 June 1986, p22.

13 SGS's 1984 profit was $10m against sales of $335m (*Business Week*, 30 June 1986, p24).

14 An important question remains as to whether Europe's 'second tier' SC producers can contribute to the strengthening of Europe's technological base. These include Matra-Harris of France, Asea and Rifa of Sweden, Micronas of Finland and in the UK, Inmos, STC, and Marconi. One company, Matra-Harris, is buying in a 1.2 micron and 0.8 micron CMOS process from Cyress SC of the US (at a cost of $1.3 million and $3 million respectively) and is aiming to build up sales in the SRAM market, (*Electronics Weekly*, 14 Jan 1987, pp16-17).

15 For technical explanations and details of market growth in ASIC technologies, *see* Hobday (1987).

16 Unless otherwise stated, information for this section was obtained during a series of interviews with the major Japanese SC suppliers during October 1987.

17 For detailed discussion *see Electronics*, 16 Oct 1986, and *Electronics Times*, 6 Nov 1986.

18 This is suggested, for example, by Soete (1985, p26).

19 This is the view put forward by Teece (1986) where he argues that in a paradigmatic (ie mature) technological phase, with the core technology being generally widely available, then technological leads cannot for long sustain competitive advantage, and 'complementary assets' become the determining factor in competitive performance.

20 By 'muscle' we mean scale of operation, access to large financial resources, engineering capacity, control over distribution, large customer base, and access to leading-edge technology.

21 For an account of the rise of the Korean SC industry *see* Park (1987), and for the progress of the Korean computer industry *see* Kim and Lee (1987).

Chapter 6

Strategic options for new telecommunications services[1]

Graham Thomas and Ian Miles

1 Introduction: new interactive telecommunications services

By new interactive services (NIS) we refer to services that are computer-mediated, that at present usually rely on text or simple graphics to convey information, and that permit users to have an influence on data delivered through a telecommunications system.

We distinguish three main types of NIS. The first involves 'accessing online databases.' The 'interactivity' here reflects the fact that the information is sent out only in response to a user request (as opposed to, say, broadcast teletext, where the user simply selects among material that is being continually transmitted); the 'telecommunications' demarcates the NIS from electronic publishing on storage media (such as, say, CD-ROM, where an optical disc containing the database is delivered). A second group of NIS involves 'messaging' of various kinds, where users can communicate with each other via electronic mail, bulletin boards, etc (as opposed to conventional mail or voice telephony, where the media have traditionally involved, respectively, non-electronic recording/display and real-time audio connections). The third type involves 'transactional activities', such as ordering or paying for deliveries online (as opposed to conventional modes of invoicing or direct payment). Most if not all NIS fall within the UK telecommunications regulation category of 'value-added and data services' (VADS). They include both specific services (such as electronic mail or Electronic Data Interchange) and broad service packages (such as the packages offered on Prestel).

The NIS discussed above are 'new' in that they are based on IT systems and typically require users to have computer terminals of some sort; they are 'interactive' in that user inputs affect the behaviour and output of the supplier system; they are 'telecommunications-based' in that they typically use public or private telecommunications networks; and they are services in that they do not directly produce material outputs - although a major part of their utility is that they overcome the traditional time and space constraints of services.[2]

NIS often compete with other modes of service delivery, both traditional (eg books, post, telephony) and IT based (optical discs, cellular telephones, and emerging systems such as voice messaging that are on the threshold of being NIS themselves, but where the user interface is a conventional telephone). This is an extremely important determinant of the evolution of NIS. The development of any interactive service is shaped by complementary and competing services delivered both by the same means and via other routes. Thus an online weather service is challenged by teletext services like Ceefax and Oracle, TV and radio bulletins, newspaper columns, and even the possibility of downloading satellite pictures into home, school or local authority microcomputers.

Why are these sectors an important area in which corporate strategy issues should be raised? There are both theoretical and pragmatic reasons. In terms of social scientific analysis, the issue of strategy in services — especially new IT services — poses particular problems. We shall devote the next section of this study to discussing the peculiar complexity of these new services. But more generally, while many of the major actors in the field are private firms pursuing their traditional objectives of long-term growth and stability and shorter-term profitability, services cannot be handled in exactly the same way as goods. Some of the main means of ensuring returns to investments put into innovation are hard to apply to services; in particular methods of intellectual property protection such as patenting and copyright are only partially applicable to many new services. Indeed, at the present time controversy is still raging about how far copyright protection can be applied to software, and the new services have yet to go through analogous battles. Thus corporate strategy becomes a study in methods of obtaining competitive advantage in the absence of such traditional instruments.

In addition, innovation theorists are now becoming more interested in telecommunications-based services. Those who see the world economy as being affected by 'long waves' of industrial innovation and who see the current wave as being driven by IT developments are paying attention to new styles of production.[3] Industrial 'best practice' at present involves the linking and integration of previously separate areas of IT use ('islands of automation'), not just in manufacturing processes but along the entire chain of production and distribution, taking in not only intra-organisational linkages but also upstream and downstream connections with suppliers and distributors. The conjunction of the necessary telecommunications links and new ways of organising and presenting information forms the core of NIS.

There are also more pragmatic reasons for interest in this area. It is a growing field, and one where there is increasing international competition, yet little has been written about it except in trade journals and consultancy reports. Issues of entry barriers, national sovereignty, and even of whether or not a country can hope to stay on the IT bandwagon without these services are raised by current service innovations. We cannot address all the implications of our study here, but hope to shed some light on the background to present developments in such a way as to inform debate.

2 Three aspects of complexity

NIS pose particular strategic problems in large part because of their 'complexity'. There are three, related, aspects to this complexity.

Firstly, NIS are part of the general 'swarming' of new IT-based goods and services associated with the precipitous development and pervasive diffusion of this new heartland technology. This means that they are only one among many candidates for investment, on the part of both financiers and financial controllers in potential supplier and user organisations. Furthermore, given that IT-based innovation is centrally concerned with improving methods of accessing and processing data, NIS are contending with other ways of delivering data to users (for instance, storage media like CD-ROM or non-interactive telecommunications like broadcast teletext). The new services are not bursting forth into a terrain populated only by traditional means of information delivery: they form only one of a whole range of new actors on the scene, and it is far from clear what the virtues and costs of different modes of utilising IT power are in practice.

In addition to the wide variety of modes of delivery of information and communication services, there are a variety of telecommunications networks in existence. This means that the same NIS can, in principle, be accessed through different telecoms channels. In practice, some NIS are exclusively available on a private network system, to which access may be marketed (although it is also possible to think of in-house NIS used solely on intra-corporate networks). Others are offered on several networks: one can access many of the best-known databases, for example, through the public telephone network, the public data network, via one of a number of specialised computer networks, etc.[4] In practice, too, it is usually possible to communicate across networks, though in some instances there are problems of incompatible standards or restrictions on access. Each network has its own particular advantages and disadvantages, has its own access conditions and imposes its own set of charges. This can only serve to make the process of choosing a mode of delivery more complicated.

Thus suppliers and users may feel some uncertainty about going down the NIS route at all. But even when the advantages of rapid interactive information access and computer-mediated communications are clearly apparent, there is a second problem of complexity. We have referred to the 'swarming' of new IT-based products. These emergent product classes are typically in the early stages of their product cycles, ie few are 'mature' in the sense of having established markets and product designs.

The innovation literature (eg Teece, 1987b) distinguishes between 'preparadigmatic' and 'paradigmatic' stages in the product cycle (at least, that of mass market goods). In the former stage, designs are relatively fluid, and suppliers compete to produce designs that will establish themselves firmly in the marketplace. In the latter stage, one design or design class becomes dominant, and competition tends to focus on price and on minor modifications within the standard design. There is a tendency with hindsight to view this process as just a matter of the natural selection of a technically superior class of product, but empirical experience and theoretical analysis suggest otherwise.[5]

Even when there does appear to be considerable stability in design — eg in personal computers with the dominance of the IBM PC — technological progress (more powerful chips) and competitive strategy (IBM's attempt to outwit clone-makers, in this case) may lead to further upheavals. Current

NIS are typically in a 'preparadigmatic' stage, with considerable uncertainty about what the features of the mature products are likely to be once (if) they become established.

The complexity of the NIS environment is not just a matter of technological evolution, but is also one of the competitive process itself. Different NIS have emerged from backgrounds with varied traditions of information search and retrieval and communications design. There has been the same sort of proliferation of procedures to use, say, different online databases or electronic mail facilities, as there has been in the field of computer software. Just as software publishers are torn between wanting to minimise demands on the user by sticking to familiar formats and commands, and wanting to highlight the particular virtues of their own system, NIS suppliers face choices as to whether to abide by de facto standards or to pioneer new approaches. In computers the balance seems to have been shifting toward the more conservative and less user-demanding approach, probably because suppliers have learned to temper the enthusiasm of their designers with some 'feel' for what the market responds best to. This sort of process may well be under way in NIS, but it is far less clear at this point that a dominant paradigm is emerging: hence uncertainty for users and suppliers alike.

The third type of complexity reinforces the two discussed above, and also reflects the difficulties of adjusting to the new modes of operation associated with IT. New IT is often described as involving the convergence of computers and telecommunications, and it is now beginning to be recognised that in practice this convergence is frequently more problematic than expected, in part because of the different cultures and skill bases of the firms and occupations associated with the computing and communications spheres. NIS suppliers and users need to find ways of overcoming this problem in order to succeed with this most convergent of products! And the suppliers face the demand for a third set of skills, too: they require 'media' skills, ie those concerned with selecting, presenting and packaging the information content of the NIS to render it useful for the intended market.

These three forms of complexity are important in shaping the strategies of suppliers and users of NIS. The ways in which their products and their corporate behaviour have unfolded in large part reflect efforts to manage complexity. Many lines of development are being followed, by different sorts of service in different sectors. Grappling with this complexity is not made any easier by the conjunction of inadequate statistical data (for example, on market size and share, customer base and profitability) and abundant hyperbole from the suppliers.

This hyperbole (and some of the uncertainty) reflects the feverish pace of development and investment in NIS. Future markets are expected to be huge, so that interactive services are seen as a strategically important terrain for competition. But apart from a few (mainly financial) services, investments do not yet seem to be reaping commensurate rewards; suppliers (who not surprisingly have a keen appreciation of the value of information to themselves and to their competitors) are reluctant to reveal how little they are making, or how few customers they really have.[6]

NIS suppliers may also keep to themselves more information on their activities than most traditional information services — for example, newspapers and magazines have to submit records to the Audit Bureau of Circulation to attract advertising revenue. Even when services are provided by public companies, their costs and revenues can often be hidden within figures which are submitted for the company's overall activities. And statisticians are unsure of how to go about defining requirements for new data on new branches of the economy — especially at a time when statistical services are under financial constraints in most Western countries.[7] Thus assessments of the size of the interactive services markets have to be based on the estimates of consultants and analysts whose access to relevant information is limited.

What these assessments do suggest, however, is that despite the hyperbole there is a sizeable market established for NIS — although it has not generally grown to the extent anticipated. The sample of UK firms recorded in *Business Monitor SDQ 9* as supplying VADS notched up billings of over £14 million in 1986; consultancy forecasts for 1990 predicted a UK VADS market of several hundred million pounds by 1990; some 800 VADS services were registered with the UK Office of Telecommunications (Oftel) in mid-1986; British Telecom's (BT's) Prestel had around 95,000 subscribers, Telecom Gold 138,000, and Istel claimed 47,000 users for its Infotrac network at the end of 1988; and so on. The scene may be a complex one, but ways of managing the complexity do seem to have been found by some firms.

Indeed, the complexity of the NIS environment is double-edged. By this, we mean that while complexity may have adverse effects on the growth of the industry generally, it can also provide some opportunities for competitive advantage. The next sections of this paper concern suppliers' efforts to turn this complexity to their advantage. (The following discussions mainly refer to British experience, unless noted otherwise: the circumstances in other countries differ because of such factors as different regulatory regimes, eg more or less monopoly power given to the telecoms administrations, and industrial policies, eg more or less subsidisation of services, equipment, etc.)

3 Managing complexity: 1 - design paradigms

Amidst the complexity, two features are apparent:

– Much of the activity in the development of interactive services is concentrated either in the area of transactional services or in transaction-related information and communication services. Here Reuters is perhaps seen as the profitable model for others to follow.

– Most of this activity is centred on business-to-business services — this is for instance where the DTI's Vanguard initiative is concentrated — rather than on services to final consumers, despite the fact that the latter offer the biggest potential markets.

These features might have come as a surprise to a commentator of the late 1970s. For the biggest single interactive services development in the UK at the time — the setting up of the Prestel videotex system and the numerous services it was to offer — was firmly targeted at residential markets. The contrast between Prestel and the different approach taken to developing mass residential markets in France with the Minitel system is striking.[8] In the UK, an engineering concept was expected to unleash mass consumer demand for 'a world of information at your fingertips' — ie access to online databases carrying topical information (news, train times) and items of less transitory significance. However, after eight years, Prestel has become largely a business service with less than a hundred thousand users, while the French Post, Telephone and Telegraph Authority (PTT) has stimulated large-scale usage of Minitel, notably for messaging purposes.[9] Prestel is perhaps the most graphic illustration of the point that successful new services cannot be conjured up simply by vision, willpower and advanced technology; Minitel is cited by proponents of the 'information society' (eg lobbyists for large-scale infrastructural investment in optical fibre networks) as demonstrating that innovative policies can promote new residential service markets.

The complexity of the environment is almost certainly in part responsible for the low uptake of consumer NIS in the UK. With the Minitel, users were provided with a standard simple computer-type terminal with VDU, and were motivated to use it by the telephone directory being put online. In contrast, Prestel (from which no doubt Minitel designers had drawn some lessons) was marketed initially as an expensive TV-based system; and though efforts had been made to create a system which would be easy for non-computer-literate consumers to use, the early numeric-only keypads made user input of more than a few symbols at a time, such as would be needed for messaging, difficult. The menu structure of the service was cumbersome, and the information provided was of uneven value and had a pricing structure that was confusing to potential users. What is more, Prestel offered services remarkably similar in appearance to the information services becoming available at the same time on broadcast teletext.[10]

This relates to our earlier discussion of 'preparadigmatic' and paradigmatic stages of product development. Prestel can be seen as an effort to establish a dominant paradigm, based on a user friendly interface employing colour and graphics, a database indexing system which required little learning by the user, and the use of a familiar piece of household equipment (the TV set) as the means of service delivery. However, the innovation literature stresses the dangers of prematurely deciding the form of a new paradigm, and the Prestel experience illuminates these dangers. Though the system was easy to learn, its usefulness was limited: it often took a long time to search through the index levels, only to find uninteresting or outdated information; and interactivity was limited by the lack of adequate communications facilities. The early Prestel system, it should be noted, was based upon an assessment of low microcomputer familiarity in the household; this failed to anticipate the explosion of personal computing or the possibility of providing a cheap and powerful terminal to consumers in the near future.

Prestel's videotex standard may not have appealed to the expected mass public, but it has found an (apparently) secure niche in the travel industry (and a few other sectors, such as insurance and the motor trade). Videotex allows relatively untrained staff to access information on flight availability or insurance rates, and to book seats or order components. In these sectors, where time-urgent information is at a premium and much time was being wasted on telephone calls, Prestel gained a significant share of business, though from its earliest days it has been faced with commercial competition from videotex services delivered over other networks. These were initially 'private' systems which could offer features not available at the time on Prestel, for instance direct links to tour operators' booking systems.[11]

Prestel represented an effort to create a paradigm in its finalised form, effectively out of nowhere. But where it is recognised that a service is in a preparadigmatic state, an alternative (and perhaps safer) approach, is to seek to maintain flexibility in the design of the service, minimising the investment committed to specific architectures from which it might prove hard to escape (*see* Gardiner and Rothwell, Chapter 11, for examples of how this is achieved for products). With NIS, this may be easier said than done: suppliers may need to maintain compatibility with existing (but possibly sub-optimal) standards, and they may also need the scale economies which can be gained by expanding the service to reach as many people in as short a time as possible. For a variety of reasons, Prestel sought to achieve quick scale economies by going nationwide before the market trials were properly evaluated. This strategy proved costly, for when the nature of the demand for new services became clearer it was difficult to alter the basic design and implement the new features (messaging, gateways, keyword searching etc) which competitors had pioneered.

But there are instances where NIS have been introduced flexibly and successfully, including services offered by organisations which have learned lessons from previous mistakes. Telecom Gold (electronic mail service) was without doubt developed with the Prestel experience in mind. From the late 1970s several attempts were made to design a sophisticated electronic mail service, but none was implemented because of design problems, heavy investment costs and (post-Prestel) uncertainty about demand. When in 1982 an electronic mail service was indeed introduced by BT, there was little of the fanfare that had been accorded to the launch of Prestel. Telecom Gold was an 'off-the-shelf' package, licensed from the then American company Dialcom. The American service had a reasonably large corporate user base, which was the market BT thought had most immediate potential. It could be hosted on relatively inexpensive minicomputers, which could be increased in number in a flexible and modular fashion as demand increased, it could be accessed from a wide variety of terminals, including almost any microcomputer, and it could transfer data on the X.25 packet switched networks which were becoming standard for both national and international data traffic.

Take-up of the electronic mail service was slow at first, but its acceptable performance and perceived value, coupled with the rapid diffusion of computers in businesses and the professions, has meant that over the last five years growth has been fairly rapid. Telecom Gold has successfully implemented its service while keeping the system modular and flexible. Its step-by-step approach was taken more because of business strategy — based in this case on a reaction to the Prestel experience — than because of the technology as such. The advantages of achieving economies of scale are just as important with an electronic mail service as with an information access service, but other considerations weighed more heavily and a more cautious path was taken.

Another major aspect of a flexible design strategy in a preparadigmatic phase of an innovation is maintaining close contact with the user community. One way in which a supplier can check its experience with its own users against more general trends is to maintain close contacts with the user community's trade associations. These can often reflect a wider spread of opinion, can provide a focus for industry-wide strategic thinking and can be a locus of standardisation activity.

Contact with users, however, also carries some degree of risk. Current users may not be those who will eventually decide on the innovation's success, they may not have the knowledge and vision necessary to perceive the key aspects of an innovation, and they may even turn out to be competitors! This has been a problem for Prestel over the years, as a number of customers have used their experience as information providers or as subscribers' suppliers of information to third parties or as subscribers to 'private Prestel' for intra-corporate communication to evaluate and prototype their own videotex systems. The problem has become more general in recent years, as the new telecommunications regulations, together with technical developments, have made it easier for firms to use their own private networks to gain competitive advantage. There is considerable fluctuation in most NIS markets; new entrants can appear from areas not previously seen as competing with existing service providers, eg in financial services, where banks, building societies, insurance companies, major retailers and other organisations are realigning and competing in newly-opened markets. This is of course by no means due only to telecommunications factors — but legislation such as the Financial Services Act, the Building Societies Act, etc, has built on the new opportunities raised by the dynamism of telecommunications.

4 Managing complexity: 2 - lock-in

There are many different suppliers of services such as online databases, for example, and it is by no means easy for users to get a comparative assessment of their virtues and limitations. This offers opportunities for suppliers to get away with providing inferior services (more expensive, less user-friendly, less regularly updated, etc). More substantially, perhaps, there is often a deliberate effort made to 'lock-in' information users with one familiar supplier. But while some suppliers have attempted to tie in users to their own standards in all types of NIS, the most severe effects are felt in transactional services. Interactive services linking manufacturers to dealers, or distributors to retailers have been the subjects of intense 'standards wars'. For instance, motor manufacturers have for some years provided links to their major component suppliers, with orders being placed and invoices sent using electronic data interchange (EDI). But since the services were run by individual manufacturers, suppliers who traded with several manufacturers found that they had to subscribe to several, often incompatible, services. The trade association — the Society of Motor Manufacturers and Traders (SMMT) — ran trials on the Motornet service (run by International Network Services — INS), and then recommended that all the major UK manufacturers should adopt Motornet for their supplier services.

Peugeot Talbot and General Motors accepted this; but Ford wanted to continue its own Fordnet service, while Austin Rover supported the Edict service of its then subsidiary, Istel (now a major independent VADS operator). In 1987, the SMMT gave approval to Edict as a second recommended standard; it urged all manufacturers to subscribe to both Edict and Motornet. After further pressure from the SMMT, which stated that its endorsement could be removed from INS or Istel if either were to block the establishment of a gateway between them, both agreed in principle to interconnect. INS had been the more wary of implementing such a link (citing not technical problems but charging and security issues) but the first effects of the SMMT's dual system recommendation have been all to Istel's advantage. For Peugeot Talbot and General Motors joined Edict as well as Motornet (GM noting that Istel had become a more attractive option since the firm had been spun off from GM's competitor Austin Rover), whilst Ford and Rover did not join Motornet. Ford is continuing to remain independent, on the grounds that communications are too strategically important to entrust to a third party.

The growing 'just-in-time' orientation of motor manufacturers means that component suppliers could be rejected if they do not fall in line with the particular EDI implementation supported by a manufacturer. It is in this context that lock-in has emerged. Once the course of following proprietary standards was set, it has proved difficult for the UK motor trade to move away from this course and towards fully standardised protocols — despite the existence of an active trade association being urged by its members to simplify matters.

This example also illustrates the risks associated with the lock-in strategy. Service suppliers who attempt to have their ways of doing things accepted as a *de facto* standard may find this rebounding on them. If the attempt fails, they are themselves locked into (their own) standards incompatible with the way everyone else is working. Thus, INS's abandonment of opposition to linking with Edict may have been prompted by Istel's having gained from the SMMT's dual recommendation. Once this link is established, it remains to be seen whether Ford is strong enough to hold to its own standard or whether it too will try to create a gateway to the other services.

Arguments about lock-in — at least via the more 'physical' means, such as special terminals or incompatible communications protocols — may attenuate as NIS become more widespread. It might be attractive for a supplier to attempt to 'capture' a customer at an early stage in NIS development — the supplier's service might then be the only one the customer is using. But as customers become more experienced with the technology and see opportunities for using, and linking, a variety of services, pressure for standardisation should grow. A service which needed its own dedicated terminal would then be disadvantaged. In time such pressure might also be applied to areas such as the interface presented to the user.

5 Managing complexity: 3 - service bundling

As noted above, the complexity of the NIS environment is increased by the fact that it is possible to access the same service through many networks. Some suppliers are attempting to gain competitive advantage by taking steps to simplify affairs via 'bundling' different services offered by a common 'host system'. A host for the NIS is roughly equivalent to a publisher, offering online information services that, like books, may be produced by quite distinct 'authors'. The host computer provides access to these different services, so it is not necessary to make contact with each service through an independent route. This terminology (and analogy), which developed along with the online database industry, is rendered more complex by the emergence of hosts incorporating communication and transactional NIS.[12] Bundling is obviously a valuable competitive strategy if the supplier can bundle together several different — if possible, complementary — services into a package which cannot be exactly copied by competitors.

Bundling has been a common practice for a long time within the 'traditional' database industry, with hosts such as Dialog, Pergamon Orbit Infoline, Datastar and ESA-IRS combining databases from a wide variety of areas with a common search language. This reflects the hosts' recognition that users were frustrated by having to 'shop around' and learn new skills. An interesting development here is the innovation embodied in 'Easylink' (an American invention, licensed in the UK by Istel under the name of Infosearch), a system wherein requirements for user knowledge of the contents and relative prices of different databases is minimised. An artificial intelligence-like interface questions the user about the sort of information required, then (at a standard charge rate) determines the appropriate databases and conducts the search.

Most of the suppliers of electronic mail are also following bundling strategies, too, enabling gateways between the computers hosting their E-mail software and the hosts of other services, and adding services other than E-mail to their own computers. A good example of this is provided by Microlink, a service run by the Europress Group.

Microlink licenses the Telecom Gold electronic mail service from BT, and aims at providing Telecom Gold access for individuals rather than corporations. Its customers are a mixture of computer enthusiasts, independent professionals and small businesses unwilling to pay corporate rates for E-mail. It offers a variety of information, transactional and communications services charged at the standard Microlink rates as well as gateways to external services which levy their own charges in addition. Microlink is a cheap mode of entry to E-mail, but users' decisions about whether to join or continue with Microlink will be based not only upon cost, but also on the value of the various peripheral services which are part of the bundle. Its main competitor is the Prestel-based Micronet package, which offers a bundle which is functionally similar in many respects but which started out from a base of home computer users.

Similar competition between service bundles can be found in the travel sector, in education, in insurance, in financial services, etc — in each case, the main aim is to provide all the interactive service functions needed by a customer in a particular market segment.

6 Managing complexity: 4 - total packages

BT itself has moved towards a bundling of its different services, including those offered via videotex and other formats. British Telecom's Dialcom subsidiary provides access into Prestel and ASCII based travel, insurance, and similar NIS.[13] The supply of NIS by network operators like BT, Mercury or Istel is more than just bundling, however; often it reflects an effort to deliver a 'total service package', ie a combination of network(s) and service(s) (and sometimes terminal equipment) rather than purely a bundle of different services.

Let us consider BT strategy here. BT's historical legacy of networks and equipment is both a source of strength and a burden. This is shown by its strategy of creating a new network to carry its value-added services. The new network — currently called Vasscom — is to run alongside BT's public data network. This is seen to be necessary, in part at least, as a response to competitors such as Istel and Fastrak, who have emphasised the value of network management as an important asset in running NIS.

This is an important selling point. Reliability and continuity of operation are vital ingredients of many (especially transactional) NIS: stockbrokers, for instance, need to react immediately to market prices, and can lose money if their communications networks are not working or if information is corrupted in transit; travel agents will lose custom if they are unable to get through to tour operators at peak booking periods. Security is another concern: users do not want to risk 'hackers' or frauds gaining access to their systems. So for many service providers, and for many customers, a robust network is a prime requirement, and suppliers of purpose-built value added networks (VANs[14]) argue that they can offer greater reliability and more sophisticated features than can BT on its public data network. BT has to cater for a wide variety of customers, and cope with, and maintain compatibility with, its inheritance of outdated technologies; its resources are spread so wide that, its competitors argue, it cannot give key business clients the close attention they need.

While disputing that its public service compares so unfavourably with the services on offer from private network suppliers, BT is creating its own parallel VAN, Vasscom. BT's intention seems to be that of concentrating its interactive services — ranging from videotex services formerly clustered under the Prestel umbrella, through the messaging and gateway services of Telecom Gold, to its database host Hotline — on to Vasscom. The rationale for BT's development of Vasscom is not only to be able to offer features similar to those of its competitors in this field; also it will seek to offer service packages where the provision of both the service and the carrier network are under its own control. (The two reasons are interlinked: control over both network and service elements facilitates the achievement of a high degree of service reliability.)

Most VAN providers strive to run a mixture of their own services and services provided by other organisations; the latter help achieve economies of scale and bring in extra revenue. The major network providers differ in the relative weight placed on the two elements, but it is unlikely that in future any large player in this field will be content with being merely a carrier. Linking service and network provision can lead to more custom, since it is liable to increase the perceived reliability and value of the service in the eyes of current and potential users. It also raises the barriers to entry for potential competitors. While a small new company might be able to develop an exciting new service concept, and even write much of the software to run the service (using increasingly cheaper and more powerful computers), there remains the barrier of getting this service distributed to the target markets. Competition between network providers reduces their power over independent service providers to some extent. But the marginal costs of developing a new service are likely to remain higher, often very considerably higher, for smaller operators than for large network/service providers.

To understand such strategies it is useful to draw upon the innovation literature again. Teece (1987b), for example, discusses the 'complementary assets' required for the commercialisation of an innovation (see Chapter 1). Such complementary assets are more often possessed by larger organisations already operating in a given field. They have been found to be important determinants of successful innovation — or rather, of who is able to score a success with an innovation. The ownership of a telecommunications network, with its body of subscribers, is readily identifiable as a complementary asset for NIS supply; and having a range of NIS products on one's network may conversely attract subscribers.

The third of the types of complexity which we identified at the outset is also germane here. A large firm should be more easily able to recruit people with new skills needed for the innovative operation, or to buy in consultancy services if it is at the stage of testing out new ground, without risking its whole financial future. Access to specialised skills is itself a complementary asset, and network providers are liable to have access to at least the computing and communications skills NIS require. However, one factor that militates in favour of small firms and new entrants is that management of the combination of the three sets of skills is apparently proving very difficult for many large organisations — whose personnel and other senior staff will tend to approach problems from the perspective of one or other of the 'three cultures'.

7 Managing complexity: 5 - specialisation

In many respects the strategies outlined above represent efforts to influence the emerging paradigm for various types of NIS (or NIS access), or to remain flexible in the face of 'autonomously' evolving paradigms. Smaller NIS suppliers who feel that they can exercise little influence on major trends may seek 'shelters' in specialist markets which are small enough to make widespread competition unviable.

While services such as Prestel were originally intended to find mass markets, the strategy behind the further development of videotex in the UK shifted to a more niche market-type approach: there was a search for trigger services which would themselves be sufficient to motivate substantial use of videotex within limited markets and, hopefully, eventually encourage these users to turn to other NIS offered via Prestel. To date, most NIS suppliers have found that niche markets are relatively easier to establish; the rapidity of change around IT does not mean that we can uncritically accept consultants' forecasts that mass NIS markets will also grow rapidly. While there are clear possibilities for mass market NIS in electronic mail, real-time messaging and some financial services (eg home banking), these are areas where competition is liable to be fierce — and where the need for more user-friendliness is high.

Niche markets are by definition smaller, so for investments to be repaid it is important that the market will bear relatively high prices (and perhaps that entry barriers to competitors are high). This latter condition will often be the case where information services are involved that draw upon a publishing or research firm's accumulated database, for example. The product also needs to be initially well-tailored to suit niches, but the possibility of gaining 'insider' knowledge of markets — ie the information/media skills relevant to a particular class of content — exists: for example, British Telecom Travel Services and BT Insurance Services have bought in people with substantial experience of the relevant sectors.

Niche markets are often (or often becoming) international in order to achieve economies of scale (national markets in Europe are often too small to support a NIS) or because the relevant information is inherently regional or global. (For example, many financial services are traded; EDI systems need to be able to cope with exports and imports.) There are still quite serious problems in 'transporting' NIS across national boundaries — different standards in the telecommunications systems, different regulatory structures, different tax regimes, and inherited differences in the stock of terminal and other equipment; not to mention the desire to protect national champions.

A niche marketing strategy requires the identification of a suitably encapsulated area which is not already over-occupied, and then the maintainance of extremely close cooperation with customers. The latter is important, because if the area is small customers may not be very numerous

— and it is vital to maintain the loyalty of each and every one of them. If the NIS supplier is successful, a mutually dependent relationship may well ensue, with suppliers gaining a sophisticated understanding of the market in which they are operating, and becoming able to sell their products on the basis of quality of service provision rather than on price. Clearly, this close customer contact fits in well with the requirement for flexible adaptation mentioned above. (For further discussion of small firms' use of niche markets *see* Dodgson and Rothwell, Chapter 9.)

This strategy can be extremely successful: one of our interviewees remarked that 'We're happy to occupy a niche — a niche that's an inch wide but a mile deep'. Examples of such successful niche services can be found in many areas, including legal services (Lexis), market analysis for advertisers (MAID) and financial information/dealing services (Reuters and others). But the difficulty is finding an area which is lucrative enough to make the exercise worthwhile, yet not so lucrative as to attract swarms of competitors. (It is just possible that certain classes of financial services may for a time have offered a market that was so lucrative that it did not matter that there were swarms of competitors, but this never promised to be a permanent situation.) The sector in question must also have a preponderance of features which are sector-specific, otherwise it would be easy for large firms supplying a wide range of services to tailor these to fit that particular area.

8 Managing complexity: 6 - skills

Firms' skill mixes are based on their past experience: media and publishing firms, for example, have capabilities for gathering information and packaging it in attractive forms, computer firms are skilled in software writing (eg for the construction of user-friendly databases), telecommunications firms have skills in operating networks and making sense of the variety of system choices available in transmitting material between two points. The contrasts sketched in here also apply to firms from other sectors who are moving into NIS: the banks who commercialise their networks, for example, may be particularly advantaged in having a mixture of telecommunications and computer staff, and some experience with packaging financial information.

Thus, any actor interested in the NIS field will need to assess what skills are a prerequisite for succesful market entry; and having done this determine how to acquire missing skills and integrate them into the corporate activity. This integration is seldom easy, as the convergence of skill bases and the introduction of new products involves a learning process which requires careful monitoring and a willingness of staff to adjust to new practices and forms of organisation.

In some instances the strategic choice has been one of external acquisition of firms with relevant skills, or entry into joint ventures with them; in other cases conventional recruitment and 'headhunting' have been adopted; and in other cases a combination of the two strategies. To some extent the uncertainty in the area has led to a 'wait and see' attitude on the part of big actors, who presumably reckon that they will be able to buy out successful small actors if healthy markets are proved to exist. Buying out NIS can also be a good way to deal with competition, as is shown by the purchase and subsequent closure of the Eurolex legal database service by Lexis, the main US firm in this field.

9 Scale and integration

One conclusion of our study is that barriers to entry with most sorts of NIS are already high, and are rising. Most successful in overcoming such barriers are large firms in 'outside' sectors which are able to find new uses for already existing IT resources. Whereas a few years ago the relatively small Bank of Scotland could see the online route ('telebanking') as a chance to extend its customer base without the need to invest in a much more extensive branch network, it is likely that once the larger financial organisations take the plunge, as they are trying to do in several interesting ways (sometimes using telephones and voice synthesis instead of microcomputers or videotex terminals), this route will no longer be so advantageous for other small banks.

The trend to increasing barriers of entry may be reinforced by the parallel tendency in the UK for network and service providers to be one and the same. In this case, network providers can have an incentive for refusing to carry the NIS of competitors — although there is room for argument between the network side of an organisation, which might wish to increase network traffic irrespective of who provides the services, and the NIS side, which might wish to protect its combination of service features and network facilities. A comparison with France, whose PTT provides data networks but acts as a common carrier could prove interesting, as this system might lead to a larger number of small-scale NIS providers easily able to link their systems to the national network through 'gateways'.

The trend towards a vertical integration of networks and services may raise barriers to entry and it may go against the grain of Oftel's pro-competitive and anti-cross-subsidisation policies, but provided that customer choice is not reduced to an unacceptably low level, it may offer some advantages to the user in that (given suitable tariff policies) it might serve to reduce confusion over network and service choice and ease the linking together of different services.

Whether a particular NIS will go down this route will be a product of many factors. A geographically dispersed firm may have already established a network as well as a competence in NIS: Istel is an example, where the dispersion of the Austin Rover group led to an elaborate network structure being set up; and where the need for user-friendly videotex services for a variety of actors in the motor trade provided experience in NIS. The high costs of establishing networks, together with the economies of scale associated with them, may make it harder for new entrants to establish their own networks: they are more likely to piggyback on existing ones. But there are exceptions to this: a few large institutions are establishing new networks (notably GEC) or exploring the possibility of so doing (eg the Central

Electricity Generating Board). And more existing intra-organisational networks are likely to be externalised as carriers of telecommunications services (for instance, British Rail has been investing heavily in its telecommunications network and has the size and the geographical spread to become a major value-added network and services provider if it chooses to do so).

Barras's description of a 'reverse product cycle' model provides us with an interesting hypothesis concerning the development of networks. Barras (1986) states that service innovation has typically involved organisations first using IT for efficiency reasons, rationalising existing activities, then exploiting the new possibilities offered by IT to enhance the services they provide, and finally using IT to provide fundamentally new services which were not previously possible. We would anticipate that large firms will increasingly gain interest in expanding their internal networks and/or linking them upstream or downstream (for instance, as in the motor manufacturers' links to components suppliers and retailers). The focus of competitive strategy will move from efficiency gains (labour saving, rapid turn-around, scheduling, etc) to enhancing the services provided (better management information systems, integration of ordering mechanisms with computer-aided design).

As the potential for new services becomes more evident, several developments may follow. Firms may wish to externalise NIS as well as networks. And firms whose internal networks are not on a large enough scale for use as general carriers may wish to export their internal NIS through 'gateways' to other networks: the aim would be to increase interconnectivity, ie to allow NIS to be accessed through more routes. This may lead to greater interest from the private sector in the development of (more or less) universal, high quality public networks, or in the expansion of, and collaboration among, private networks that might carry NIS (which might involve regulations that would force some measure of 'common carrier' behaviour upon integrated network suppliers).

10 User problems and strategies

In this chapter we have mainly concentrated upon the problems and strategies of NIS suppliers. But the three types of complexity described above also create problems for users which can prove just as difficult to manage. The complexities of NIS adoption may result in avoidance of NIS, or the locking in of users to suppliers of a service which in retrospect prove to be an expensively wrong choice. This is particularly problematic when many consultants are in some way tied to particular suppliers. To help overcome these problems, the DTI's Vanguard initiative has been set up to offer free advice and consultancy to firms reluctant to dip more than their toes in the water.[15]

Other factors that are seen as inhibiting user uptake of NIS include:

– The need for more education, and the lack of general awareness of the potential benefits of new services.

– Legal problems, often to do with the verification of an 'electronic signature', with who bears the cost of false intelligence or the failure of a transaction, or with questions of intellectual property rights — and almost never to do with issues such as privacy or data protection (an interesting contrast to the debates in West Germany and Scandinavia).

– Accounting problems, for instance the fact that use of interactive services does not always fit easily into organisations' existing budget headings; this is a specific indication of the more general problem of organisational adaptation to new IT-based operations, and is beginning to be addressed in the technical accountancy literature.

– 'Ideological' problems, in particular the view of many online database services that they have difficulties convincing potential customers that they should pay for information which might be available more cheaply on other, more familiar media, or which are 'value-added' repackaging of official statistics or public domain material.

– Regulatory problems, which take very different forms in different countries. In the UK, some large telecoms users, generally those with their own private networks, were of the opinion that the present regulations were too restrictive, as some of the services they would like to offer or use contain elements of (currently prohibited) resale of voice capacity, although they also were of the opinion that the worst of the current restrictions could be mitigated through informal bilateral agreements with regulatory authorities.

Our research has left us with the strong impression, in connection with this last point, that, apart from universal grumblings about tariff structures and complaints about the slowness and expense of the procedure for equipment approval (especially modems) most NIS suppliers and users do not find the present UK regulatory environment unduly restrictive. Most of the problems facing the introduction of NIS into new areas of economic life have more to do with processes of organisational adaptation and with suppliers failing to match services to markets than they do with battles against inappropriate regulation.

The strategies which need to be adopted by NIS users in order to manage complexity in general mirror those of suppliers. Close contact with potential suppliers is essential in order to gain knowledge of what is available; trade associations can help to maintain this contact and use research facilities to increase the knowledge base, as well as helping to negotiate favourable deals; skills bases must be extended and integrated; organisational change and friction must be managed - a process which is aided by setting clear lines of responsibility for the introduction and management of new services and by the appointment of integrated IT managers at board level.[16] Two areas where users have special interests, however, are tariffs and standards.

Tariffs are a source of considerable confusion amongst users, and often a significant inhibiting factor affecting NIS take-up. The most glaring examples of inscrutable tariff practices lie in the area of international data traffic, although telecommunications operators are now coming under increasing pressure from users and transnational regulators such as the

EEC. But other examples can be easily plucked from database directories, where a brief look at the charging systems reveals that database providers and hosts seem to delight in making the costs of searches unpredictable.

This is, however, not a matter of pure obscurantism or complexity for its own sake. It is in part a response to the burgeoning of different methods of accessing NIS: the growth of multifunctional terminal equipment, and rapid changes in the number of different speeds and network routes whereby a given service can be accessed. The response of service providers has often been to try and break down their service into as many elements as they can separate out — connect time, time of day, data transmission speed, number of data packets sent and/or received, number of references 'hit', number of references printed out, etc - and to make separate charges for each element, so that whichever access mode is used no customer gets anything too cheaply.

Such practices may seek to be fair to all users (or to ensure that suppliers have no anomalously loss-making modes of NIS delivery), but they have the effect of deterring all but the most knowledgeable, convinced and determined. Users require fewer mysteries and more sense of control over costs — thus simple tariffs and 'one-stop billing' are desirable. Simplification of tariffs would be likely to lead to longer-term benefits for both suppliers and users which would outweigh any short-term losses or imbalances. Users with significant power, either independently or via their trade associations, can often force suppliers to offer simplified or reduced tariffs, for instance, as a result of trade association pressure, the network costs of travel and insurance services are frequently borne by the tour operators and insurance firms rather than by the independent agencies retailing the services.

Standards form another area where the interests of users lie firmly on the side of simplification. Particularly for smaller users who do not have the power to affect the direction of the major service providers, there is a need to work with standard protocols and interfaces so that the dangers of lock-in, of wasted investment and of expensive readjustment are minimised. It is understandable, then, that user organisations are supportive of the efforts of governments and international regulatory agencies to enforce compliance with open standards, despite the admitted difficulties of defining these quickly enough to keep up with technical developments (and in the face of the prevarication of large suppliers and governments which wish to protect proprietary offerings and national champions).

11 Conclusions

The development and use of new interactive services cannot be the sole element of corporate technology strategies. Mostly, these services will be a means to an end — the more efficient production of goods, the enhancement of other intermediate and final services, etc — and at least equal attention must be paid to the other means of achieving the desired outcomes. However, given the current trends towards integration of the different components of production processes, integration which involves communication between organisations as well as within them, it is safe to predict that telecommunications-based interactive services will in future play an increasingly important role in the strategic concerns of most firms. Both suppliers and users will need to take seriously the challenge of integrating their internal communications and information systems with external networks and services. Both will need to develop new forms of organisation in order to take advantage (or prevent others taking more advantage) of the new opportunities.

It is likely that the growth of NIS will be encouraged by further liberalisation of telecommunications regimes, especially in the more traditionally PTT-oriented countries of continental Europe. The efforts of the EC telecommunications directorate to facilitate the creation of one element of the 'single European market', even if not totally successful, will aid the process of the internationalisation of service markets — a process already well under way, given the international scope of many of the firms best placed to offer certain elements of NIS packages, notably the provision and management of VANs. Although there is still much scope for local expertise and market knowledge (for instance, the peculiar extent of the UK package holiday business, and the effects this has had on the development of some NIS), the challenges to firms in the near future are likely to have a strong international dimension. This is the basis of the fear, expressed in some quarters, that the liberalisation and modernisation of British telecommunications might pave the way for the domination of UK telecoms service markets by foreign suppliers.

The main challenge to firms in this area, then, is to overcome the obstacles of complexity described above so that suppliers can create a strong presence in interactive services markets and so users can take advantage of these in order to improve the competitive performance of their own products and services. One question for UK firms, which if answered in the affirmative would lead to another challenge, is whether it is necessary to extend rapidly the use of NIS from the current rather narrow business-oriented base into mass markets. The argument here is that mass-market supply and use of interactive services would provide the population with an extended skill base (in telecommunications, software, information management, graphical design, etc) from which further advances could be made. [17] Whether this can be achieved by firms following their own strategic interests, or whether there is a need for more central, political direction, is a question whose answer lies outside the scope of this chapter. The comparison between the 'private', niche market orientation of the UK and the 'dirigiste', mass market, developments in France should prove interesting over the next decade.

While we have here tried to cast light on the strategies employed in the NIS field, we are aware that in many respects we are raising more questions than we answer. What is clear, however, is that this is an important area of economic development and the arena for substantial corporate competitive struggles; that the development of the area requires overcoming some obstacles that presently confront users, and that the sum of the individual interests of suppliers does not always provide the force necessary to overcome these obstacles; and that there may well be issues of entry barriers and oligopolisation in NIS as well as in network provision. All of these factors are liable to affect the prospects of individual countries for transforming themselves into 'information societies': and to condition the sort of 'information society' that they eventually develop.

Notes

1 The work on which this paper is based was supported by the Leverhulme Trust, as part of a project entitled 'The Emergence of New Interactive Services'. Thomas and Miles (1988) provide a fuller discussion of its results.

2 While many accounts of the service economy note that services are typically consumed when and where they are produced, Information Technology (IT) makes it possible to store a great many information services in electronic media, and to deliver them in locations remote from their production. This increased space-time utility is an important feature of IT-based services innovation (Riddle, 1986, Miles, 1988b).

3 *See* Freeman and Perez (1988) for a concise summary of some of the ideas involved.

4 Since the privatisation of British Telecom (BT) in 1984 the use of such terms as 'public' and 'private' in connection with telecoms networks and services has become problematic. The distinction is no longer one of ownership but one of access. Thus BT is obliged to connect to the 'public data network' anyone who will pay the fees and who is using equipment which conforms to standards set by regulators, but may set further conditions on the use of its other data networks. Services may be open to anyone, to anyone who will pay the fees, to customers possessing particular attributes (eg members of a professional or trade association), or to members of a particular firm or organisation. The first two categories are roughly 'public'. Another feature of 'public networks' is that they are often, at least in principle, servicing the whole of a national geographical area — but while the public telephone network in the UK goes a long way toward this, the public data network is geographically very limited (as are Istel, etc.).

5 The cases of IBM personal computers and VHS video recorders are often cited as examples of non-state-of-the-art products gaining dominance simply because of the market power of the supplier; for a more theoretical analysis see Metcalfe (1986).

6 There are several reasons for this. In addition to the usual factors such as share prices and loan equity, users are attracted or repelled by their perception of network externalities (how many other people will I be able to reach via this system?) and futureproofing (will I have to learn a new set of protocols if this supplier fails to achieve market dominance?).

7 An enquiry into the operations of the VADS, attempted in Britain in 1987, had to be revised and scaled down after suppliers protested that they did not organise their business in ways which would provide official statisticians with the data they sought.

8 Strictly speaking, the system is called Teletel and the terminal (or rather, one kind of terminal) is called Minitel. However, many people now speak of 'the French Minitel system' and the two terms have become somewhat interchangeable.

9 The French success is often ascribed simply to the decision to give terminals to home users. In fact it is due to an interrelated set of decisions: the free and easy-to-use terminals, the provision of a well-designed 'trigger' service in the form of the electronic phone directory, the decentralised database concept, the choice of a packet-switched network shared with other services, the use of simple gateways which allow small organisations to operate services cheaply, the integral messaging facilities, the absence of extra subscription costs, the simple 'kiosque' tariffing system which gives the user 'one-stop billing', etc.

10 This was no coincidence: considerable effort had been taken to ensure that the formats of teletext and videotex were similar ones, enabling the same chips to be used in TV manufacture, and hopefully leading to more consumer familiarity.

11 For a study of private videotex systems in the UK *see* Yates-Mercer (1985).

12 Perhaps a better analogy would be between the host and a bookshop; in this case, the addition of more services would resemble a bookshop beginning to deal in other commodities as well as books — or even offering post office and banking services!

13 ASCII stands for American Standard Code for Information Interchange, a character set which differs (though not greatly) from that of most videotex systems. ASCII-based services tend to be 'scrolling' rather than page-based, though this is not necessarily so.

14 VANS are value added network services; the term has been replaced for official purposes in the UK by VADS, as noted earlier, but still has considerable currency.

15 Accordingly, the DTI has recently published a report entitled *The Economic Effects of Value-Added and Data Services* which sets out the use of various NIS for competitive advantage in a number of sectors of the UK economy. It is interesting to note, however, that an interviewee from one of Vanguard's five sponsors (British Telecom, Istel, INS, Midland Bank, IBM) declared that one of Vanguard's main functions was to act as a 'cabal' to protect the interests of the 'insider' suppliers.

16 *See* Feeny and Brownlee (1986) and Earl and Runge (1987) for some empirical studies of the adoption of telecommunications-based information services. Keen (1986) puts forward arguments for treating telecommunications as a central object of corporate strategic concern.

17 *See* Miles (1988a) for further discussion of these issues.

Chapter 7

Benetton: a case-study of corporate strategy for innovation in traditional sectors

Fiorenza Belussi

1 Introduction

This chapter analyses the main features of the rapid growth of Benetton, the world's largest woollen knitwear maker, exploring the main factors underlying the expansion of the firm, and suggesting some interpretative hypotheses for its growth, particularly with regard to the role of its strategy for technological and organisational innovation.

Since the influential works of Schumpeter, the importance of technological change and innovative activity for industrial dynamics and for economic growth have been widely discussed. The Benetton case study is conducted within a Schumpeterian perspective.

The chapter will provide a very detailed picture of the complex interdependence of innovative activity among product and process innovations and the firm's organisational changes. It will argue that the creation of a firm specific technological trajectory, even in a traditional and low technology sector, is influenced by existing technological know-how, capabilities or expertise developed during earlier periods of growth. The features of what can be described as a 'business milieu' are also analysed in a broad sense. The empirical analysis presented puts a great deal of emphasis on the historical origin of the firm, on the formation of local entrepreneurship, and on the social environment.

Another important point which distinguishes the approach is the divergence from the traditional, orthodox neoclassical vision of the firm. Following the works of Nelson and Winter (1977, 1982), Baumol (1959) and Marris (1963, 1964), and bearing in mind their criticism of profit maximisation theory,[1] the paper tries to outline a much more realistic model of firm behaviour, whereby long-term expansion of output is sustained by the necessary demand conditions and by a continuous flow of innovations. Within the analysis, and based on the work of Porter (1980), the concept of the firm's strategy plays a fundamental role. In terms of this analytical framework, Benetton's competitive advantages over its rivals were gained by being a highly innovative firm which maintained a cumulative competitive leadership over time.

The relationship between market structure and the firm's conduct and its performance (Bain, 1968; Caves, 1964) is also analysed, describing the induced process towards an increasing domination of the market by the firm. The Chandler (1962) strategy-structure model, and some recent comments by Williamson (1985; 1986), have also indirectly inspired some considerations of the advantages of the Benetton organisational structure which extends its boundaries, incorporating strong linkages among the agents involved in the production and distribution systems (suppliers, subcontractors, agents, retailers).

A further element, which is a major focus of analysis, is the impact of new technologies on the firm's pattern of growth.[2] The approaches adopted by Freeman and Perez (1986), and by Freeman and Soete (1987), regarding information technology (IT), have been considered in order to describe the more recent evolution of Benetton.[3] It will be argued that it is the utilisation of IT that is the real motor sustaining the latest (and more intensive) phase of Benetton's development. On the one hand, it is widely applied within the production system, increasing the productivity of all productive factors and production functions (capital, labour, space, raw material, inventory, buffer stock, energy, managerial coordination), the flexibility of the system as a whole, quality control and product differentiation. On the other hand, IT played a crucial role in the development of the distribution system. Here lies the novelty of Benetton's model: the information system allows the linking up of a network of wholesalers and retailers with a large constellation of producers.

2 Fast growth

Benetton was formed in 1965 as a general partnership, under the name of 'Maglificio di Ponzano Veneto fratelli Benetton' (Gruppo di Lavoro IRES, 1984). Although a relatively young company, Benetton is today the biggest Italian fashion firm, and with twelve factories and 4500 outlets in 60 countries is the largest woollen knitwear maker in the world.

Benetton's story began with Luciano Benetton and his sister Giuliana. Luciano was a shop assistant in a textile shop in Treviso and his sister was working in an artisanal knitwear producing factory. In 1957 they decided to work together. Giuliana had discovered a talent for designing and making knitwear; Luciano would collect orders and Giuliana would produce them at home. The origin of Benetton's organisational structure lies, therefore, with the ancient local putting-out system, which was never fully superseded by the factory mode of production.[4]

In 1965 they established a small factory in Ponzano (in the Veneto region of North-East Italy) with 60 employees. At that time the other two Benetton brothers (Gilberto and Carlo) joined the company. The division of labour among the family was clear-cut and it is the same today: Luciano deals with the marketing; Giuliana with the design function; Gilberto with administration and finance; and Carlo is in charge of production. As shown in Table 7.1, during the 1970s there was a gradual expansion of the firm's activity. By 1978 Benetton was already considered an important firm in the textile/knitwear sector with around 1000 employees and with an export market which amounted to 26 per cent of total sales. There followed a period of rapid growth between 1978 and 1981; in this period total sales increased from 55 to 322 billion lire. The increase in exports was clearly the leading mechanism in the growth of sales. In only four years the export share rose to 40 per cent of total output.

Table 7.1 Benetton Group performance

	1970	1978	1980	1981	1982	1983	1984	1985
Sales (billion lire)	33	55	190	322	400	475	623	880
Export (per cent)	5.3	26.6	33.0	40.0	44.0	54.0	55.0	59.9
Employees	912	1019	1287	1677	1538	1565	1504	1446
White collar workers (per cent)	n.a.	n.a.	20.6	20.2	26.0	28.4	30.0	33.3
Total sales								
Export knitwear				43.0	52.0	61.0	63.0.	n.a.
Export cotton				30.0	38.0	53.0	53.0	n.a.
Export jeans				31.0	37.0	46.0	46.0	n.a.
Exports (percentage of total sales)								
France			16.1	21.3	16.6	17.6	15.5	11.9
Germany			8.6	11.1	10.0	14.2	14.2	13.4
UK			–	–	3.6	5.2	5.2	7.4
Benelux & Switzerland			3.1	3.0	5.6	6.1	5.4	n.a.
Sweden			0.2	0.5	0.8	0.6	0.5	n.a.
Spain & Portgual			–	–	–	–	3.0	n.a.
US	0.8	0.5	0.1	2.4	7.7	13.4		
Domestic Benetton shops					11625	1227	1253	1393
Foreign Benetton shops					752	1069	1391	1967
France					283	287	430	491
Germany					168	233	285	347
UK					44	63	85	198
US					36	66	190	401
Benelux					25	44	49	56
Japan					n.a.	38	36	–

Source: Benetton SpA, Ufficio Marketing, 1986

This second take-off began when Benetton started operating abroad on a large scale and when it filled the remaining gaps in its coverage of the Italian market. Three main factors can explain this new phase: Benetton's leadership on costs which made its products very competitive in relation to its competitors; rapid expansion in the market for informal clothes; and the existence of a protectionist policy implemented by the industrialised countries to stop (or at least to reduce) the competitive pressure of commodities from Newly Industrialising Countries (NICs), formally concluded with the Multi-Fibre Agreement.[5]

Benetton chose from the beginning to create a 'subcontracting system', so a consistent part of the total value-added, which is estimated to be at least 70 per cent, is made by small artisan firms (about 300 firms), which are located near the Benetton plants.

This strategy of 'decentralisation' of some production phases to subcontractors is not at all specific to Benetton firms, but had been a widespread phenomenon in many Italian companies in the 1970s. What is specific to the Benetton case is the combination of this production strategy with its commercial strategy and with the technological innovations to be discussed below.

3 Creation of the retailing system

Benetton was the first firm in Italy, and possibly in the world, to introduce a system of franchising in the textile and clothing industry.[6] This system is a special form of franchising which is informally regulated. Retailers which sell Benetton's products do not pay any royalties, but have rigid controlling terms. No other make of clothing can be sold in the shop.

The first shop was opened by Benetton itself, with other financial partners, in 1968 in Belluno, a small city near Treviso (in the Alps). During the 1970s the chain of Benetton shops grew rapidly, firstly in Veneto (the region where Benetton is based) and later throughout Italy. The financial resources to develop such an imposing structure were found outside the firm, through partnerships with several commercial companies. Benetton moved from jerseys, cardigans and other knitted clothes, to denim jeans in time for the great jeans boom of 1975-76, and then started to make cotton clothes and T-shirts.

By 1975 it had about 200 shops in Italy and was opening more at the rate of 100 or so a year. Throughout this period of growth Benetton ensured that it kept direct control of its outlet markets.

Benetton's exports are 'pushed' by the creation of shops with the Benetton name. In Italy, as well as abroad, Benetton does not sell its products to other outlets. In essence it exports the entire selling strategy: not only its products but also the Benetton style, shop organisation and marketing strategy. In other words, 'product with shops' (Rullani and Zanfei, 1984).

In relation to competitors in the fashion industry, this gave Benetton considerable advantage: it was an organisational innovation of great significance.

4 Subcontractors

Subcontractors are involved in all labour intensive phases of production: assembly, ironing and finishing. The subcontracting firms can be divided into four main categories:

— those under the financial control of the Benetton family (through various financial companies);
— 'affiliate' firms;
— independent firms; and
— homeworkers.

'Affiliate' firms are those belonging either to former employees or to actual Benetton managers or clerks. Benetton has directly promoted the creation of such firms with the guarantee of orders in the start-up phase.

This subcontracting system has two main advantages for Benetton: use of external managerial resources; and a significant reduction in labour costs (in terms of unit labour cost the saving is about 40 per cent). Subcontractors agree to work exclusively for Benetton because of the stability of demand and the guarantee of a 10 per cent profit margin on their sales. The typical subcontracting firm is small (20-40 employees), but there are also firms with 80-100 employees. Workers are not unionised but there is an agreement signed by local trade unions and Benetton about observing the same pay and conditions for Benetton workers and subcontracted workers.

Labour productivity in subcontracting firms is estimated to be 10 per cent higher than that which could be achieved through in-house manufacturing (this is due essentially to management's greater control over the workforce and their ability to enforce a faster working pace).

5 Other 'actors' involved in the Benetton system: sales agents, retailers and labour force

Benetton attained its retail distribution network through an unusual arrangement with 'sales agents' both in Italy and throughout Europe. An individual sales agent may supervise and hold an interest in a number of stores. Late in 1982, Benetton conducted its business with 35 such agents. They are not employed by Benetton. Sales agents were paid by Benetton on the basis of a commission of about 4 per cent of the factory sales of goods sold through their retail outlets, in addition to their share of the profits of the store in which they hold ownership shares. The functions of these sales agents are crucial in the Benetton 'information system'.

Sales agents present the Benetton collection to shop operators in their own regions, and collect orders for the initial stock and re-orderings during the season, thus playing a vital control function for the whole system. The agents are also responsible for coordinating the high level of advertising funded by Benetton. In 1985, sales commissions amounted to nearly 40 billion lire, which is considerably more than internal labour costs.

Both the Benetton shop and the retailing system can be considered fundamental Benetton organisational innovations. The retailing system has been modified over time, and different patterns of ownership exist. In the first period of the company's growth the Benetton family directly invested in the retailing area. Later on they disinvested their capital from this business area in Italy and shifted it to foreign countries. In other countries the share of shops owned by the family, or by the Benetton Group SpA, has risen.

The shops, which conform to an image and style of management decreed by the company, are called by various brand names, such as Jeans West, Sisley, Tomato, 012 (for children) and, increasingly, only Benetton. Benetton, or its agents, choose the sites for the shops with great care, looking for the more prestigious locations, and often ending up with four or five Benetton shops in the same street.

The typical Benetton shop is standardised. This allows for a centrally determined 'optimized' lay-out for the display of goods and the selling system. In a Benetton shop it is the colours, the window displays and the open shelves that strike you most, as they are designed to do by the now famous architects Afra and Tobia Scarpa. Organisational and labour costs are much lower than in other typical clothing shops.

Another advantage, also in terms of space, is the absence of warehousing: indeed all stock is displayed on the shelves. It is the use of IT and the flexibility of the whole production cycle which enables the system to work without high stock levels.

Benetton's commercial strategy is to stay ahead of competitors in costs, and thus on prices; both in Italy and abroad, Benetton determines the selling price of each item for the retailer.

Expenditure on advertising and even more so, for promotion (eg Benetton Formula One), increased markedly between 1984 and 1985 (in 1985 it amounted to 36 billion lire). In 1984 the total cost of design and redesign of products was relatively low in comparison with advertising costs: the cost of services related to styling and coordination of product distribution amounted to 18,600 million lire, which is nearly 2 per cent of net sales. This notwithstanding the high level of new designs in total production (about 1200 in 1984).

A major feature of the Benetton system is a sharp division in the labour market between the 'internal' labour force, of around 1600, and the external labour force, of around 15,000-20,000 workers (it is impossible to assess this number precisely). It is important to note that these forms of 'black labour' are not directly organised by Benetton, but by the subcontractor firms. The total internal labour force is divided into eight production units, and the number of employees per plant is small.

Benetton's industrial relations system is rather simple and is characterised by:

— a rate of unionisation similar to the Italian average (40.7 per cent);
— a strike rate lower than in other firms in the same industry; and
— comparatively low union bargaining activity at the firm level.

6 The formation of a 'technological trajectory'

The following section will focus on the determinants and the effects of the introduction of innovations and their relationship with Benetton's corporate organisation. According to the traditional distinctions in innovation literature (Freeman, 1982), innovation can be oriented to: product changes; process changes; and organisational changes.

Table 7.2 illustrates the main innovations introduced since 1965 (the year the Benetton company was established). Benetton's expansion is characterised by a corporate strategy for the systematic coordination and complementarity of innovative efforts in each of these dimensions (product-innovation; process innovation; organisational innovation). The list of major innovations introduced by Benetton in Table 7.2 shows four major phases in a shifting focus of innovation and adaptation efforts.

In the first phase, from 1965 to 1970, three dominant features can be observed: the introduction of in-house incremental innovations in machinery through minor, but effective, changes in ordinary secondhand machines bought in the market and adapted by the firm itself; the building up of Benetton's particular retailing system (discussed earlier), which made available a major resource for the general growth of the firm; and a product differentiation strategy of introducing light colours (eg 'pastello') in casual and sports fashion.

Table 7.2 Major innovations introduced by Benetton

Innovation	Year	Description	Cost	Main characteristic	Source	Reason for introduction	Effects of innovation
Modification of knitting machinery	1965	Modification of machines for manufacturing women's seamed stockings	low	Process/product innovation	In-house (modification of existing machinery)	Availability of cheap second-hand machinery due to depreciation	Reducing investment costs
Machinery for striking wool	1965	Machinery with wooden arms that soak wool in water	low	Process/product innovation	In-house production of machinery	Effort to use less expensive material (recycled wool or hard and rough wool)	Reducing input costs
Use of light colours (eg 'pastello') in casual fashion good	1965		low	Product innovation	In-house		Product differentiation
Franchising system for the chain of shops	1968	Invention of the Benetton chain of shops		Organisational innovation in retailing	In-house	Direct knowledge of the consumer's preferences. Use of shop for advertising and marketing. Reducing uncertainty about the market Assuring outlets to the production and easier planning and coordination of the productive process	Improve competitive position. Establish brand loyalty and exclusive niches in the market.
Internal organisation and layout of shops	1968	Invention of the Benetton shop. Reduction of *space* and *labour*. Rationalisation of the layout	low	Organisational and process innovation in retailing	In-house (carried out with external expertise)	Reducing costs for the retailers	*Ceteris paribus*, lower prices. Uniform 'Benetton image'
Dyeing product in final phase	1972	Dyeing centre (with washing machines)	n.a.	Process/ Organisational innovation	In-house (adaptation of existing machinery and improvement)	Allowing production of knitwear following the market requirements for specific colours. Sharp reduction in warehousing	Marginal increase in production costs, but with major improvements in the competitive position
Knitwear stretching	1972	Knitwear stretching through rotation in order to return the item to its original size after dyeing	low	Process innovation	In-house adaptation of machinery	Solution of 'Technological bottleneck' caused by after-production dyeing	

Innovation	Year	Description	Cost	Main characteristic	Source	Reason for introduction	Effects of innovation
Automation of knitting	1979/ 84	Total replacement of the old looms with automatic looms	high	Process innovation	Bought (with in-house improvements)	Reducing labour costs: six looms for each worker instead of two	Higher labour productivity and higher quality of product
Introducing CAD system	1980	Automatic size grading	high	Process innovation	Bought (CAMSCO)	Labour productivity growth (one operation that previously lasted 24 hrs, now can be done in 15 mins). Material-saving from a utilisation rate of 75-76% to 85-89% of the fabric	Reducing unit costs Improving product-quality (diversification)
Information network	1980/ 85	Hardware based on four mainframe computers	high	Process/ organisational innovation	Bought (three units of Siemens-Fujitsu 7865, and one Olivetti 5330)	Easier management control on the system. Improved speed and quality of management information. Reducing the time for shops order and re-order	Dramatically improved the competitive position
Office automation	1980/ 84	Personal computers	low	Process innovation	Bought (IBM)	Improve the productivity of clerical workers	Reducing organisational delays
Automation of the spreading out of the fabric prior to cutting	1982	Extension of the work tables (from 25 to 35 metres) and lifting up of fabric by air	n.a.	Process innovation	Bought	Reducing physical effort required of the workers, improving productivity	Reducing costs
Automation of dyeing	1982	Automatic dyeing machines	high	Process/ organisational innovation	Bought	Reducing dyeing time (-20%) from 2½ to 2 hrs Improved quality control	Reducing time lag of adaptation to demand
Automation of cutting phase (jeans and cotton)	1980/ 85	NC machinery. Attempt to introduce laser cutting (partial failure)	high	Process innovation	Bought		Reducing costs and standardisation
Automated warehouse	1984	New fully automated establishment concentrating all the storage activity	high (36 billion lire)	Process/ organisational innovation	Bought from Comau on custom order	Reducing delivery time. Improving control of orders.	Improving the competitive position

Source: Benetton SpA, Ufficio Marketing 1986

During this period Benetton showed considerable entrepreneurial skills in its ability to utilise already existing resources and knowledge, for example, in the adaptation of secondhand machines which were originally used to manufacture women's seamed stockings (unfashionable at the time) to produce knitwear. These machines, then provided 90 per cent of Benetton's knitting capacity, were purchased for approximately $1000 per machine, and were converted for an additional $4000 each: the same machines were valued at roughly $470,000 each in 1982 (Harvard Business School, 1985).

Another example is the adaptation of a very old and well known system of 'beating' and dyeing wool in the final manufacturing phase of production. This process was adopted by Benetton after a trip by Luciano Benetton to Scotland, where this process is used in artisan shops. However, Benetton was the first company in the world to transform this into an industrial process, and was thereby enabled to follow more closely demand variability.

Using the concept of a technological trajectory (Dosi, 1982), Benetton's development involves a complex process in which a significant role is played by: tacit knowledge about the production process; the capacity to link innovations to a systematic 'vision' linking production and distribution (that is, an integrated innovative entrepreneurial strategy); and cumulative advantage coming from an innovative lead.

Much research has explored diversity of patterns of technological change (*see*, in particular, Pavitt, 1984 and Pavitt et al, Chapter 4). Clothing firms are considered 'supplier dominated' with only a limited tendency towards innovation. According to Pavitt, in such firms: technological change comes (exogenously) from suppliers' equipment and materials; and technological trajectories are defined in terms of cutting costs. However, in Benetton two phenomena can be observed. First, there are 'non-technological' innovations directly linked to design, trademarks, advertising and so on. Second, there are process-related innovative activities, which are complementary to purchases of equipment from outside.[7]

This last aspect appears to be linked to specific knowledge about the production process, and is based on the engineering capabilities of the entrepreneur. (Giuliana Benetton even now goes daily to a factory, controlling and making minor modifications to the looms.) This technical know-how precedes the constitution of the firm (and in fact it can be considered a condition, necessary if not sufficient, in explaining the creation of the firm and its success). Historically, Treviso is an important textile area in Italy. The young Benetton brothers worked in the textile industry as blue-collar workers (they came from a poor family and were forced to leave school because of economic circumstances). Their knowledge of the production cycle came directly from the shop floor.

In the intermediate period, in the 1970s, Benetton's growth was not characterised by the introduction of major innovations: the firm was in a process of 'learning by doing' (Arrow, 1962), 'learning by using' (Rosenberg, 1982), 'learning by learning' (Stiglitz, 1986), and 'learning by failing' (Maidique and Zirger, 1985).

In a third phase (approximately between 1977 and 1982), the distinguishing element is the introduction of process innovation aimed at a higher level of automation in some production processes (cutting, knitting and dyeing). This phase is characterised by acquisition of external new technology supplied by machinery producers. The rate of growth in the internal and foreign markets required (and allows for) an increase in the scale of production, and relatedly, an acceleration in the rate of adoption of new and expensive automated machinery. More than in the first period, the introduction of innovations was a response to outside technological opportunities and based on the use of microelectronics in industrial machinery.

Certainly, this technological 'leap' appears to be a consequence of (or at least allowed by) the expansion of the firm. However, right at the origin of Benetton's technological trajectory there are some incremental improvements of machinery and some 'innovative' procedures and behaviour.

The most recent phase of Benetton's technological development is characterised by a wider use of new information technologies, involving: the building up of an information network, connecting production and commercial activities, the first application of CAD; and a new automated warehouse. Benetton's strategic thinking about the opportunities provided by IT explains much of the company's success.

7 The use of information technology

The antennae of Benetton's information system are its shops. They must be in close contact with head office, reporting weekly takings and detailed sales trends to Ponzano.[8] In Ponzano, a private information network initially set up by Benetton in the 1970s and continuously modified, deals with three fundamental functions namely: collecting orders by Benetton's sales agents; collating detailed orders by shops (colour - size - model), to be used for long-term planning; and financial accounting.

It must be recalled that nearly the whole of Benetton's production is in response to orders from the retailers.

These characteristics represent the heart of the Benetton's system and its real novelty. So, unlike other firms in the fashion sector Benetton does not produce for stock. This has an enormous influence on total costs, and on the ability of the firm to follow market trends.

The pattern of sales and extent of re-orders are regularly fed back from the shops to Benetton, and in this way the time required for the final decision on the distribution of work among subcontractors is markedly reduced. This allows for optimisation of the total production cycle and better utilisation of capital equipment in the whole system.

The information network built up by Benetton and investment in IT have decisively strengthened the firm's competitive position. A major source of Benetton's success since the 1970s has been its ability to adapt quickly to new and changing markets.

Because of its information system Benetton is able to reach the market six to eight weeks before its competitors and, thanks to the flexibility of the system, it is able to respond within a very short time (about ten days) to the re-orders of domestic and foreign shops. In this way, it almost 'interacts' directly with its consumers.

This 'real time' planning of production based directly on shops' orders has been remarkably successful in reducing the typical seasonal peaks which characterise this industry. Moreover, a large reduction is obtained in the size of inventory and in the average length of time that a single item spends in the warehouse. As mentioned above, the use of so private and exclusive an information network was tied to a very specific organisation of production.

8 Towards a pattern of automation

For a better understanding of the role of new technology within Benetton's model, four main elements can be identified: the design function; the production function; the coordination function; and the entrepreneurial function.

8.1 Design function

The first product innovation, was the use of light colours in casual fashion goods. This low cost innovation, made in-house by Giuliana Benetton in 1965, substantially increased the firm's competitiveness. Benetton was immediately involved in a product differentiation strategy, enforced by feedback from the market easily identified, as we know, by the creation of the Benetton retailing system.

The rate at which such efficiency improvements could be put into effect was considerably enhanced by using technology bought from outside the company. Another jump in productivity occurred with the recent automation of design, using a CAD system. As a result of this investment, high level productivity growth, a consistent level of material saving, an improving product quality and increased product differentiation were attained.

The focus of attention is now moving towards coordinating design with computer aided manufacture (CAD-CAM) and coordination with managerial functions.

8.2 Production function

A large number of improvements associated with process innovation have been identified. Minor modification in secondhand machinery occurred in the first phase of development, greatly reducing investment costs, and some minor adaptation of existing machinery saved total input costs.

Since its beginning, as discussed above, Benetton chose to create a 'subcontracting system' based on local entrepreneurs. This enhanced the system efficiency of Benetton's model achieving: a significant reduction of labour costs; and a significant saving of managerial resources.

The dominant features of the company's technological trajectory can be summarised in the following way: predominantly incremental technological innovations in the 1960s; a learning process in the 1970s; and a shift towards automation and IT from 1977.

The third phase includes a convergence with a global coordination function (by, for example, the restructuring of delivery through an automated warehouse).

8.3 Coordination function

This emerged as a distinct element in parallel with a wide range of organisational innovations.[9] A major novelty of Benetton lies in the creation of its own retailing system; building up a chain of shops using franchising. These enormously improved the firm's competitive position over its rivals. The main advantages realised were: direct knowledge of consumer's preference; the use of shops for advertising and marketing; guaranteeing outlets for production; easier planning and coordination of the production process; and finally, and very importantly, reducing uncertainty and risk in the market.

As a result of other organisational changes outlined in Table 7.2, and in particular as a result of the adoption of a post-dyeing process, Benetton's system became more and more flexible: ready to capture minor changes of demand identified by shops, and ready to distribute new orders within the network of subcontracting. IT was the enabling tool for sustaining such an impressive performance, and the organisational model, shaping every production and distribution stage, can be described as an integrated just-in-time system.

Other characteristics are worth noting. IT bound up different parts of Benetton's structure, allowing a strategic global control over: the firm's available resources; its current activities; and the process of long-term strategic planning. The main effect of IT was not a simple reduction in the cost of existing functions. It has made possible the development of new functions linking information channels and economic nodes and increasing the capability for communicating, processing and storing information.

An important level of coordination is related to financial activity. The franchising system is linked with external venture capital and with Benetton's financial lending system and financial accounts. These links are important because Benetton is a firm which increasingly is becoming a 'service centre' for the entire system.[10]

8.4 Entrepreneurial function

In previous sections an overview of the business milieu in which Benetton developed was presented. There has been a growing awareness in recent years of the importance of non-market factors in influencing the behaviour and performance of firms. Particularly important in this case are factors associated with the origin of entrepreneurs. In Benetton the entrepreneurial role was, and is, based on an entire family (three brothers and a sister) which acts as a 'collective' entrepreneur. Within the family, the division of labour is clear cut and has been the same since Benetton's establishment. This model is clearly linked to the Italian family system.

The Benetton family was, and is, deeply involved in the process of product innovations (ie the design function) and process innovations (ie the production function) especially in the earlier phase of development. The role of such entrepreneurship was also instrumental in the firm's organisational changes and in building up the franchising and subcontracting system. This coordination dramatically enhanced the ability to realise the latent productivity made possible by the use of new technology, and put Benetton firmly in the forefront of technological developments in the international textile and clothing industries.

9 The domination of the market by the firm

In Italy, and in other countries, one of the characteristics specific to the fashion industry is the dominance of small firms, due mainly to low entry barriers and lack of economies of scale. Another feature is the segmentation of national markets due to differences in taste and culture. Benetton's strategy has aimed at reducing the impact of these factors upon its growth of market share.

The effects of Benetton's organisational revolution, matched with a high propensity to innovate, has deeply modified pre-existing market structure. Benetton is the leading knitwear firm (5 per cent of total Italian production) and the leading jeans producer (6 per cent of total Italian production). However, some data indicate that there is a tendency towards a rapid and continuing process of concentration.

The strength of this pattern of development is revealed by the considerable number of Benetton's imitators which have now achieved leading positions (Stefanel, Maglificio Calzificio Torinese, Gruppo Tacchella). Among the competitors, the Maglificio Piave, located in Treviso and using the brand name Stefanel, is the most impressive, because of its competitive position close to the same market segment as Benetton (having the same cultural and economic background, the same kind of products and similar image).

10 Conclusions

Some conclusions can now be drawn. This chapter started by presenting the Benetton story as an interesting case of an innovating firm within a traditional sector. A discussion of the characteristics of the expansion of the firm, related the pattern of growth to innovation strategy: in product innovations, process innovations and organisational innovations. The innovation strategy developed by Benetton cannot be conceptualised either as an inventive 'act of insight', or as an adaptation of a particular fundamental radical innovation. In contrast, it reveals a flow of interrelated improvements both in products and in processes. Whereas much emphasis has traditionally been placed upon technological innovation, the Benetton study stresses the fundamental importance of organisational innovations, both in production and in distribution.

In the discussion, an attempt has been made to delineate the formation of the firm's specific technological trajectory. In contrast with the widely-held view that traditional firms are dominated by the producers of technology, Benetton shows a consistent history of autonomous generation of innovations and incremental technological change. Based on peculiarly local circumstances and embodied within the entrepreneurial function, the technological trajectory of the firm started with some incremental improvements in machinery and in product design. However, a shift from internal to external technological generation occurred over time.

The second part of the story involves assimilation of IT and a movement towards automation. Benetton's increasing competitiveness can be explained by a particular form of 'system efficiency' in 'producing' and 'selling'. In other words, Benetton's organisational structure built up flexibly and interactively with demand, used a strategy of a 'just in time' system in manufacturing combined with a 'just in time' system in selling.[11]

The chapter argues that the rapid shift of the firm towards a new 'technological regime' has become possible because of the social and institutional conditions existing and historically ingrained in the area in which Benetton originated. There are also other, more general but significant features of Benetton's production system which are worth highlighting.

First, growth of the firm does not happen through internal expansion (Penrose, 1959) but through the development of a network of controlled firms. Thus, the group becomes a 'flexible' system. This flexibility does not necessarily involve small overall size but involves a network system with a propulsive 'core' and an 'adaptable' periphery.

Second, the Benetton case shows that manufacturing based on electronic technologies does not imply a trend toward smaller firm size (as suggested for example by Piore and Sabel, 1984). On the contrary, Benetton clearly shows the growth of new forms of oligopoly.[12]

Third, the firm appears to become a 'mobile' system of both economic transactions and organisational links: certainly the activity of the firm is not limited to simply 'buying or doing' (Williamson, 1985, 1986). Moreover, it can rapidly modify its organisational borders through a 'recentralization' or a 'decentralization' of the production process.

Fourth, from a sectoral point of view Benetton's system is highly vertically integrated (from raw material production to marketing outlets, across the boundaries of the textiles/clothing industry). Nevertheless, the firm appears to have been able to construct market and non-market relationships within a 'quasi' disintegrated system combining the efficiency of market discipline with the security of hierarchical structure. This pattern of re-organisation seems to be close to the idea of a firm as a 'governance structure' (Williamson 1975, 1979, 1981) which minimises: the level of uncertainty; the degree of risk involved; and the costs of using purely market forces.

Fifth, a double level of entrepreneurship is generated following a hierarchical pattern of division of labour between the 'core' and the 'periphery' of the system. The specific activities of the dominant firm are the strategic functions of total control and coordination of the whole cycle: planning, marketing and those manufacturing phases that require the most complex technological know-how. At the same time, the least skilled functions are carried out by a 'new generation' of subsidiaries which concentrate entirely on production tasks. The Benetton strategy maintains complete control over these firms. Each of these subsidiaries is responsible for only a particular phase in the production process and never responsible for the production of any complete item. However, Benetton's strategy also tends to induce a propulsive interaction with the local environment and plays a very active role in the internal organisation of production in these firms: it advises on the management of the firm, on the layout of machinery, and on the most efficient methods of production. But the technical knowledge and the market access of subcontracting firms are very limited.

Sixth, this process of dividing labour amongst firms appears to have important implications for more general industrial dynamics. The growth of a new generation of small firms feeds on the growth of the entire system. The latter is organised, loosely speaking, like a pyramid: the apex is highly concentrated, and the more the system grows the wider the base of small firms becomes. Furthermore, the tendency towards small average firm size cannot be totally considered a 'spontaneous' aspect of the evolution of the industrial environment; it is the result of a complex strategic reorganisation (associated with the exploitation of the economies of specialisation) of the production cycle led by some innovative firms. A dynamic efficiency[13] is assured, in a Smithian way, by the expansion of the market and therefore, by an increasing division of labour[14] among the different parts of the system.

Seventh, the possibility of developing and quickly expanding such a complex network is strongly connected with the external environment of the firm. We are referring, in the widest sense, to the institutional context and to historical conditions. These 'externalities' appear to be based on three fundamental factors:

– The diffusion of skills amongst workers, which in turn is both a local consequence of the historical existence of textile and clothing artisanal companies, and the effect of the recent diffusion of technical knowledge about textile machinery linked to recent developments in Italian industry.
– The specific labour market structure of the Veneto region and the lack of industrial conflict there. (This implies also a social acceptability of the labour conditions often linked to work in small firms and in the putting out system of production: insecurity of employment, comparatively poor working conditions, and so on).
– The existence in the social structure of what the sociologists call 'propensity to social mobility'.[15] The swarm of 'new generation' small firms is driven by that particular entrepreneurship based on manual workers who start up companies. In Italy in general, and not only in the case study analysed, the 1970s showed a fortuitous coincidence between on the one hand, the production requirements of flexibility and decentralisation, and on the other hand, the market mobilisation of large groups of skilled workers highly motivated by upward social mobility.

Notes

1 Dosi (1986) remarks that in an environment which is complex, changing and uncertain, firms do not and cannot adopt maximising behaviours; under conditions of frequent technological change their behaviours are more adequately represented as routines, strategies, metarules and search processes.

2 Freeman and Soete (1987), Freeman and Perez (1986), and Pavitt (1986a) provide an extensive contribution to this debate. For an intersectoral and broad view on this topic see also Bessant, Guy, Miles and Rush (1985) and, referring to the service sectors, Barras (1986).

3 We define IT as involving a combination of new technological developments in microelectronics, computers, opto-electronics and communication systems.

4 There are a number of European forms of industrialization, apart from the capitalist factory system, which have been largely neglected until now, especially within the field of industrial organisation studies; and the influence of historical elements in determining the pattern of accumulation and the trajectory of growth, has also often been ignored. The use of a historical perspective can more suitably explain the observed increasing variety and specialisation of regional/national industrialisation models. Two elements are worth analysis. The external environment of the firm can be seen as a resource of great importance both for the acquisition of skill and technological know-how by the local labour force and for the emergence of different levels of entrepreneurship. Recently some investigations have dwelt at length on this historical aspect of growth (Sabel and Zeitlin, 1982; Zeitlin, 1984). However, these important contributions tend to see the modern development of a new pattern of small firms as simply the 'revenge' of a historically pre-existing 'flexible specialisation' model upon the mass production system. As we discussed in the conclusions of this case study, the divergence in our analysis refers to the final outcome of this phenomenon of industrial decentralisation, which does not necessarily determine a structure dominated by small firms. On the contrary, it can conceal new forms of oligopolistic power.

5 The international regulations had their origin with the long-term arrangement on cotton textiles (LTE) in 1962 and increased with the Multi-Fibre Agreement (MFA) in 1974 and in 1977 (Correale and Gaeta, 1982).

6 The system of franchising was well known and had been established in the US for some time (eg McDonald's fast food chain) but the traditional system and relationship between franchiser and franchisee was radically modified by Benetton. With regard to the UK, for example, there is a famous forerunner, Marks and Spencer (Tse, 1985) a chain of large 'high-street' shops which established a close relationship between retailing and production through subcontracting since 1930. However, this set-up is considerably different from the Benetton system because the emphasis is placed on quality control of the products through close control of new materials carried out directly by the technologists employed by the company (Rees, 1969). Benetton, by contrast, emphasised the colour coordination and design of their garments, based on an innovative system which narrows the gap between producer and consumer. In addition, Benetton began as a producer (and only later entered retailing); Marks and Spencer, on the other hand, began as retailer and only later took an interest in production.

 7 A significant invention by Benetton (see Table 7.2) was dyeing knitwear
    at the end of the production cycle, in order to follow market demand.
    This process can be applied only to one-colour garments and represents
    an area of increasing technical know-how for Benetton. Nevertheless, it
    is calculated that total production costs rise nearly 30 per cent. For that
    reason Benetton utilises this 'post-dyeing' process only for a reduced
    number of items (about 30 per cent of the total volume of wool knitwear
    produced in one season) and particularly only for the re-order phase, in
    which a time-saving technology becomes more efficient than a cost-
    saving technology.

 8 Because labels are applied directly by Benetton during the last phase of
    the production cycle, they are standardised for all shops (including those
    in foreign countries). They contain duplicated information. Once the
    product is sold the label is divided in two parts, one remains in the shops
    and the other will be sent through agents directly to Ponzano.

 9 This hypothesis has also been proposed by Kaplinsky (1984).

10 For further discussion of this and other features of Benetton's
    development, *see* Belussi (1987).

11 This term was first coined for describing the Japanese industrial model.
    The existing literature on this topic is now widespread. *See* for instance
    Schonberger (1982) and Sayer (1986).

12 In recent decades this issue has received growing attention. However, to
    understand the origin of 'industrial dynamic' we have to turn back to
    Joseph Schumpeter. Linking up with the classical tradition, Schumpeter,
    in his seminal works of 1934 and 1947, was the first modern economist to
    develop a theoretical approach to the process of the capitalistic dynamic.
    More recently on the relationship between growth and market structure,
    interesting hypotheses are suggested by Bain (1967), Kamien and
    Schwartz (1982) and also Pavitt, Robson, Townsend (1987).

13 This idea is largely based on Rosenberg and Frischtak's (1985) criticism of
    the Pareto-efficient allocation of resources within the development paths
    of NICs (preface pp. XIV-XV). For a more general approach *see also* Klein
    (1977) and Kay (1979).

14 The advantage of small size can be seen in two directions. First, a system
    based on a network of small firms allows rapid changes in the product-
    process mix (Sabel, 1982). For this reason this model can cope with a high
    level of innovative activity. As the illuminating analysis of Abernathy
    (1978) has shown, within big firms and mass production, there exists a
    'fundamental dilemma of innovation versus productivity'. Second,
    thanks to a set-up strategy of flexibility and specialisation (using, in other
    words, economies of scope) this system grants a growing exploitation of
    economies of scale and permits production based on increasingly high
    volumes. As Scherer pointed out in the 1970s, economies of scope can be
    associated with economies of scale. In industries such as knitwear and
    garment making the manufacturing process may be fragmented without
    resorting to inferior techniques. That is to say that small production units
    may largely benefit from economies of scale. On this point *see also* Brusco
    (1975). An interesting survey can be found in Gold (1981). However, note

that in the case of Benetton economies of scale have not completely vanished but focussed on the initial and final phases of the production cycle. As seen in previous sections there are also pecuniary economies of scale linked to marketing, financial accounting, purchasing raw materials, etc.

15 For an extensive discussion see Bagnasco and Trigilia (1984) and Brusco (1982).

Chapter 8

Food retailing, technology and its relation to competitive strategy

Jacqueline Senker

1 Introduction

British supermarket chains have become increasingly sophisticated in the use of technology. They have not only introduced innovation in systems for the distribution and handling of food but have also been responsible, through close collaboration with their suppliers, for some important food manufacturing innovations. Since the late 1970s, competitive success in food retailing, as measured by market share, has been achieved by several multiples which have adopted a technological strategy. This chapter will demonstrate that this strategy was only open to firms with a long tradition of company investment in in-house technological expertise, and will emphasise the importance of cumulative technological skills for companies which wish to adopt a technological strategy.

Three theoretical models will be described, and their ability to explain food retailers' involvement in food manufacturing innovation, and increasing use of technology examined. The models are based on concepts drawn from analyses of manufacturing industry. After a brief discussion of these models, they will be set in the context of recent developments in the structure and strategy of British food retailing and the food legislation which played a part in influencing retailers to set up in-house food technology departments. The relative merits of the three models will then be assessed by reference to details of methods by which retailers use their food technology departments. This assessment throws new light on the use of technology as a competitive weapon.

2 Three theoretical models

Concepts developed by Rosenberg (1984), von Hippel (1982) and Porter (1980, 1983 and 1985b) in relation to analyses of manufacturing industry appear to be relevant to explaining retailer involvement in food manufacturing innovation. The concepts are presented in turn, together with my extrapolation of each concept to retailing.

Rosenberg has suggested that increases in scale create a vast range of problems and opportunities for firms that require control of inputs and their qualities to a degree which had not previously been nearly so significant. It also requires careful attention to new production processes, and final products have to meet precise specification characteristics. Scientific knowledge is applied not only in new industries based on recent breakthroughs in basic science, but the larger body of scientific knowledge has applications throughout industry, specifically in large-scale industries (Rosenberg, 1984, pp15-18).

Applying this concept to retailing would suggest that the increased scale of retailing requires retailers to exercise increased control over the food products they sell, and their quality. Changes in production processes at the factory and changes in the final product have required retail involvement to ensure that products meet precisely defined performance characteristics and are correctly stored and distributed to meet the demands of large-scale retailing.

Von Hippel tried to identify the locus of innovation, after his empirical studies had found that in some industries innovations emanated from user firms, whilst in other industries they came from product manufacturers. After a review of available evidence he concluded that the ability to appropriate the benefit of output-embodied innovation can help to identify the locus of innovation. Trade secrets and 'response time', ie the time it takes for imitators to copy an innovation, are important mechanisms for the capture of innovation benefit (von Hippel, 1982).

Applying this concept to retailing suggests that retailers have become involved in innovation because they believe they can appropriate the benefits of this activity.

Porter's early work recognised that competition arises not only within an industrial sector, but may also take place with buyers, suppliers of similar or substitute products or new entrants to the industry (Porter, 1980). Subsequently, he suggested that technology as a strategic variable can change the competitive rules of the game, by impacting on all the forces driving competition; and can be employed to implement a firm's chosen strategy - whether it be cost leadership, differentiation or focus (Porter, 1983). Technology is embodied in every 'value activity' within a firm, and Porter calls the collection of these activities 'the value chain'. This includes not only core technologies encompassed within a firm's products and production processes, but also those in support activities, for instance procurement, office technology, transportation or design. Technological change can affect competition through its impact on virtually every activity in the 'value chain' (Porter, 1985b).

We can recognise the technological activities of retailers as one dimension of their competitive strategies, which can be focussed on various parts of the 'value chain'. Their technological activities can be connected with attempts to build retailer brand image to differentiate themselves from competitors, or to fill market niches.

3 Structure and strategy in food retailing

Concentration in food retailing began to gather pace in the 1960s, fuelled both by the spread of self-service supermarkets and the abolition of resale price maintenance. By the 1970s a difficult trading environment had developed for the multiples. The volume of food being purchased was almost static, and profit margins for packaged groceries were eroded by strong price competition. These conditions were exacerbated by inflation, increasing commodity prices and Government prices and income controls. The major grocery retailers responded by adopting strategies to increase sales volumes to compensate for low margins, often by merger or acquisition of less successful chains. Substantial economies of scale could be achieved from increased sales volume, particularly through the exercise of purchasing power to negotiate considerable discounts from suppliers, but also in store operations. Other strategies for coping with slim margins involved diversification into fresh foods and non-foods, and opening larger stores to house the wider range of products offered. The multiples found that larger stores had the advantage of lowering operating costs. As a result many small units were replaced by outlets with increased selling area. Rapidly increasing floor capacity in the grocery trade created an over supply of retail grocery services, which led to a major price war between the multiples. The cumulative effect of these developments increased concentration in food retailing. Multiples' share of grocery shop sales was estimated at 20 per cent in 1950 (Beaumont, 1982a, p9). By 1982, they accounted for over 72 per cent of packaged grocery sales (Davies et al, 1984). Not only do multiples account for increasing market share; fewer of them exist. Renewed acquisition activity in the mid 1980s led to an estimate that over 57 per cent of all grocery sales were accounted for by the seven major food multiples (*Financial Times*, 24 Jan 1987, p1).

Price competition is a valid strategy when the rate of inflation of the prices of goods being sold outstrips inflation in selling costs. This was the case up to 1980, but subsequently when selling cost inflation became greater than inflation in merchandise, price competition lost its appeal as a competitive strategy. The demise of this strategy was confirmed in a speech given by the Chairman of Tesco's in 1985:

> It is very clear that no company will get a price advantage for long. A very low price advertised today is bettered within 24 hours by a competitor. This is all very well short term, but in the long term it cannot be in anyone's interest. (Reported in *The Grocer*, 23 Nov 1985.)

The exhaustion of price competition created the need for the large multiples to develop new competitive strategies. They adopted a variety of strategies, designed primarily to differentiate themselves from one another. One strategy to increase market share, based on the belief that consumers are now more interested in novelty and quality, has been to enhance store image by its identification with exclusive own label products and high quality fresh foods. Table 8.1 gives details of the leading multiples' market share, but it must be interpreted with caution.[1] Sainsbury and Tesco are clearly market leaders. The position of Marks & Spencer is more difficult to pin down, until it is recognised that by comparison to the other companies its major activity is not food retailing and that it does not stock a full range of food products.

Since about 1980, the role of distributors' own brands[2] has begun to change. Though some own labels provide a low price alternative to branded

Table 8.1. Retail multiple shares of the national food market 1982 (percentages)

Company	
Tesco Stores	8.5
J. Sainsbury	8.3
Asda	4.7
International Stores*	4.3
Fine Fare	4.0
Marks & Spencer	3.4
Argyll	3.1
Safeway	2.1
Kwik-Save	2.1
Waitrose	1.5

* International's market share is grossly overstated because it includes turnover from Argos Distributors.

Source: Business Monitor 1982 Retailing and annual reports

goods, others are in 'direct competition with the main brands, equal in quality and consumer perception. Here their function is inextricably bound up with the development of a retailer brand image' (Beaumont, 1982b, p34).

Table 8.2 shows fluctuations in own label packaged groceries' share of turnover since 1975. However these figures conceal the absolute growth in sales of own label products that has occurred because they omit fresh and chilled groceries and increasing floor capacity means retailers carry more branded as well as more own label products. Furthermore the two brands with the highest value in the UK are owned by retailers, namely Sainsbury and St Michael (van Mesdag, 1985, pp72-3).

Table 8.2. Own label sales as a percentage of turnover: packaged groceries

	1975	1978	1981	1983 (first 6 months)
Asda		7.6	6.4	6.5
Safeway		31.8	27.7	33.8
Sainsbury	64.1	63.0	53.2	53.3
Tesco	22.1	23.3	21.6	30.3
Waitrose	38.9	40.9	45.2	47.7
All multiples		22.9	22.9	26.2
Co-operatives		33.0	21.5	33.8
All voluntary Groups		17.3	15.4	15.4
Average	41.7	30.0	26.7	30.9

Source: Davies et al, 1984, p38a

Detailed statistics do not exist on the degree of concentration in food manufacturing and its change over time. However, the many mergers in this sector give grounds for believing that concentration has been increasing. The *Census of Production* statistics for the number of food and drink manufacturing enterprises employing over 100 persons provides one indication of increased concentration;[3] between 1958 and 1985 they fell from 918 to 552. In 1980 it was estimated that Britain had 22 of the 100 largest food businesses in the world, ranked by turnover, and 15 of the 21 largest European food manufacturers, ranked by food sales (*Economist*, 1980). These large, diversified food businesses compete in many processed product markets, which led to an estimate that 40 per cent of total food sales in Britain are accounted for by 30 firms (Beaumont, 1982a, p7). In most processed product markets, five or less firms have a major share (Watts, 1982, p21).

Concentration is not thought to be related to technology. The technological processes necessary for the preparation of food products are not particularly enhanced by large-scale methods: '...most food-processing is technologically straightforward and efficient even on a small scale. ...Plant size may be important in a few cases, such as corn oil refining or instant coffee processing, where economies of plant size may limit competition' (Horst, 1974, p74).

Scale economies for food processing firms relate to potential savings in sharing a common distributional network, or in advertising (Horst, p87).

Concentration in food retailing and the development of distributors' own brands has upset the balance of power between food manufacturers and retailers. It goes further than the exercise of countervailing power, which suggests that oligopolistic retailers will be able to extract price concessions from oligopolistic sellers (Galbraith, 1963, pp132-3). In addition to seizing the marketing initiative with innovative own label products, some retailers have taken control of the organisation of physical distribution, and, by centralising buying decisions, have curtailed the role of food manufacturers' salesmen. The control by the food multiples over physical distribution and the concentration of retail buying power is distancing food manufacturers from the final consumer.

4 Food technology in retailing

The Food and Drug Act, 1955, was similar to earlier food legislation in placing an obligation on retailers to ensure that the food they sold was not injurious to health or adulterated in any way. The new legislation also included regulations concerning minimum standards of composition for certain foods. No offence was committed until a retail sale had been completed. The only statutory defence for the retailer was that the food had been supplied by a branded manufacturer. The brand name on the invoice amounted to a warranty that the product could lawfully be sold (Cranston, 1984, pp273-4). No such defence was available to retailers who sold own label products. Growth in the sales volume and range of own label goods since the 1960s has placed retailers under a very strong obligation to ensure that these goods meet the requirements of the law. Accordingly, multiples selling own brands have employed food technologists, to check on the hygiene of suppliers' premises, and to sample own label products to ensure they meet health and compositional standards.

Thus by 1970 food technology departments were to be found in most of the leading food multiples which sold own label products. One notable exception was Tesco Stores, which did not establish a department until 1973. This grew quickly to become one of the largest in the country. The size of retailers' food technology departments ranges from three or four technologists up to as many as 100 technical staff. Although legislation accounts for the existence of some food technology departments in food retailers, it cannot completely explain the growth of these departments, particularly those which predate the Food and Drug Act. Large, established food technology departments, like those in Sainsbury and Marks & Spencer, reflect company cultures which incorporate the belief that benefits are gained from investment in technical expertise.

Interviews carried out in 1984-85 with the heads of the food technology departments of eight leading food multiples[4] on the size and activities of their departments showed that there has been a steady increase in their size over time, as shown in Table 8.3. The table also shows that the market leaders have considerably larger numbers of technical staff than their competitors.

Table 8.3. Technical staff employed by food retailers

Company (date laboratory founded)	1970	1975	1980	1985
J Sainsbury (late 1920s)	100	100	100	130
Marks & Spencer (1948)	30	43	56	69
Tesco (1973)	–	9	40	112
International (unknown)	3	3	3	3
Argyll (1930s)	11	9	8	11
Safeway (1964)	8	14	20	27
Asda (1970)	8	15	21	27
Fine Fare (1965)	4	5	8	12
Total	164	198	256	391

Details of the work carried out by these technological departments indicated that they could be divided into two groups – 'accepters' and 'interveners'; accepters have small technical departments, whilst interveners — Sainsbury, Tesco and Marks & Spencer — have substantial in-house technological capability. The size of the technological department was the major factor affecting its capability to undertake the various tasks described below, but there was much variation among companies.

The accepters carry out the minimum of tasks necessary to cover themselves under food legislation: They carry out quality control and sensory evaluation of own label products through spot checks on samples selected at random from the shelves of their stores, and factory inspection of prospective own label suppliers to ensure they comply to good hygienic practice. Some try to conduct regular follow-up inspections on current suppliers, but lack of qualified personnel creates problems. In the procurement of own label products, accepters rely on manufacturers who are able to produce imitations of branded products. Manufacturers are provided with a layman's specification, perhaps specifying quality and price, or by reference to a branded product, and might include taste criteria or mouth feel. Suppliers are expected to carry out any reverse engineering necessary, which generally does not present a problem, given the information provided by the statutory list of ingredients. Suppliers are chosen on the basis of samples produced, after which specification details are firmed up with the chosen supplier. Finally, the accepters have limited recourse to external sources of technical expertise. They seek advice from the Research Associations to which they belong to cope with legal, labelling or analytical problems, ie problems they could cope with themselves with a larger staff.

The interveners, by contrast, cover a much wider range of activities. In addition to carrying out the necessary tasks to safeguard themselves under food law, the food technology departments provide in-house services to their stores and warehouses, adopt methods which impose requirements on their suppliers of own label products, and have diversified in new directions. Interveners' food technologists supply technical information for their buying and marketing departments, and in some companies they are even fully integrated into the work of the buying department. Hygiene in stores and warehouses is checked, covering such matters as pest control and sanitation, and staff in stores are trained on correct food handling procedures. With the growing importance of the cold chain (in which foods are handled at between $0°$ and $10°$ C to avoid spoilage) tests are made throughout the distribution chain to check that the correct temperature has been maintained. In addition to these in-house services, interveners work closely with their suppliers to ensure the quality of own label products. Suppliers of own label products are required to carry out regular microbiological tests on production runs and supply results to the retailer. The retailer compares these results with tests on random samples taken from their stores. As well as quality control, these checks can improve standardisation and reproducibility, and give information on shelf life.

Interveners' food technologists liaise very closely with their suppliers. They spend a great deal of time in their suppliers' factories, providing analytical and technical help when necessary. They visit factories worldwide, which often makes them more knowledgeable about developments in food manufacturing than the manufacturer. Factory visits provide the basis on which to assess the performance of available plant, and retailers' food technologists can advise their suppliers on the selection and development of process plant. Interveners use customer complaints as a source of information about failures in quality control, and seek to develop procedures to overcome such problems. They carry out comparative testing on branded goods and competitors' own labels and are often able to identify recipes of competitive products. They are active in developing new products in their test kitchens. In procuring own label products, they draw up rigorous technical specifications for both manufactured and fresh foods. Specifications vary in detail between companies and for different products, but the range and extent of detail which may be included in a specification is indicated below:

> [The specification] will have a description of the product to be provided, eg its appearance and taste. It will also have, for manufactured foods, a full breakdown of ingredients by percentage composition and ... the source of the ingredients; manufacturing details are likely to be included in the specification, eg times and temperatures of heat processes; nutritional composition ... physical, chemical and or microbiological standards are likely to be an important part of the specification and, most important, it is likely to include details of the quality control procedures to be carried out by the supplier ... (Griffiths, 1984, p14).

Retailers who develop own label products try to delay imitations by getting their suppliers to sign exclusivity agreements. After an agreed period of exclusivity, they allow their specifications to be used by suppliers as the basis for competitors' own label products. However, exclusivity agreements are not legally binding and it is very easy to copy food products.

Interveners have also been responsible for passing on the information they acquire from their membership of Research Associations and other sources to their suppliers. In-house technological capability not only affects the methods for procuring own label products, it also affects the choice of supplier. The interveners demand that their suppliers have high hygienic standards, modern production plant, in-house technical expertise and quality control capability. They prefer small firms, so long as they are able to supply the necessary volume, because they are more flexible and prepared to work closely with the retailer. They use large companies for products which involve trade secrets, for instance corn flakes or Coca Cola, or where large volumes are required.

Most significant, however, is the fact that the retailers with large, established food technology departments — 'the interveners' — have been able to implement the new competitive strategy of offering high quality fresh foods and exclusive own label products to their customers. They have been responsible for developing new methods of distribution and storage and for introducing innovative products to market in collaboration with their suppliers. Such collaboration has resulted in the development of frozen and chilled chicken; low fat milk; controlled atmosphere packaged (CAP) meat and gas flushed fish; myco-protein pie; chilled pizza; chilled recipe meals. Many of these retailer-influenced innovations have occurred in fresh and chilled foods, an area traditionally neglected by manufacturers of packaged groceries. Multiples who gain expertise in these products can develop their store image through its association with high quality fresh foods, pioneering new products, or own label products of a higher quality than branded goods. This is important in an environment where food multiples all sell more or less the same brands of food at more or less the same prices. A store able to differentiate itself from its competitors can build market share of total food sales. This is reflected in the market shares of the interveners shown in Table 8.1.

Detailed case studies of these product innovations have shown that retailer involvement was overwhelmingly governed by the need to sell products appropriate to their retailing methods. The problems encountered, for example, with the mass marketing of chicken, focussed retailers' minds on: how to turn it into a grocery product; how to eliminate space and labour costs; and how to minimise wastage from putrefaction of unsold stock. Sainsbury and Marks & Spencer, with cooperation from their suppliers, came up with different solutions to these problems, which led to two parallel innovations — frozen chicken and the 'cool chain' for chilled chicken. Similar considerations dictated the need for Tesco to define very closely the appropriate manufacturing, packaging and palletising methods for chilled pizza. In these instances retailers were largely responsible for the introduction and diffusion of new process plant for the processing of chicken, and for new distribution methods (Senker, 1988).

Retailers who have influenced innovation all have strong food technology departments, but the benefits of such departments do not appear to accrue until several years after their establishment. Sainsbury, with long-standing food technology expertise, related primarily to its manufacturing interests, was able to exploit this expertise for the benefit of its retailing activities when the need arose. Marks & Spencer had traditionally sold food, but did not want to sell it under the St Michael brand name unless it carried the same assurance of quality as other St Michael products. It therefore set up a Food Technology Department in 1948, which was called upon to perform the same task for the company's food products that the Merchandise Development Department had performed for textiles (Rees, 1969, p174-176). It did not reap the benefits of this strategy fully until the 1960s, when all the food sold had reached a sufficiently high quality to bear the St Michael brand name. The example of Tesco, in particular, shows that even companies who only aspire to be 'followers' need to have cumulative expertise. Setting up a technology department in 1973 gave Tesco the opportunity, when the nature of retailing competition changed in the 1980s, to follow Marks & Spencer's and Sainsbury's example of developing and selling quality own label products. By contrast, the 'accepters' can only offer alternatives to branded products.

Unlike manufacturers, who produce commodity-like products for the mass market, these retailers are able to offer a constantly changing range of foods, obtained from numerous suppliers, and are able to tailor the products to meet the needs of the market segment they seek to attract. They minimise the risks attached to innovation by having better access to information on changing consumer demand than food manufacturers. Both undertake market research, but retailers can monitor what is actually happening in their stores. In addition, retailers test market new own label products in selected stores, without having to bear the heavy launching and promotional costs incurred by food manufacturers.

5 Conclusion: assessment of the models

This chapter identified three theoretical models to explain the technological activities of retailers. The information presented shows that a variety of motives govern these activities. Perhaps most significant in terms of innovation was the need to ensure that grocery products were appropriate to changing retail methods. Large scale retailing of traditional packaged groceries did not require retailers to become involved in innovation. When, however, retailers extended their range of products to include frozen, chilled and fresh foods which had limited shelf lives, and were vulnerable to spoilage if incorrectly handled, the need for retailers to define performance characteristics became pressing. Many of the activities of food technology departments, in particular rigid specifications and checks throughout the distribution of chilled food, seem to relate directly to the Rosenberg-derived model. This model, however, suggests that retailers get involved after the introduction of new production processes at the factory. The evidence has shown that retailers have been responsible for the introduction and diffusion of new process plant.

The von Hippel-derived model predicts that retailers develop innovative own label products because they can appropriate the benefits of this activity. The weakness in this model is its failure to acknowledge that firms require in-house technological expertise in order to innovate. Retailers involved in innovation do not appropriate the benefit of specific innovations directly. By stocking exclusive products, however, they are able to build store image and market share. The exclusivity agreements demanded by retailers appear to support von Hippel's ideas that 'response time' may be an important variable in explaining the locus of innovation. The ready availability of process equipment, the lack of patenting and the ease of copying new food products reduce the lead-time before competitors stock the same item. This is exacerbated by retailer dependence on their suppliers for the introduction of the innovation, and the limited power of exclusivity agreements. Because of the short lead-time enjoyed, the introduction of new own label products must be a continuing process.

From this point of view, it is possible to understand retailers' involvement in innovation as part of their competitive strategy. This relates to the model based on Porter's ideas about the technological dimension of competitive strategy. The evidence provides strong confirmation for his idea that competitive threats and opportunities arise from within and without an industrial sector, by showing how the technological expertise of some buyers has promoted innovation by their suppliers. It also provides evidence that implementing a technological strategy in support activities (ie in procurement and transportation) has given some retailers a competitive advantage. However, it highlights two weaknesses in Porter's approach: the need for established in-house technological expertise as a prerequisite for adopting a technological strategy, and consideration of the risks and uncertainties of undertaking innovation. Only retailers with a long tradition of investment in technical expertise are in a position to adopt a technological dimension to their competitive strategy. By monitoring consumer reaction to new products in selected stores, they are able to deploy this expertise so as to minimise the risks associated with innovation. Technological strategy can be an important source of competitive advantage, but competitive success in such a strategy depends on cumulative technological expertise, and on the ability to minimise the risks and uncertainties involved.

All the models presented at the beginning of this chapter provide a partial explanation for retailers' involvement in innovation. The Rosenberg-derived model, which suggests that the application of technology is a response to the problems and opportunities presented by increases in the scale of retail operations, however, is most significant. The development of cumulative in-house technological capability is a prior condition for becoming involved in innovation, whether for von Hippel or Porter type motives. Only the companies which had made a technological response to the challenges of large scale retailing, the 'interveners', had learned that they were able to derive benefits from this approach and were able to deploy a technological dimension to their competitive strategy when the situation so demanded.

Notes

1 Market shares of the food market are usually presented as shares of the packaged grocery market, which only accounts for 35 per cent of grocery outlet turnover. It ignores provisions, fresh fruit and vegetables, and it omits the food sales made through large mixed businesses, such as Marks & Spencer. This table assesses multiples' market share by relating their food turnover to national retail food trade as a whole. This approach has limitations in that the turnover figures for most food multiples includes non-food items, such as alcoholic drinks, sugar and chocolate confectionery or light bulbs. And for some multiples such as Asda and Tesco it includes turnover from clothing and household goods sales. This means that the share of the food market for multiples with large non-food sales tends to be overstated compared to multiples who concentrate on food sales, or who break down their turnover to show the contribution from food, for instance Marks & Spencer and Sainsbury.

2 Distributors' own brands have been defined by the Economist Intelligence Unit as 'consumer products produced by, or on behalf of, distributors and sold under the distributor's own name or trade mark through the distributor's own outlet' (O'Dochartaigh, 1974, p4).

3 This method has been adopted for two reasons. The total number of enterprises is not available for 1958, except by summing enterprises in each 3 digit classification, a total of 7359 enterprises. This is an overestimate because some enterprises appear under more than one heading. During the 1970s and 1980s better methods of identifying very small enterprises led to an apparent increase in the total number of enterprises to 9173.

4 Argyll, Asda, Fine Fare, International, Marks & Spencer, Safeway, Sainsbury and Tesco. (By 1987 Dee Corporation had taken over International and Fine Fare; and Argyll had taken over Safeway.)

Chapter 9

Technology strategies in small and medium-sized firms

Mark Dodgson and Roy Rothwell

1 Introduction

The development and realisation of strategy implies to many an effort and long-term view inappropriate to the circumstances of small and medium-sized firms (SMFs). Managers of such firms are far too concerned with fire-fighting and immediate business tactics, the argument goes; and the opportunity for, and necessity of, strategy formulation are considerably greater in large rather than small firms (Birley, 1982). This chapter will argue that technology-based SMFs need, and increasingly are developing, corporate strategies for technology. Evidence will be provided to show that in some cases these smaller firm strategies are just as sophisticated as those in large firms, if not more so.

Some recent commentators such as Friar and Horwitch (1986) point to the convergence in the strategic directions of large and small firms. Large firms, they argue, increasingly are attempting to emulate the conditions of organisational flexibility and entrepreneurial stimuli of small firms, and small firms are improving 'professional' managerial practices, for example, for accessing technology from external sources. This chapter will argue that such sophisticated strategies were characteristic of a number of Europe's most successful high-tech SMFs. These strategies will be described, and their importance for the successful management of corporate growth and technological change discussed.

2 The importance of high-tech SMFs

SMFs are an important component of many high-tech sectors, and firms in these sectors are often amongst the most successful SMFs. In a recent review of the best twenty US small firms — according to growth in sales and earnings and return on invested capital — fifteen were found to be high-tech based companies (*Business Week*, 25 May 1987). In another recent review of Britain's high-tech 'stars' — adjudged by a panel of experts — one-third of the 33 companies selected had a market capitalisation of below £100 million (*Management Today*, Apr 1987). New technology based firms (NTBFs) are, and have been for some time, a significant feature of US industry, and there is evidence to suggest they are growing in significance in Europe. While a 1977 report by Arthur D. Little found only 200 such firms in the UK, and fewer in West Germany, a 1986 report by Segal, Quince and Wickstead in Cambridge and the ISI Institute in West Germany estimated that in 1985 this number had increased to between 6000 and 7000 NTBFs in the UK, and around 3000 in West Germany.

Figure 9.1 presents firm size/innovation share data for Britain. It plots, for different time periods between 1945 and 1983, the share of important innovations introduced by British firms in five firm-size categories. The data are taken from the SPRU Innovation Databank which contain details of 4500 significant British innovations. Perhaps the most notable feature of the data is the increasing share of national innovations by firms in the 1-199 employees size category. For SMFs (employing below 500) the innovation share increased from 22.6 per cent during 1965-69, to 29.2 per cent during 1975-79, to 38.3 per cent during 1980-83. Using the SPRU database, Wyatt (1984) derived time series data on the ratio, innovation share/employment share. She found that between 1955-59 and 1975-80, the relative efficiency of firms increased from 0.46 to 0.53 in firms employing below 200, and from 0.66 to 0. 82 in firms employing between 200 and 499. Wyatt further found a greater relative R&D efficiency in SMFs (Wyatt, 1984). From these data it appears that SMFs are achieving an increasingly important share of national innovations.

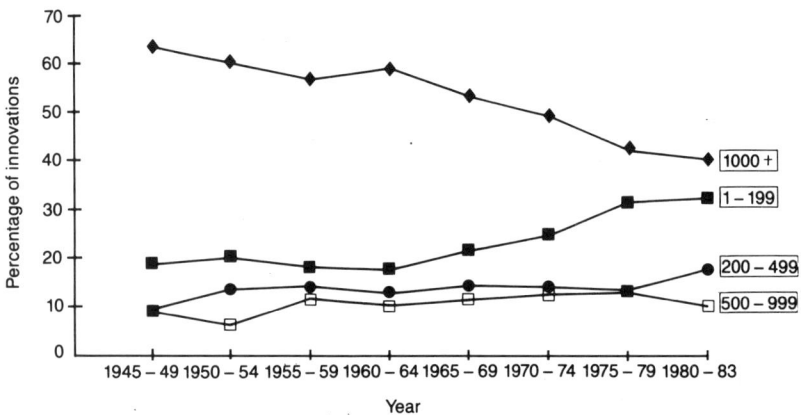

Source: SPRU Innovation Databank
Fig 9.1 Trends in the size distribution of innovating firms 1945-83 (unit employment in boxes)

Various factors explain this rapid growth in the numbers and importance of NTBFs and high-tech SMFs, including: opportunities provided by information technology (IT), biotechnology, new materials technology and the developing software industry; the creation of new capital markets such as the Unlisted Securities Market and the Third Market in the UK, and the growth of available venture capital; improvement in public policies directed towards such firms; and a general improvement in attitudes towards the entrepreneur (for further discussion of these points see Rothwell and Dodgson, 1987; and Dodgson, 1987). The research reported here examined some of the most successful of these companies, focussing in particular on the relationship between their technological mastery and growth patterns. The study highlights that even long established firms can enjoy renewed levels of high performance if they adopt appropriate techno-market strategies based on in-house technological accumulation mixed with effective accessing of external expertise coupled to a strong market orientation.

3 The companies in the study

The research on which this chapter is based was conducted for the EC's Industrial Research and Development Advisory Committee. The chapter will primarily refer to the research conducted by the authors as part of a larger study. The research focussed on studying the strategies, commitment to R&D and economic performance of twelve leading technology-based SMFs in Britain, Denmark, Holland and Ireland. Particular attention was directed towards understanding the factors underlying the success of these companies. This sample was part of a larger sample of 38 such firms throughout the EEC. Not all the firms in the smaller sample (referred to throughout the chapter as the sample) were recent start-ups: the oldest firm was established in 1874, the youngest in 1981. Three firms were established before 1920, four between 1950 and 1970, and five after 1970.

More recently, the sample companies showed remarkable growth in their annual turnover between 1983 and 1985. The average (mean) rate of growth of each company during this period was 127 per cent, and in two cases it was over 300 per cent. Collectively, the twelve firms had annual sales of 212 million European Currency Units (ECU) in 1983. This increased to ECU 261 million in 1984 and ECU 322 million in 1985; a growth rate between 1983 and 1985 of 51.8 per cent. Total employment grew by over 1000 between 1983 and 1986. It grew by 11.2 per cent between 1983 and 1984; by 18.7 per cent between 1983 and 1985; and by 30.7 per cent between 1983 and 1986.

Data on profitability were incomplete. Two firms' accounting procedures did not reveal profit before tax, only after tax (because of complex tax procedures). Generally, profit levels were high. Excluding one company (which was only a few years old and had planned losses), average profit before tax as a percentage of turnover in 1985/86 was 13.3 per cent. This figure does not include the two firms reporting average after tax profits of 8.7 per cent. Three firms reported zero profit or losses in 1983: they were all recently established; two have now moved into profit, while the third is rapidly moving towards profitability. The companies generally were highly export-oriented. Export ratios varied from 5 per cent to 100 per cent of sales, with an average export ratio of 68.7 per cent (these figures do not include one company which, because of complex international transfers of semi-finished items, could not calculate precise export ratios). By far the most important overseas market was the US. Seven companies exported to the US where, in 1985, they exported goods and services worth ECU 88.1 million. The second most important markets were European. Three companies had significant Japanese and Korean export markets.

3.1 Technology

All the companies in the sample were highly technologically advanced. Some were world leaders working at the 'leading edge' of their technology:

in biotechnology, new materials, scientific instruments, and IT-related technologies such as minicomputers and image processing. All the companies were reliant largely on internally-generated knowledge, claiming that their in-house R&D activities are the major source of technical know-how and the main basis of their technological accumulation. Nevertheless, they all enjoyed a variety of often very strong external technological links with universities, research institutes and with other industrial companies, usually suppliers and customers.

A considerable percentage of resources, both financial and manpower, were devoted to R&D activities. The actual R&D expenditure as a percentage of sales varied from 5 per cent to 40 per cent, with an average (mean) of 12.4 per cent. (The data are for eleven firms; one firm declined to reveal its R&D expenditure). These figures are for internally-generated R&D expenditure, and do not include the often large amounts of R&D undertaken for external concerns.

The high level of resources dedicated to R&D was matched by the high number of R&D personnel employed. While noting that one company estimated that all its employees were involved in R&D, the other eleven had 593 employees (or full-time equivalents) working on R&D in the firms; 17.2 per cent of the total number employed. The average intensity of R&D employees/total employees within the eleven firms was 25.6 per cent.

Within the numbers employed in R&D were a high percentage of graduate scientists and engineers. In ten of the firms, 270 out of the 489 employed in R&D were graduates or had postgraduate qualifications (55 per cent). One of the remaining two firms, which claimed all its staff worked on R&D, employed 200 graduates, while the other had 150 science graduates working in the firm, 'most' of whom worked in R&D (it was impossible to obtain a precise figure for R&D employment within this firm).

3.2 External orientation

Most of the firms initially gained technological expertise — and began their movement up the technological learning curve — on the basis of externally acquired know-how. External linkages were still very important: nine firms claimed important technological links with universities; four claimed links with government research institutes; two used licensed-in technology; two created joint ventures; and two made acquisitions in order to access external technology. Four British companies were participants in the Alvey Programme of collaborative research into advanced information technology (*see* Chapter 12).

Three companies began their lives as university spin-offs, and while two no longer have strong technical links with their old university, they have forged strong links with research groups in other universities. Two other companies began their lives dependent on technology from government institutes or departments, with which they retain very strong links. One company, started as a joint venture, initially obtained all its technological know-how from its US partner. Two firms gained their initial technical competence through licensing US technology.

Among the most important continuing sources of external technical information was feedback from users and suppliers. All the firms paid particular attention to feedback from customers, while eight firms specifically mentioned this source as being of key importance in the company's technological development. In a number of cases, user feedback was formalised: in one firm, for example, senior management paid annual visits to all main customers to discover how service could be improved.

The external orientation of innovative firms was confirmed in parallel research at SPRU on a sample of SMFs contained in the Unit's innovation data bank. Of the 103 firms surveyed, 89 per cent had a significant technical and/or market and/or manufacturing relationship with an external institution that involved know-how transfer, and 84 per cent of these links were with other firms (Beesley and Rothwell, 1987). Forty per cent of the firms had some form of technical link with other firms, usually a supplier, a customer or both.

For a small firm, developing a new product can be a high risk activity. It demands a commitment of a large proportion of investment funds to a single project, together with the opportunity costs involved in committing scarce time and skills to one activity rather than another. Anything which can be done to lessen that risk is of great benefit to any size of firm, but is perhaps more crucial to small firms with fewer resources. Engaging in external technical and other linkage activities to increase technical manufacturing, market and sometimes managerial know-how, was an important aspect of the strategies adopted by the highly successful firms described in this chapter.

Links with suppliers were also extremely important, particularly in the electronics area, where firms took great pains to identify new developments in microprocessors which they could incorporate in their products, and new advances in manufacturing methods which they could profitably adopt. External technical expertise and internal knowledge generation were seen in all cases as necessary complements in the overall process of technological know-how accumulation.

4 Management of growth

While all the companies in the sample currently are highly successful, their development towards commercial viability and technological and market leadership has not been without its problems. Access to start-up finance was not a particular difficulty, primarily because of the competence and credibility of the firms' management, but funds to assist subsequent growth or to facilitate vertical integration were often extremely difficult to obtain, especially for the independent companies in the sample. Companies in particular experienced problems in obtaining finance for: long-term R&D; to assist the move to manufacture; and to support major changes and expansion in manufacture.

The companies that have experienced severe financial or market difficulties, did so largely because of poor or complacent management. Three companies were rescued from insolvency through changes in management; one company attributed much of its success to the early appointment of a talented manager; another company had to appoint a new manager to oversee dramatic changes brought about through rapid growth. A company that was formed as part of a public policy initiative attracted private sector funds mainly because of the exceptional quality of its founding management team; and one small company has gained considerably through its access to managerial and financial advice from its shareholding bank.

Different kinds of management skills are needed at different stages in the growth of companies. These can best be analysed by identifying some of the key transitional phases the companies in the sample faced. These phases are very much ideal types and they do not represent a strict chronological model for company growth; they may run concurrently, but each marks a critical threshold in the company's development. The transitional stages are:

– Start-up
– Technological and scientific consolidation
– Internationalisation of markets
– Professionalisation of management
– Vertical integration
– Product and business diversification

As mentioned above, the companies had very different histories, and they were started up by a variety of means and from a variety of sources. They commonly began, however, with an individual, or small group of people, convinced of the potential of a new business based on a particular high technology. The management of this phase is mainly concerned with the process of convincing others — primarily financiers — of this business opportunity. The younger companies in the sample, as we have seen above, successfully attracted early capital investment to start-up their companies on the basis of their managers' technological and business credibility.

Having established a company, a crucial early but continuing phase is that of technological and scientific consolidation. To be at the technological forefront, companies have to amass and master levels of know-how often non-existent elsewhere. Working, marketable prototypes may have to be developed from scientific ideas which previously have produced nothing tangible. Existing technological artefacts may be redesigned and improved using recent scientific developments. Scientific and technological competence is developed to enable the company to attain comparative advantage over other companies. The management skills required at this phase are considerable and diverse. The manager not only has to identify which technologies and scientific developments offer business opportunities through comparative advantage and are to be pursued, but he has also to ensure that the requisite skills to realise that comparative advantage exist in-house or can be obtained and assimilated from external sources.

It is rare for any high technology company to exist entirely on domestic markets. This sample of companies had, on average, over two-thirds of their sales in export markets. Many found marketing overseas to be not only an extremely costly exercise, but one which took up a considerable amount of senior management time. Yet it was essential; in one case the Californian market for one company's products was twice the size of the entire European market. The chief executive officers in the sample claimed that marketing overseas was often their greatest management problem, particularly in the first few years of the company's life, and that the inability to recruit suitable marketing managers was one of the major constraints on future company growth.

The companies in the sample had all undertaken the process of the professionalisation of management. Founders of such companies, although imbued with significant technical and scientific skills combined with entrepreneurial ambition and flair, are not always best equipped to handle the more formal aspects of management, ie creating financial control and reporting systems, personnel management, creating effective organisational structures; nor are they much given to delegating responsibility. These are, however, all essential requisites for young companies wishing to grow rapidly. In three firms the founder/technological entrepreneur consciously and systematically acquired and applied professional management skills, through reading, attendance at seminars and learning from peers and consultants. Other firms recruited professional managers, who, as we have seen above, have been instrumental in overcoming many of the problems facing the company and rebuilding the company's growth pattern. The managerial transition was often a traumatic time for the companies, with the founder/entrepreneur finding it difficult to share control. Most, however, realised the necessity of utilising new skills.

One of the major problems perceived within these companies was a future shortage of available entrepreneurial managerial talent. This reflected the concern that company development and expansion would be limited by the lack of personnel capable of the dynamic leadership required to develop new products aimed at new market niches. Part of the professional manager's skill, it was believed, had to lie in providing the opportunity and incentive for such entrepreneurial development. The most explicit strategy for this was found in a company which had stimulated a number of spin-offs to market new product developments. The person responsible for each product development was awarded with the opportunity of being the managing director of the new company.

Two types of integration strategies were found in the companies: a move to manufacturing, and towards the incorporation of proprietary products with other company products in the form of systems. The move to manufacturing has obvious advantages; greater control over supply, less reliance on subcontractors, attaining more value-added in-house. It also has obvious disadvantages; considerable cost (we have seen that financing this investment often proved difficult), lack of appropriate skills and need for extensive recruitment. The firms that had begun to manufacture did so primarily to realise greater added value; firms that did not manufacture tended not to because of fears of being unable to attract the required skills. The latter type of systems-based integration was less common, although some firms made considerable efforts to extract as much cash flow as possible from in-house developments through incorporation into larger products or systems. Both these types of integration require novel management skills.

The product life cycles in some of these companies were very short; sometimes as short as one to two years. While the high commitment to R&D assisted the updating of products, many companies were actively seeking to diversify into new products. The strategies of the companies were to diversify into areas related or complementary to existing areas of competence. The R&D process was, of course, a major means through which diversification was to be achieved. However, accessing external sources through links with universities, forming joint ventures and acquisitions, was often as important. The decisions of when to diversify and how to select appropriate diversification targets both involve considerable managerial skill — skill which was to be found in these well-managed firms.

The firms in the sample were all successful at managing growth. An important component of this was the successful management of technology. An underlying reason for this was the existence of effective strategies for technology.

5 Technology in a strategic framework

Most of the chief executives in the sample firms had a good knowledge of the technology in which their firms operated, and eight possessed formal technical qualifications. They were all acutely aware of their companies' technical strengths, their competitors' technical strengths, and hence of their comparative technical advantage. This technological awareness underpinned the chief executives' sophisticated strategic plans for technological development. These strategies involved the identification of future strategic market niches and the active planning of the accumulation of technological advantage needed to achieve a sufficient share in those markets. Technological competence and advantage was to be obtained either through internal R&D, licensing, joint venturing, by acquisition, and most commonly by employing a combination of these. Additionally, companies kept abreast of scientific developments in universities and research laboratories. Many of the firms did, however, report that lack of funds to support long-term research was a major problem, and several firms experienced considerable difficulties in identifying suitable R&D partners elsewhere in Europe.

Technology strategy was only one component of the overall strategies of the companies. We have already seen that their market strategy involved concentrating on niche markets, primarily international, where the company competed on technological leadership. The overall business strategies were directed towards rapid growth through organic development and partnerships with, and acquisition of, related and complementary technology businesses.

Another key strategic issue was that of personnel. The success of these companies, as explained by their chief executives, was based on the quality and commitment of their employees. The disadvantages the companies felt because of their inability to match the salaries offered by larger firms, were to some extent counterbalanced by the provision of a stimulating environment in which employees had possibilities for career progression. It was the aim of these firms to provide opportunities for individuals, and at the same time to ensure that this benefited and complemented the needs of the firm. This synthesis between the needs of the firm and the needs of the individual required considerable managerial skill.

6 Conclusions

Technology-based SMFs are an increasingly important part of Europe's industrial structure. Nation states have developed a plethora of support mechanisms for small firms (Rothwell and Zegveld, 1985), and they have become an important policy target for the EC. Much of this policy, particularly until recently in the UK, has been directed towards the role SMFs play in the process of employment creation rather than their ability to generate new technological products, processes and services (see Dodgson and Rothwell 1988). Yet the potential of European SMFs to develop and utilise new technology is virtually limitless. In his chapter in this volume, Hobday describes the growth in the number of small and medium-sized semiconductor manufacturers in Europe, and their strategic significance. Belussi's chapter charts the rapid growth of an Italian clothing company based in a major part on technological innovation. Without suggesting that SMFs represent a panacea for industrial regeneration in Europe, these two examples highlight their efficacy and importance both in key new industries and in traditional industrial sectors.

How do policy-makers assist the development of technology-based SMFs? Already much is being done: universities are becoming more active in encouraging technology transfer, schemes ranging from consultancy support to tax credits for R&D are in place, and venture capital is increasingly available throughout Europe. Sharp, in Chapter 13, describes the high number of SMFs participating in the EC ESPRIT programme. Much still needs to be done: more long-term seed corn and development capital is needed; procurement policies need more SMF bias; far greater effort is needed in education to produce more highly-skilled manpower; and, very importantly, European markets need liberalising to produce a large and truly common market (Rothwell and Dodgson, 1987).

The majority of these policies are universal in their approach. They aim at increasing the population of high-tech SMFs in the hope that by supporting the many they will assist the few which contribute greatly to the process of technological development and which might grow into the large firm league. What is required, however, is more targeting of measures to companies with obvious and outstanding growth potential. SMFs of the type described in this chapter should be viewed as national and European strategic assets. Their development should be nurtured and supported by technological, market, financial and management assistance. A key defining criterion of future growth potential is the existence of a coherent strategy for technological development. Its existence could be one of the major factors which determines which firms should receive specific targeting. Explicit strategy documents could be reviewed, assessed and influenced.

The companies studied for the research are, of course, exceptional. The major factor underlying their success and growth is the quality of their management. While technological entrepreneurs are 'born entrepreneurs' and cannot be reproduced, professional managers, aware of all the limitations and possibilities of small firms, and capable of identifying, encouraging and nurturing entrepreneurship can be trained. Yet very little effort is devoted to management training. In Britain, at least, most managers lack formal education and training (Constable and McCormick, 1987), and in the case of high-tech SMFs 63 per cent have no management training at all (Mangham and Silver 1986). If Europe is to take seriously the possibilities provided by high-tech SMFs, then considerable resources have, as a matter of urgency, to be allocated to management training.

One important facet of that training would be concerned with strategy formulation. The research reported here has highlighted its importance for determining the patterns of growth of high-tech SMFs. Yet these strategies need to move beyond the emphasis on niche markets. No European technology company has emulated the phenomenal and rapid growth of a US company like Digital Equipment, or a Japanese company like Sony. For a European firm to prosper in such a way, global markets need to be addressed. Few European SMFs have the confidence or ambition to approach such markets. It should be a priority for researchers and policy-makers in the future to assess how strategies might be framed, and how best to identify those companies in which such a strategy might be realised.

Chapter 10

Corporate strategy: skills, education and training

Peter Senker and Tim Brady

1 Introduction

In this chapter we shall argue that traditional economic analysis takes no account of relationships between firms' strategies and policies and their demands for skills. Because of the uncertainties which industrialists face, and the incompleteness of the information which they have at their disposal, few of the key strategic decisions which industrialists make are entirely determined by market forces as orthodox economists would have us believe. We suggest an alternative model to describe the real world in which industrialists operate: one in which firms have discretion to decide whether to innovate or not, and to decide on their recruitment and training policies. Using case study material, we try to show that this alternative model provides a better explanation of the relationships between firms' strategies and policies and their demands for skills.

We argue that, in an environment of rapidly changing technologies and markets, systematic human resource development, including career development planning and continual periods of education and training, is crucial to effective strategic planning.

2 Theoretical background

The neoclassical theory of the firm assumes that businesses — individual entrepreneurs — respond automatically to shifts in the relative costs of inputs, and to changes in the relative prices that they can secure for the products they produce. Businessmen are assumed to have perfect knowledge of market conditions, to know and use the best production techniques and materials, and to select and buy other inputs — including the manifold types and grades of skilled labour, in order to maximise profits in the short run.[1]

The elements of the model relevant here can be summarised as follows:

– the entrepreneur has perfect knowledge of market needs;
– the firm makes products which the market demands;
– the entrepreneur uses the lowest cost production methods from the techniques available, and the lowest possible cost combination of materials to make products; and
– the entrepreneur chooses the least cost combination of skills.

It is impossible adequately to condense Routh's review of the sorry history of classical and neoclassical economics (Routh, 1975) into this brief chapter. However, salient points which impinge on the issues central to our thesis are set out below.

Routh suggests that Kuhn's concept of scientific paradigms (Kuhn, 1962) has application to economics: 'once it has achieved the status of paradigm, a scientific theory is declared invalid only if an alternative candidate is available to take its place.' He argues that neoclassical economics is only likely to die when an alternative paradigm is available to take its place. Routh concludes that blocking the way to the establishment of a new paradigm are 'powerful vested interests with the qualities of a self-perpetuating religious order' (Routh, 1975, pp196, 311, 24).

Routh cites John Kenneth Galbraith's Presidential Address to the American Economic Association in 1969. Galbraith points out that the three legs on which neoclassical economics stands — consumers' sovereignty, maximisation of profits and subordination of the firm to the market — 'tax capacity for belief'.

He goes on to suggest that orthodox[2] economics:

> ...ignores facts as irrelevant, bases its constructs on axioms arrived at a priori, or 'plucked from the air', from which deductions are made and an imaginary edifice created. It inhabits a world of purely economic phenomena, of universal validity yet, or because of this, without history; therefore subject to mathematical treatment, its variables and constants unaffected by the passage of time. Man and society are stripped of their attributes, as if they could exist without psychological, legal, historical or moral dimension. Thus verification is both impossible and regarded as unnecessary. In effect, then, orthodox economics becomes a matter of faith and, ipso facto, immune to criticism (Routh, 1975, p25).

Routh concedes that, prior to consideration of the evidence adduced in the rest of his book, defenders of orthodox economics 'would have no difficulty in outlining a rebuttal', on the grounds that 'there is no such thing as a paradigm common to all orthodox economists, and, indeed the term "orthodox" is itself a misnomer for those who accept certain standards of rigour in the teaching and examining of economics' (1975, p27).

Routh is by no means alone in the vigour of his condemnation of orthodox classical and neoclassical economics. For example, Kay has written in a similar vein in relation to neoclassical economics. He suggests that 'The insulation of neoclassical theory from empirical reality and competing paradigms has been virtually complete...mainstream economics has continued to be a fertile source of sterile theories...It represents an intellectual tragedy of the first order...If the neoclassical theory of the firm had remained in Nirvana, and somebody today published a theory of the firm based on omniscient owner-managers of single product firms, the absurdity of this concept would guarantee it a brief life cycle' (Kay, 1974, pp187-9).

In the 1930s, Berle and Means published a pioneering work which considered some implications of the separation of ownership and control in the modern corporation (Berle and Means, 1932). This was followed by an extensive literature which developed managerial and behavioural theories of the firm.

This literature does not yet amount to a concerted attack on the neoclassical fortress, which survives the continuing multifarious and uncoordinated sniping to which it has been subjected since its formulation some three hundred years ago. The approaches of theoreticians such as Simon (1961), Cyert and March (1963) and Galbraith (1972), to name but a few, have been diverse. But no coherent theory is yet available to replace neoclassical economics.

For the purposes of this chapter, the principal limitations of neoclassical economics as a mode of analysis may be summarised as:

— The nature of the entrepreneur as a short run profit maximising and cost minimising 'automaton'.
— The absence of consideration of product change. There have been even greater changes in the products made between the turn of the century and now than in production processes.[3]
— In the neoclassical model of the economy, there is no possibility of businesses deciding whether to make high technology products incorporating IT or low technology products; whether to make their products from metals, plastics or ceramics; no need for them to decide whether to make products by conventional manual methods, or to automate; whether to seek to enter new markets, or to remain serving traditional ones.
— Neoclassical economics considers skill shortages in terms of insufficient people available to fill vacancies.
— Recruitment policy is condensed into the grossly inadequate 'least cost combination of skills' formula.

Neoclassical economic theory makes the assumption that businessmen subject to market forces make perfect decisions based on complete and accurate information. The ideology of market forces extends and distorts this into the belief that businessmen actually make perfect decisions in the real world.

Real firms, whether private or nationalised, face strategic decisions: the messages they receive from the marketplace are important inputs to decision-making. But the market information which businesses obtain does not and could not provide complete data for the decisions about developing new technologies and markets which businesses have to make. Such decisions have profound implications for the skills which firms demand.[4]

Below we summarise the main assumptions of an alternative to the neoclassical economic model in which firms have discretion to decide whether to innovate or not, and to decide on their recruitment and training policies.

— Management can acquire knowledge of market needs. Market

information, even though it is imperfect, provides important inputs to decision-making.
— Management decides which products to develop and make.
— Management decides which production techniques to employ: they may develop some of their own production methods.
— Management selects, recruits and trains in accordance with its work organisation policies, perceived skill needs and with the traditions and prejudices of the society, industry, locality and firm. Recruitment, work organisation and training policies may be influenced by negotiation with workers and trade unions.
— Choice of products developed and made, production methods and materials used may be constrained by availability of skills.

Using case study material, we shall now show how this 'alternative model' allows a better explanation of firm strategy and analysis of some of its education and training policy implications.

3 Education and training as strategic issues

In order to achieve competitive success, firms need to acquire and develop the manpower resources necessary to achieve their product/market goals. They have to determine what skills they need in order to cope with markets and technologies say five to ten years into the future. Involved in this are forecasting, planning and implementation. The development of markets and technologies needs to be forecast. The firm's role in these markets and in relation to the technologies has to be planned. Appropriate recruitment and training policies need to be devised and implemented.

The need for new skills is not generated by market forces. It is generated by the decisions of businesses on the products they make, the production processes they install, the materials from which they decide to make their products, and by decisions about organising work. And businesses do not and cannot make these decisions 'perfectly'. A firm which wishes to continue to make the same products by the same production methods from the same materials is unlikely to demand new skills. However, a firm which wishes to make new products and/or adopt new production methods and/or incorporate new materials may well demand and train workers with new skills to conduct R&D, to design the new products, to select the appropriate new materials and to operate and maintain new production equipment.

If firms fail to secure and retain the resources of skilled labour they need to implement their product/market plans, then those plans will fail. A shortage of engineers and scientists can result in failure to develop, or delay in developing, the planned products and the production processes by which they are to be made. Failure to recruit and train sufficient production workers can result in failure to achieve production targets. A failure to retain key skilled workers will be detrimental to the long-term competitive position of companies. Proper human resource development, including career development planning and continuous education and training to meet changing skill requirements in the face of technological and market developments, is a crucial element of strategic planning.

Firms in other nations appear to plan and operate on this basis to a far greater extent than their UK counterparts: the introduction to a 1984 study on vocational training and education in West Germany, the United States and Japan describes how '...all three see a clear link between investment in education and competitive success' (Institute of Manpower Studies, 1984, piii). In contrast, a recent report on employers' attitudes towards training in the UK reveals that 'few employers think training sufficiently central to their business for it to be a main component in their corporate strategy' (Coopers and Lybrand, 1985, p4). The following case study illustrates these points.

Case Study 1: The washing machine manufacturing plant

The relatively poor performance of the British washing-machine industry cannot be laid entirely at the door of poor corporate strategy within the industry. Nevertheless, some part of the failure of major UK manufacturers such as Hoover and Hotpoint to make a greater impact on European washing-machine markets in the 1960s must have been due to inappropriate corporate strategies and decision-making.

Technological change in both the products and the production processes used in the domestic washing machine industry has been relatively slow during the last several decades, and the British industry has generally lagged behind its European competitors. Hoover was successful in beating off the challenge from John Bloom in the market for twin-tubs, but was slow to change to making automatics. Hotpoint was early into the market for automatics, but retrenched sharply in the face of very difficult market conditions and lost the possibility of making a substantial impact on European markets in the subsequent period.

Although British firms have generally been slow to incorporate new technical developments in their production processes, the vast majority of washing machines now made by the British industry are automatics, and microprocessor controls have been introduced on some 'up-market' washing machines.

Various means for automating the operation of presses have been adopted, including microprocessor control. The use of plastics has been increasing gradually — including the substitution of plastics for metal in the manufacture of the complex outer tub; and a leading British manufacturer has pioneered the use of precoated metal for the outer casing of the machine, eliminating the need for a paint shop. The use of electronic automatic washing machine test facilities is now common in British washing machine plants.

Nevertheless, it is questionable whether all British firms have equipped themselves with skills adequate to cope with the present technology in the machines they make, or in the production processes which they operate. Problems arise in relation both to product design and production process implementation.

The case of one British washing machine plant in the course of a major investment programme illustrates the problems of making decisions about work/organisation and training in the absence of clear strategic policy guidelines (Senker et al, 1988).

The company insisted that Expenditure Proposals should include provision for training. However, a major materials handling project they started ran out of money before any had been allocated to training, and the training requirements had not been thought through. New automatic test equipment had been installed and debugged. New models were being introduced and this needed the automatic testing machines to be reprogrammed. The work was subcontracted back to the manufacturer of the test equipment at considerable expense, since the company lacked the skills needed to do this in-house.

Shopfloor people were inadequately trained. The plant relied on (professional) engineers to deal with day-to-day 'firefighting' problems on the shopfloor computerised equipment. This diverted the engineers from work on product and process development.

This lack of a clear policy in relation to work organisation and training had left the company with several unresolved questions:

— With new equipment, should you man up, eg employ technologists; or should you upgrade current skills? Should skilled jobs be deskilled, or will unskilled jobs be reskilled? For example, a supplier of automated machines had offered courses. The company had yet to send anyone away on the training course: it was not sure whether to send supervisors, setters, quality control or maintenance staff.
— In general, was it sensible to plan increasingly on the basis that one person should be trained to deal with all aspects of complex items of equipment? (Programming, setting, operation and maintenance.) Management was concerned that if such a policy were to be adopted, it would challenge their current policy of employing flexible semi-skilled workers who are able to work on a range of jobs throughout the plant. Similarly, training a small group of technicians able to fault-find, and perhaps reprogram computer-controlled machines would challenge their current policy of employing craftsmen able to perform a range of tasks from the relatively simple to the highly complex.

They had made an attempt, which failed, to introduce production craftsmen who would combine maintenance, toolmaking, fitting and electronics work.

Exceptionally, some major British firms have recognised the significance of education and training to their future success. Our second case study shows how education and training has been used as an agent of change in the reorganisation of manufacturing in Lucas Industries.

Case Study 2: Lucas Industries[5]

Lucas Industries is a large engineering company founded in the last century, which evolved to become a supplier of automotive components, and subsequently into a world-wide group supplying systems and components to aerospace and industrial markets in addition to the automotive market. In the 1970s, shortcomings in corporate management led to a lack of awareness of changes in market conditions faced by the company. By 1980, the domestic market had contracted severely, whilst there was increased competition in the international market. These external factors were compounded by internal problems. The manufacturing methods in many of the company's plants reflected the classical narrow production engineering of large volumes and a small degree of product variety, which had become the norm during the 1960s. The pattern of demand had since shifted towards smaller volumes but greater variety of products. Lucas had reacted to these changes in demand by incremental adjustments in its manufacturing methods, but something more radical was required to make the company competitive again.

In 1981, Lucas made the first financial loss in its history. A new strategy was devised to make the company more competitive in the changed market environment. The total strategy consisted of several elements — a marketing strategy; a product engineering strategy; a manufacturing systems engineering strategy; and a business systems engineering strategy — overlaid by a financial control strategy. The development of this strategy was an iterative process. Only once targets were established and set for the various businesses could the next stages of the strategy — product engineering, manufacturing and business systems engineering — be developed.

Each business unit was required to produce a competitiveness achievement plan (CAP). This involved comparing its performance with that of its best international competitor, and if its own performance was inferior, specifying how it intended to close the gap. Businesses with CAPs considered feasible and affordable were provided with the necessary financial and manpower resources; those without credible CAPs were earmarked for closure or disposal. Concurrent with the introduction of CAPs, the company undertook a 'bottom-up' exercise among their product engineers asking them how they thought their roles might be changed in the new market circumstances and what organisational and personal barriers there were to improved performance.

At an early stage in this process it became clear that a major reorganisation of manufacturing processes would be needed if businesses were to become more competitive. In 1983, Lucas appointed a new Director for Manufacturing Technology to achieve this reorganisation which involved moving to a manufacturing systems approach. Because of a shortage of manufacturing systems engineers from academia, the company had to devise its own training schemes to retrain its existing manufacturing engineers.

The changes in moving to a manufacturing systems approach were on such a scale that they have taken place over several years and virtually no one in the company has been left untouched by them. A resource intensive awareness training scheme was developed to explain the need for the changes and to gain the commitment of the people involved. This was the first task for the training department. A top-down approach was used for this process because of the need for top management commitment to the changes before they were implemented.

Two main mechanisms were adopted to force the changes. The first was the use of 'task-forces' in the individual businesses to bring about the changes in manufacturing methods. The second was the redevelopment of the central training department into an agent of organisational change. In addition, an internal Systems Engineering Contracting Unit covering manufacturing technology development, manufacturing systems engineering, and business systems engineering, was established. This was staffed by young graduate generalist manufacturing systems engineers and business systems engineers.

The task forces are multidisciplinary teams of people drawn from functions in the individual business units, such as marketing, finance, design and personnel as well as production engineering and manufacturing systems engineering. These are supplemented by engineers from the Systems Engineering Contracting Unit to provide systems engineering expertise and assist in training the in-house members of the task force. Following initial training, the task force redesigns the business unit and its manufacturing strategy.

A crucial role has been played by the central training department in developing appropriate training courses and inputs to facilitate the changes. A new training framework needed to be established, and a new training strategy devised, to ensure that all training — whether provided centrally, at company level, or individual site level — formed an agreed and integrated programme. The scale of the task was such that new delivery mechanisms had to be developed in addition to new courses. A modular structure of training has been evolved over a period of three years providing flexibility, individual tailoring of training for specific needs, training on the basis of when the need arises, and realistic operations support to allow people to divide the time spent on training into smaller elements with less disruption of their normal operational role.

A number of new delivery techniques including computer-based training aids, factory simulation case studies and videos have been used. Despite these, traditional facilities were unable to cope with the scale of the retraining task and the company turned to open learning. The development of open learning courses has enabled the company to reach many more people in a shorter time than would otherwise have been possible.

4 Skills implications of commitment to innovation

While Lucas recognised the significance of education and training to their future, in general there is a gulf between the thinking of UK industrialists and some of their major overseas competitors in relation to innovation and skills.

There are very considerable differences between the various sectors of British industry in their commitment to technological activities. The commitment of British industry to innovation has been questioned by Patel and Pavitt (1987) who have shown that industry-financed R&D in the UK had the lowest rate of growth amongst ten major advanced nations, between 1967 and 1983. They present evidence that British industry has not only declined in its commitment to innovation relative to the US and Japan, but also relative to other major European countries such as France and West Germany. In particular, the innovative strengths of British electronics firms in the 1960s have been eroded, reflected in a declining share of world exports and rapid growth in imports. We believe that part of the reason is because British industrialists' decision-making has often been unduly influenced by short-term considerations (see Chapter 1).

Just as managers decide what to invest in R&D, and whether to incorporate new technologies — such as IT, or high technology materials — in their products and production processes, they also have the discretion to decide what education and experience they will require of people who are recruited to perform particular types of work; and what training to give them once recruited.

Case Study 3: High technology ceramics

The case of high technology ceramics shows how British industrialists' lack of commitment to innovation can feed through into lack of demand for new skills. The last 25 years has seen the emergence of a range of new structural materials including advanced ceramics, polymer composites, and strong engineering plastics. The importance of these new materials goes beyond the advantages to be gained from improvements in performance and the availability of new products. Potentially there is a 'multiplier effect' which may enhance the future economic performance of those countries which can achieve a significant market presence in new materials (Brady, 1988).

In Japan, where the advanced ceramics sector is more mature than in other countries, there is already evidence of such a multiplier effect. Not only is the production sector growing, but peripheral industries are emerging, such as those which produce advanced ceramics manufacturing equipment and those which design materials with specific properties.[6] Japanese user firms are also heavily involved, and their role is critical: Pavitt and Thomson (1987) make the general point that the growth of innovative small firms depends on 'large and dynamic user firms willing and able to be innovative and efficient in their own production technologies'.

Thousands of graduates and other research workers are employed on advanced ceramics R&D in other Western industrialised countries, especially in the US. The Americans now appreciate the strategic importance of advanced ceramics and have launched a number of R&D

programmes in efforts to try to match the Japanese. But the resources being expended by British firms on R&D on advanced ceramics appear to fall far short of what is necessary for the UK to gain any strategic advantage from their production and use.[7]

The availability of appropriately trained, skilled personnel will be a major constraint on realising the opportunities offered by advanced ceramic materials, *only if* UK firms decide to embark on more ambitious R&D programmes in advanced ceramics, and secure the resources necessary to do so. At present, British demand for these specialised high technology skills is low. This reflects the fact that few British industrialists appreciate that, to remain competitive, they need such skills. At present, their strategies do not envisage the prospect of using the new materials on any significant scale and they are not making plans to recruit accordingly.

Industrialists' failure to innovate results in loss of economic activity to overseas competitors, it does not always result in skill shortages in the economists' sense. Traditional economics tends to assume that 'if there was a shortage in any particular occupational group, relative pay levels in that occupation would rise...after a lag while the market adjustment took effect, a new wage level sufficient to remove the shortage would be reached' (Brady, 1989).

But failure to innovate can actually *prevent* skill shortages, as vacancies for new skills are not created, and the lack of economic activity in new technologies can detract from economic growth. This does not reflect 'market forces': it reflects conscious decisions made, or perhaps not made, by industrialists.[8]

It is clear from the case of advanced ceramics described above, that the demand for ceramics skills will increase *only if* British industrialists decide that they want to make use of these new materials. Similar arguments apply elsewhere: it is only advisable to educate more electronics and software engineers to the extent that industry plans to modernise its products and production processes.

5 Training policies in Britain and Japan

Once employees have been recruited, employers need to decide what training to give them. Employers' strategies, attitudes and policies are more important in determining the extent and nature of training than 'market forces'. Earlier, we mentioned a recent report which criticised attitudes to training in British industry (Coopers and Lybrand, 1985). In summary, it was found that few British employers saw training as an issue of major importance. Training was more likely to be seen as an overhead to be cut when profits were under pressure, rather than as an investment in the company's future (the case of the washing machine manufacturer reported above clearly shows the lack of priority given to training in comparison with capital investment). The report's authors found pervasive negative attitudes towards training amongst British top managers. They regarded the reasons given to justify management reluctance to invest in training as mainly rationalisations of generally negative attitudes: factors mentioned include uncertainties about future markets, prospects and technological developments; risks of poaching; demarcation problems and problems related to the responsiveness of external training suppliers.

Attitudes to vocational education and training are very different in Japan. Japanese employees typically commit themselves to a particular firm when they leave the education system, and employers try so far as possible to retain their employees. Japanese firms prefer to recruit young and inexperienced workers and to instil positive attitudes towards working for the employer at the same time as training in specific job skills. Japanese employers are highly committed to training employees 'on-the-job' in the range of skills needed for their current job. There is no problem in persuading employees to train for changes in their job, or to do new jobs, the need for which arise as a result of technological change. Workers and management are strongly committed to the goals of the organisation, which includes strong commitment to transferring skills from senior to junior employees.

Ronald Dore (1987) analysed the differences between the 'organisation-oriented' system of employment in Japan and the 'market-oriented' system of employment still dominant in the thinking of British firms. Some of the points he makes are summarised in Table 10.1.

Table 10.1. British and Japanese employment systems

British system	Japanese system
Market-oriented	Organisation-oriented
Individuals take their skills to the market looking for new employment whenever it seems advantageous to them: possibility of mobility often in the thoughts of both employer and employee	The marketability of their skills is of little concern to employees who do not normally expect to be in the job market
Employers see training as an alternative to buying in skills	Employers see training as a means of getting their employees to do their present jobs better

Most UK firms conform to the market-oriented employment approach outlined above, and our previous two company case studies both fall into this category, even though one has successfully used training as a strategic tool while the other has afforded it little importance. Our fourth case study is a rare example of an organisation-oriented company (in Dore's definition) in which the concept of continuing education and training is completely integrated with operational goals and strategies.

Case Study 4: IBM UK Ltd[9]

Education and training is seen as a vital and integral part of IBM's competitive strategy — they maintain that it is not separable from the other elements of its strategy. Investment in education and training is given a high priority because it is considered fundamental to the achievement of the company's goals. Without an appropriately resourced education and training policy, IBM's employment and career development policies — central planks of IBM's strategy — would be unworkable.

The training and education policy takes account of both short- and long-term requirements. In the long-term IBM needs its workforce to be able to react to changing technological and market circumstances and it sees an educated workforce as the best way to facilitate this. Many of the shorter-term requirements relate to skills implications of changes in product mix and process technology.

The commitment to the long-term needs is exemplified by IBM's employment and personal development policies. IBM tends to recruit people for a career rather than for a specific job — with the exception of some production jobs in manufacturing and some jobs where a particular skill or expertise is required. People are recruited for their potential as much as for their immediate usefulness to the company. Each employee has a career development plan, continually updated, which covers personal and professional development. Promotion is on the basis of meeting performance targets in annual appraisal rather than on the basis of qualifications. Thus there are links between education and training plans, employee development plans and the appraisal system. It is in the individual's interest to acquire new skills which will enhance his/ her usefulness to the company, and in return for security of employment (provided by the company's employment policy) employees are expected to be flexible in terms of the types of job they do and the skills they acquire.

Education and training in IBM are largely functionally based. There are some centrally developed programmes addressing the long-term requirements of the company — Management Personnel Development (MPD), and Technical Personnel Development (TPD). These specify the number of hours training each manager (in the case of MPD) or technical person — engineers, scientists, systems engineers, programmers, systems analysts, and technical managers — (in the case of TPD), is expected to receive in the year.

In addition to the central programmes is plant level education and training. Manufacturing plants base their training provision on the centrally developed programmes, but tailor them for their own operational requirements. About 80 per cent of this training reflects short-term operational requirements with the remaining 20 per cent relating to strategic requirements. Identification of future skills needs takes place at two levels - plant level skills and individual skills. The former result from changes in product and process technology likely to take place over the next five years. The second level is covered via the procedures already discussed - the appraisal system and employee development plan in which individual skills needs (and hence training requirements) are noted.

As with Lucas Industries, a wide range of delivery mechanisms and techniques are employed. Distance learning is being used increasingly and is found especially useful in the manufacturing plants operating a three-shift system.

6 Conclusions

Neoclassical economics assumes that firms recruit a lowest cost combination of skills in order to minimise the costs of producing a given range of products. In this model of firm behaviour, there is no scope for the exercise of corporate human resource development strategy.

This chapter has indicated some of the limitations of the neoclassical economists' model. Employees are not recruited just to make existing products out of the materials used at present by current production methods: some employees are recruited — and trained — explicitly to develop new products, sometimes out of new materials, and to devise and implement new production methods. Deciding to manufacture new products, to use new materials, to implement new production processes inherently involves explicit policies for skills and training which should be integrated into corporate strategies (this also applies to new services; *see* Thomas and Miles, Chapter 6).

In a competitive capitalist economy, market forces ensure that the production of some products ceases because customers refuse to buy them. Market forces direct economic activity away from the production of unwanted goods and services. Market forces also provide incentives for businesses to meet consumers' demands. Centrally planned economies lack this mechanism for eliminating gross inefficiency. But, no matter how strong the incentives, market forces cannot operate by themselves to ensure that businesses anticipate consumer requirements and demand the skills necessary for their satisfaction.

The examples of the UK washing machine plant and Lucas illustrate these points. Lucas was producing products no longer demanded by the market, or, because of inappropriate manufacturing methods, at costs which were too high in relation to those of its competitors. But it took several years for signals from the market to translate themselves into consolidated action because there was no strategy linking market requirements to product development, production engineering and business planning. Once Lucas had decided to adopt an integrated strategy, the role of education and training became crucial in its implementation. The washing machine manufacturer was pursuing a market-led product and production engineering strategy but had ignored the question of skills. As a result it was unlikely to be able to produce its products competitively.

Treating investment in education and training in the same way as capital investment is also inappropriate. IBM maintains that a full economic assessment of its education and training policies is not feasible. They have sought a definitive measurement in terms of return on investment for many years, but without success. Some job-related training has yielded measurable benefits in terms of productivity or improved quality: both IBM and Lucas attribute improvements in their manufacturing performance to training. But assessing the benefits of education and training which are not directly linked to specific job requirements is less easy.

IBM and Lucas differ sharply in their attitudes towards the provision of education and training that are not directly job-related. In IBM, education is seen as providing the more strategic and fundamental skills while training relates to the skills and knowledge required to carry out specific jobs. IBM holds the position that no education is wasted as it contributes to career development, and that it makes their employees 'better people'. In Lucas 'a key aspect is training provision in support of projects as distinct from training supplied in the hope it might be useful' (NEDO, 1987). In this respect it mirrors the job-specific training at IBM. At Lucas, the pressing need across the Group for new manufacturing techniques and the long-term development of engineering management expertise are seen as examples of strategic skill requirements. But Lucas views the broader IBM concept of education as superfluous.

We are not suggesting that IBM's concept of education and training is superior to that of Lucas. But it would appear that both firms' attitudes towards education and training are superior to that of the washing machine manufacturer (Case Study 1). Both IBM and Lucas view education and training as central to their corporate strategies. In Lucas, the main thrust of recent strategy has been the reorganisation of the manufacturing process: much of their training has been directed towards achieving this successfully. But there is a continuing commitment to education and training in other areas — in product engineering, in marketing and business systems engineering. IBM's commitment to education and training is clear — in their opinion, to neglect it would be commercial suicide. We believe that these case studies provide some useful lessons for many companies.

Uncertainties about future markets, prospects and technological developments should not deter firms from educating and training their workforces — indeed failure to provide adequate and relevant education and training may destroy opportunities for moving into new markets, for enjoying new prospects and for benefiting from new technology. Education and training should not be marginal activities to be cut when profitability falls. Rather, they should form key components of and be fully integrated into overall corporate strategies.

Notes

1 'In the modern world nearly all the means of production pass through the hands of employers and other businessmen who specialise in organising the economic forces of the population. Each of them chooses in every case those factors of production which seem best for his purposes. And the sum of the prices which he pays for those factors which he uses is, as a rule, less than the sum of the prices which he would have to pay for any other set of factors which could be

subsitituted for them: for, whenever it appears that this is not the case, he will as a rule, set to work the less expensive arrangement or process ... if there are two methods of obtaining the same result, one by skilled and the other by unskilled labour, that one will be adopted which is the more efficient in proportion to its cost' (Marshall, 1961, pp404-5).

2 Routh criticises both classical and neoclassical economics under the umbrella term of orthodox economics.

3 'The fundamental impulse that sets and keeps the capitalist engine in motion comes from the new consumer goods, the new methods of production or transportation, the new markets, the new forms of industrial organisation that capitalist enterprise creates' (Schumpeter, 1950, p83).

4 'We are talking about a world in which decisions to employ and to produce are at the discretion of thousands of decision makers, each in a state of doubt about what the others are going to do and as to the outcome of his own decisions' (Routh, 1975, p298).

5 The information here is derived from a case study by Tim Brady published in *Education and Training in Lucas Industries*, NEDO, September 1987.

6 Illustrated, for example, by the recent demonstration at the Milan European Machine Tool Show of a prototype grinding machine for ceramic components developed by Yamazaki. The new machine, called Ceratech, was developed with assistance from Tokyo University's production engineering institute and is claimed to resolve many of the difficulties that have held back the widespread use of ceramics in engineering (*Financial Times*, 12 Nov 1987).

7 UK expenditure on ceramics R&D in 1983 was estimated to be £33.1 million in comparison with something between £320 million and £430 million in Japan in 1984. The British Chamber of Commerce in Japan, *Research and Development in Japan*, 1987.

8 It was the absence of the link between industrialists' strategies and the demand for engineers in the arguments of the Finniston Committee's Report which laid it wide open to criticism by conventional economists. The Report forecast unequivocally that 'Total demand for engineers....will increase' (*Engineering our Future: Report of the Committee of Inquiry into the Engineering Profession*, HMSO cmnd 7794, 1980, p761). Finniston did recognise the need for appropriate industrial strategies, but failed to emphasise that, in their absence, the forecast demand for more engineers would not materialise. This failure led to the accusation by economists that it represented special pleading on behalf of the engineering profession.

9 The information here is derived from a case study by Tim Brady, published in *Education and Training in IBM UK Ltd*, NEDO, September 1987.

Chapter 11

Design management strategies

Paul Gardiner and Roy Rothwell

1 Introduction

Design management strategies are an essential element of overall corporate technology management strategies. In order to manage design strategically, it is necessary first to understand what is meant by 'design', and here we are concerned about design not only as the aesthetics of shape and form, but also, and more importantly, as engineering design and product development. Given these different senses of design, it should be noted that there is a very wide range of ways in which these notions can be applied in practical company-based situations. Nevertheless, the main point is that design can and should be managed in all its senses and its areas of application. With regard to the design of products, manufacturing processes or systems, the strategic management of design requires knowledge of a wide range of issues including, centrally:

— where the firm and its fundamental technologies and products stand in relation to competitors and their products;
— knowing where the firm wants to go, and equally importantly where it does not want to go in terms of technologies, products and markets;
— knowing what are the technological options and the realistic (achievable) pathways that should be considered given the firm's relative strengths and weaknesses (technological, manufacturing, design, marketing, financial);
— stimulating the dialogue between product development, production, marketing and financial personnel concerning the market potential of existing designs and of possible new designs; and
— making the idea of 'good design' and innovation part of the corporate culture, which is necessary if the company is to be successful and profitable.

The implementation of design strategies requires:

— taking steps towards the accumulation of the requisite design and technological know-how to enable the firm (profitably) to satisfy evolving user requirements;
— the long-term support and commitment by senior management to the implementation of design strategies.

In each decade there emerge only a very few really radical, landmark-type innovative designs, such as the jet engine, the transistor, the jumbo jet, the laser, or the personal microcomputer. While these designs and the tremendously powerful intellectual ideas embodied in them are unquestionably extremely important, the significance of much smaller design changes should not be underestimated. Arguably, the vast volume of all product-embodied technical change is accounted for by the accumulation of relatively small design modifications (*see* Figure 11.1).

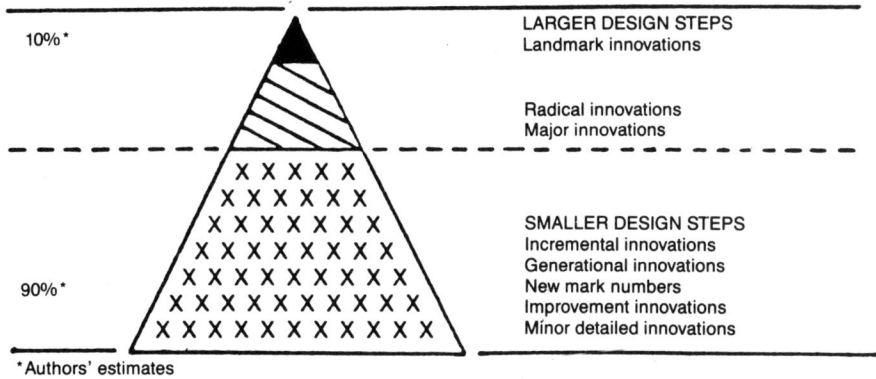

* Authors' estimates

Fig 11.1 Technical change

In terms of corporate strategy, this means that while there should always be corporate receptiveness to the strategic possibilities of the really radical landmark-type of opportunity, most day-to-day (tactical) thinking will of necessity be on those smaller design steps which together act to improve product and process performance, maintain competitiveness and generate profits.

Strategically managed designs and design processes are inseparable from strategically managed innovative products, processes and systems. For industries across the technology spectrum, there are a number of common, specific design processes linking invention, innovation and re-innovation (Rothwell and Gardiner, 1983; *see* Figure 11.2). The financial and intellectual resources required, and the management techniques employed, are significantly different at each stage. For instance, the risks and the degree of commitment for a 'design for demonstration' leading to invention, are at a much reduced scale when compared to that of 'design for marketable production' leading to commercial introduction. With established products, where markets are both evolving and demanding, the dynamics of the redesign process leading to reinnovation are also varied and can be highly complex. We have identified twelve main patterns of redesign leading to reinnovation (*see* Table 11.1). This richness and variety of design and redesign processes is what makes their strategic management so challenging and so necessary.

Underlying this complex situation, there are two crucial considerations for the successful strategic management of the design/innovation process. (Some of the concepts introduced here will be examined in greater detail later.) First, is the target product, process or system part of an existing

CENTRAL DESIGN
ISSUE

BASIC IDEA

DESIGN
PROCESSES

Is it feasible
scientifically
or technically?

Models

Design for
demonstration

INVENTION

Can it be built
commercially?

Prototypes

Design for
marketable
production

INNOVATION

Can it be
made better
or cheaper
or both?

New mark
numbers

Redesign

REINNOVATION

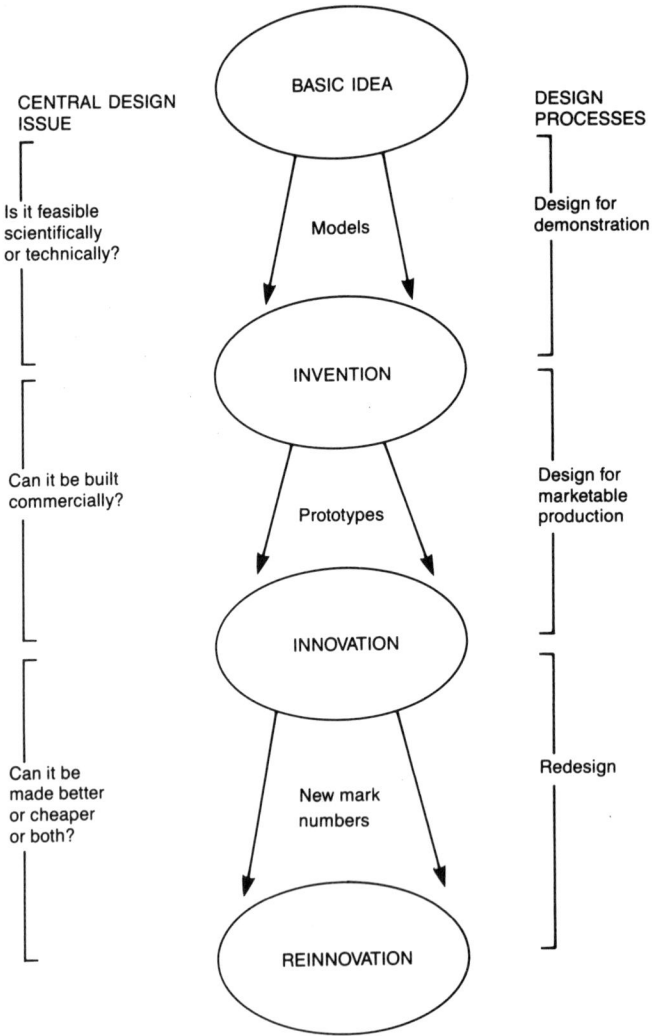

Fig 11.2 States of technical change

Table 11.1 Twelve patterns of redesign and reinnovation

Redesign at	**Conceptualisation stage** (eg the planned permanently manned US space station was first based on a single power tower concept, next around a dual keel design, and more recently on a somewhat simplified and reduced version of that previous configuration).
Redesign at	**Prototype stage** (eg BMX type bikes developed out of small wheeled 'shopper' type bicycle designs by Alex Moulton. Originally the small wheeled prototype bikes had a monocoque or unitised metal body structure. This worked satisfactorily but was like riding on a tin drum, and so it had to be replaced by the more traditional tubular steel frames).
Redesign with a	**'Leading edge' supplier** (eg Rediffusion has been one of the world leaders in flight simulators. Part of the reason for this has been the advanced 'leading edge' computers supplied by Gould to Rediffusion. Each new generation of computer allows for a new redesign of flight simulators with increased sophistication).
Redesign by	**Technical diffusion** (eg the innovative wide chord fan blade design for Rolls-Royce's RB211-535E4 is now being scaled up and scaled down to be diffused into the redesign of bigger and smaller engines).
Redesign using a	**Succession of minor details** (eg following the fuel crisis of the early seventies, locomotive diesel engine designers were able to improve fuel efficiencies by about 2 per cent per year over a sustained period of years).
Redesign with	**Incremental subassembly changes** (eg compared to Boeing's 747-300, the new 747-400 will have an increased wing span of more than 18 ft due to extensions and the addition of winglets, additional variable camber leading edge flaps, a new 3000 US gallon tail fuel tank to increase the range by 320 nautical miles, and a regauged wingbox to increase the maximum brake release gross weight to 850,000 lb. Also there is a new, two man, digital cockpit pioneered in Boeing's 757/767s).
Redesign of a	**New generation** (eg British Hovercraft's AP1-88 is a total redesign with a simpler welded aluminium structure, separate lift and propulsion systems with industrial diesel power units, rubber belt drives and shrouded fixed pitch propellers).
Redesign using	**Hybrid technologies** (eg fully digitalised watches appeared some time ago, but more recently there have appeared watches that have a traditional face and hands but with a digital drive thus combining old and new technologies).
Redesign using	**Radical technologies** (eg conventional inertial navigational systems based on gyroscopes are being replaced by new ones using ring laser technologies, and shortly new fibre optic based gyros will be introduced).
Redesign a	**New integrated package/system** (eg Rediffusion's very advanced flight simulator for Boeing's 747-300 combines enhanced visual displays, computing and instructional systems based on sophisticated Gould computers using the latest reflective memory techniques).
Redesign using	**New materials** (eg automotive bumpers are frequently now just one large ABS moulding which combines structural, styling, aerodynamic qualities and mounting points for accessories - formerly these features could only be obtained by using a mix of different materials and subassemblies).
Redesign for	**Retrofitting** (eg the Didcot electric power station needed to be refurbished. With new computer-aided-designed turbine blades, and instrumentation and control systems overall thermal efficiency has improved and millions of pounds are being saved annually).

'design trajectory', or is it at the threshold of a newly emerging one? The leading price and non-price parameters and the direction of technological pathways have to be understood and constantly re-examined for radical new departures. Second, does the product, process or system have an intrinsic 'robustness' which allows for the creation of an uprated, rerated, and derated 'family' of variants? Not all of these variants will need to be in production at any one time but, as markets evolve and user demand shifts, these 'design families' allow for a considerable degree of flexibility in responding to changes in user requirements. Design robustness, in turn, leads to economies of scale, combined with economies of scope, and even of the technology itself, thereby increasing the likelihood of sustained competitive success.

In Figure 11.2 we indicated that there were different design processes linking invention, innovation and reinnovation. To this sequence must be added the ever-increasing role of users in influencing designs (*see* Figure 11.3). At the invention stage, the role of potential users is generally relatively weak, although there are marked exceptions to this pattern (von Hippel, 1976; Shaw, 1985 and Rothwell, 1986) whereas, at the re-innovation stage, their role is much stronger simply because they have had past experience with earlier models which forms a basis for informed feedback, and they can

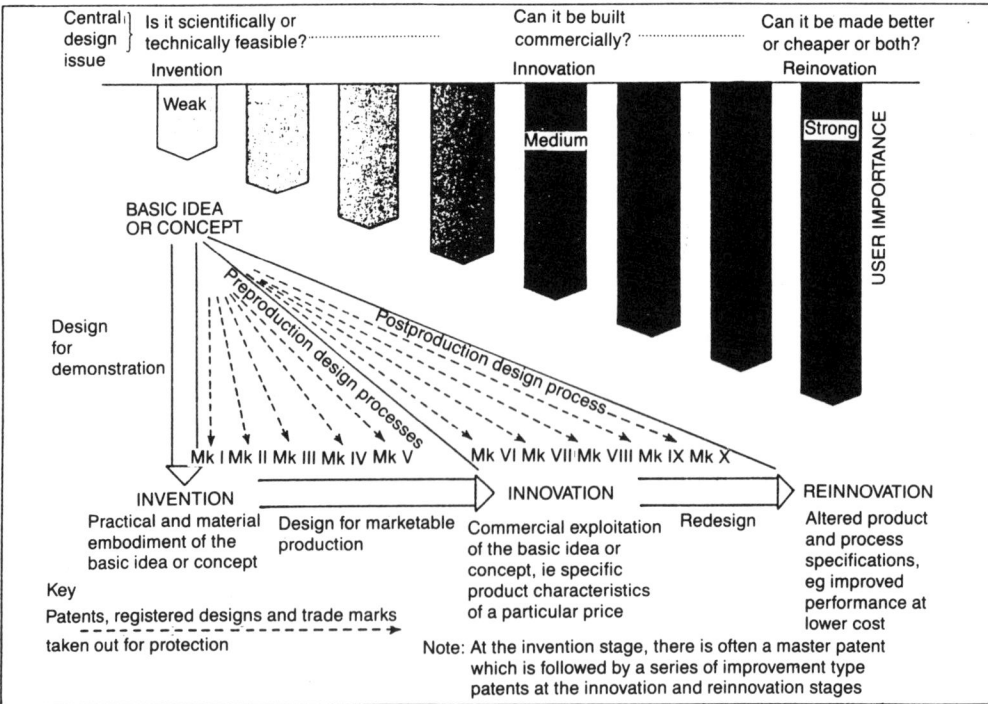

Fig 11.3 Engineering innovation as an iterative design process and the changing role of user importance (an idealised spectrum)

then more accurately describe the various strengths and weaknesses of a particular design. The identification and involvement of leading-edge users should be an important element in any firm's design strategy.

2 Design trajectories

As stated earlier, it is of strategic importance to the firm to be able to determine the position of its products along the prevailing 'design trajectory'. The notion of the design trajectory has parallels with the Nelson and Winter (1977) concept of the 'technological trajectory', but it is rather less abstract, the current 'state-of-the-art' design being embodied and identified by a series of specific working models (Gardiner, 1984a). The current state-of-the-art model represents the design target for competitors, or the point of departure for the leading manufacturer in either moving further along the existing, or shifting to a new, trajectory. For example, at the start of the Ford Fiesta development programme, the state-of-the-art target to meet or exceed was the Fiat 127; just prior to the Fiesta's launch in 1976, the design was retargeted on the later Volkswagen Golf, which then represented the new state-of-the-art design along that particular design trajectory.

A major advantage of utilising real design objects to define a design trajectory is that whole 'packages' of dimensions are implicitly taken up. In general, technological or economic trajectories have only a few dimensions, such as maximum speed vs time, or vehicle weight vs time, or cost per mile. A design trajectory with state-of-the-art models, in contrast, is multidimensional, containing a variety of characteristics and performance parameters with major compromises made between them to achieve the 'best' or most appropriate working combination at a given moment in time. As demand shifts and technologies develop, some characteristics are de-emphasised while others are reinforced and new ones added, leading to a new 'best practice' model representing a shift along the design trajectory.

The shift from one dominant design trajectory to the next frequently occurs following the emergence of a new technological capability; for example the shift from the propeller to the jet engine. And it is not always the design leader along the first trajectory that successfully shifts first to the newly emerging trajectory. Thus, the aircraft manufacturer Douglas, whose DC7 was the leading-edge propeller aircraft design, became a follower for the new commercial jet aircraft trajectory when Boeing introduced the jet-propelled 707 in 1958. At about the same time, new innovative firms such as Fairchild Semiconductor and Texas Instruments established a new integrated circuit-chip-design trajectory. They quickly left behind more conservative firms such as RCA who remained committed to the older vacuum tube and discrete semiconductor design trajectories. Clearly it is strategically important that firms do not become 'locked-in' to the prevailing design trajectory and that they take considerable pains to assess the strategic implications of emerging technologies. Identifying and entering emerging design trajectories at an early stage can offer a firm a considerable strategic advantage over its more slow moving competitors.

3 Redesign strategies

Successful designs undergo constant modifications in order to continue to satisfy evolving user requirements, and in Table 11.1 we listed a number of observed characteristic patterns of redesign and reinnovation for a variety of products, processes and systems. What is perhaps less widely appreciated is that redesigns employing largely existing technology and components can open up new applications and user segments; or that proven components can be combined with radical technology to yield greatly improved or 'new generation' devices. The recombination of existing equipment and products, or the imaginative combination of the 'existing' with the 'new', can greatly reduce design and production costs for the introduction of new devices, while at the same time reducing customers' perceptions of the risks involved in the use of the new combinations. Two recent examples of redesign using hybrid technologies are the Black and Decker paintstripper and the Canon laser copier.

Case Study 1: Heatguns

For both amateur and professional decorators, paintstripping using chemical treatments is an unpleasant, messy and potentially hazardous operation. The various types of radiant heater and flame-type strippers, while somewhat less hazardous in use, also have a variety of drawbacks. Tradition, however, is strong in the decorating business and at the beginning of the 1980s, when Black and Decker saw the opportunity to make a new type of heatgun for paintstripping, there was considerable uncertainty concerning whether or not consumers would adopt a new tool. The design of a wholly new tool would have carried with it high development and production costs, and market failure would have resulted in financial losses to the firm.

For Black and Decker, the solution to this high-risk situation was to adopt a deliberate strategy of 'designing something new from something old', ie a heatgun derived from an electric drill. As things transpired, this represented an extremely shrewd piece of strategic design management. In order to transform the drill into a heatgun, Black and Decker simply replaced the transmission and chuck subassemblies with a new heater element and nozzle. This meant that the new tool contained a motor, fan, case and switch which were all reliable and well-proven electric drill components. Because of this, the heatgun was a marginal cost design since two-thirds of it derived from existing drill production lines operating with high economies of scale and learning curve economies. In addition, two-thirds of the parts for servicing and repairs were already inventoried and only a few new parts for the heater subassembly needed to be added. And finally, development and safety testing requirements could be met by concentrating only on the few new additional components.

As things turned out, the heatgun rapidly gained acceptance in the marketplace, but Black and Decker resisted the temptation to rest on its laurels. The firm did not attempt to maximise short-term profits on its inexpensive, low entry risk design, but quickly embarked on a vigorous programme of redesign. Two years after the introduction of the first hybrid model, a second generation model was introduced. A custom-designed smaller, lighter and cheaper motor was employed because the heatgun required a less powerful and simpler motor than the drill. In turn the balance and ergonomics of the tool could be reoptimized with a new design for the case. This redesign was so complete that the new model contained virtually no parts in common with the drill derived version and, more importantly from the point of view of commercial manufacturing, the number of component parts was halved. The heatgun, now in its third generation via a process of continued redesign, has evolved into a comprehensive design family of variants, ranging from a basic single temperature/air flow version to a top line version with five electronically controlled heat settings and two airflow rates. In both consumer and industrial versions, a wide range of user price and nonprice requirements are being met. The heatgun family has grown into the most rapidly established power tool segment that Black and Decker has ever been instrumental in creating.

Case Study 2: Photocopiers

Photocopying machines are for most companies a major capital expenditure just like mini/micro computers and word processing work stations. Technologically, there has been one big difference between conventional photocopiers and these other types of machine. Word processors and mini/micro computers are at their core electronic machines; whereas, conventional photocopiers are essentially electromechanical machines. This does not necessarily make them any simpler. Having a working design lifetime ranging from tens of thousands of copies for the smallest machines to many millions for large machines, and having to handle dusty toners and paper, there are quite severe requirements on electromechanical designs if the machines are to operate reliably even with routine servicing. One of the best ways of handling these demands, in a market characterised by a very broad range of user requirements, is to develop a basic robust design and then have variants of it by offering a limited number of add and drop option packs or modules. This has been successfully achieved by firms such as Canon.

The gap between the conventional electromechanical type office machines and the more electronically based one has substantially narrowed. The more recently introduced digital laser copiers are much more 'electronic' in nature and employ digital signals rather than the analogue ones characteristic of conventional photocopiers. This means that the digital electronic signals generated by the laser copier can be handled like all other electronic signals: slave printers can be multiplied and visual information can be digitally processed, stored or transmitted simultaneously to a number of distant printers. Because of this, laser copiers represent a significant shift along the photocopier design trajectory. Laser photocopiers can now also be electronically integrated with office computers and word processing equipment.

Figure 11.4 illustrates a number of the differences between Canon's conventional (analogue) copier and its recently introduced laser (digital) copier. This laser copier retains the well proven paper handling and scanning systems, and the developing, transfer and fixing corona assemblies of the print mechanism of Canon's conventional copiers. To develop this new type of copier an additional digital electronic information processing step (involving a highly innovative toric lens and amorphous silicon drum) has been inserted between the original optical and print systems. In this way the traditional photocopier technology (familiar to service engineers and supported by distributed inventories of spare parts) is carried a step forward and made more 'intelligent' for office users, while preserving its proven robustness in use. This is again an example of a design strategy that successfully combines the 'existing' with, in this case, the radically new.

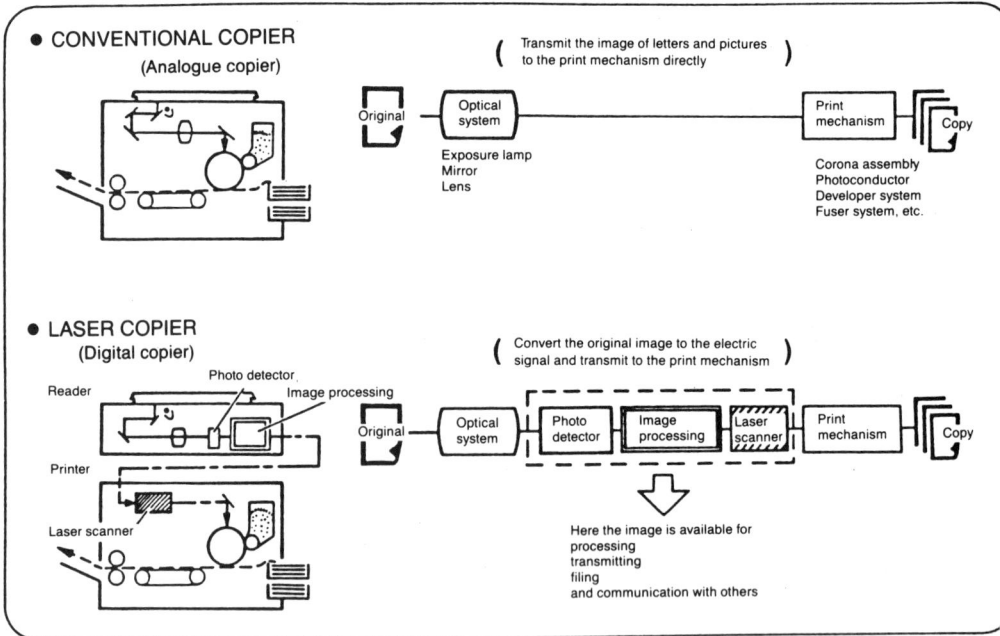

Source: Canon Laser Copier, 1986 unpaged

Fig 11.4 Difference between conventional copier (analogue copier) and laser copier (digital copier)

The phenomenon of producing something radically new by combining new elements with old ones has a long and honourable history. Over a century ago, steam engine pistons, cylinders and cranks were converted to working with internal combustion processes. In turn, these new internal combustion engines were combined with horseless carriages to produce the then new radical form of transportation – the car!

4 Robust designs and design families

Traditionally the term 'robust' is taken to mean reliability in use and the ability to handle harsh treatment. Here the term 'robust design' has a different and rather special meaning: a robust design is one that has sufficient inherent design flexibility or 'technological slack' to enable it to evolve into a significant 'design family' of variants. Essentially, a robust design is one that can satisfy the evolving needs of a 'set' of user segments. For the manufacturer it offers economies of scale combined with economies of scope; for the user it offers maximum choice from among a set of well-proven products (Gardiner and Rothwell, 1985). Our model for the robust design is given in Figure 11.5 and it can, perhaps, be best illustrated with a number of practical examples.

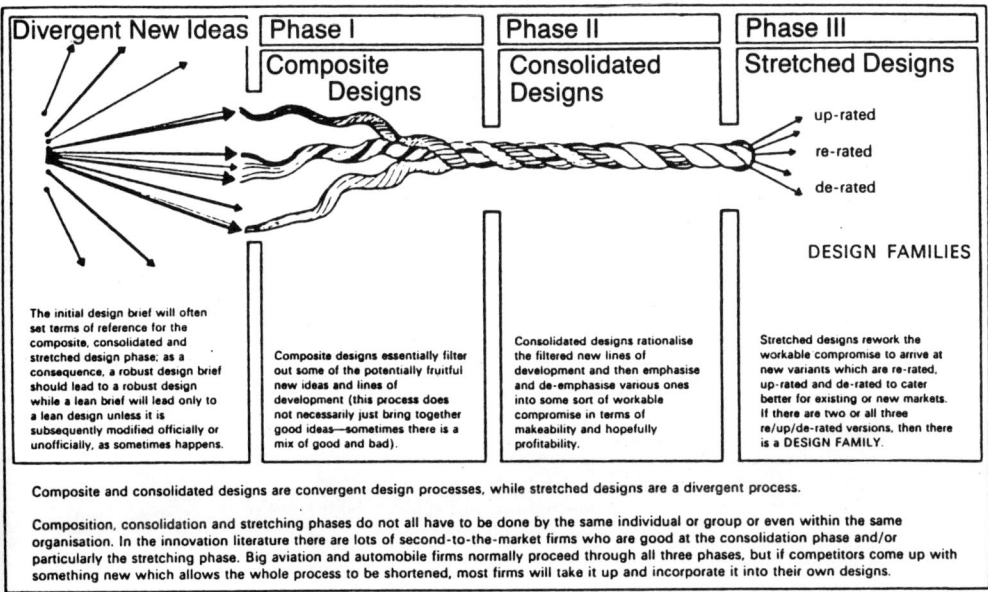

Fig 11.5 The evolution of robust designs

Figure 11.6 shows the evolution of the original Rolls-Royce RB211 aeroengine into a design family of uprated, rerated and derated variants. For production and servicing reasons, the RB211 configuration was a 'simplified' design consisting of seven basic modules. This modular configuration inherently allows for different modifications to meet a variety of user thrust and performance requirements. Thus, by removing the large, front, low pressure fan module and replacing it with a scaled-down fan, it was possible to produce the highly successful derated (ie lower thrust) 535C engine. The subsequent introduction of a new wide chord fan blade in the front low pressure compressor module resulted in the improved 535E4 engine. This innovative wide chord blade design is currently being diffused back into the RB211 family to improve further the fuel and thrust ratings of the uprated variants. The designed-in robustness of the initial RB211 was crucial in enabling these major modifications to be undertaken. The family concept has clear advantages for Rolls-Royce in terms of R&D economies, production economies, spares supply, customer credibility (design familiarity), customer support services and general learning economies. The customer gains the advantage of wide model choice, rapid producer response to satisfy evolving requirements, parts commonality and cumulative learning effects in both the use and servicing of the engines. Even now the story has not yet ended. The RB211-524D4D engine with a thrust of 58,000 lb is to be certified in 1988, and there is now a distinct possibility of evolving the 524D4D into the RB211-524L in the 65,000 lb thrust class.

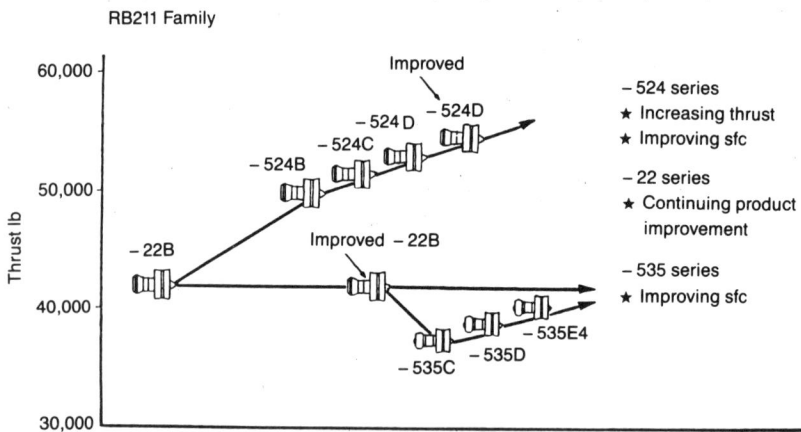

Source: RB211-22B Technology and description, Rolls-Royce Limited, TS2100, Issue 20, July 1980. Updated and revised by authors to 1987 figures.

Fig 11.6 The evolving RB211 aeroengine family

Often in the past, design stretching was achieved more or less on an *ad hoc* basis when the original product had been over-engineered. Today, an increasing number of companies are deliberately designing 'stretch' into their products. The IBM PC personal computer, for example, is in reality a family of products; because of the deliberate adoption of an 'open architecture' it has proved possible to expand and modify the original model and there are now six main variants on the market. IBM's most recent generation of computers, the Personal System/2, is again a family of machines designed to meet a wide range of user requirements.

Other robust designs are the Boeing 707 and 747; the Ford Cortina; Canon photocopiers; and Rediffusion's BAe 146 flight simulator. A number of 'lean' designs, ie designs that lack built-in stretch, have also been identified, examples being the Comet aircraft and the British Leyland 1100 car (Rothwell and Gardiner, 1982). And, through a comprehensive redesign which effectively decoupled the critical relationships between various operating parameters and subsystems, British Hovercraft Company's SR.N6 hovercraft — an essentially lean design — was transformed into the AP1-88 robust design family (Rothwell and Gardiner, 1985). Clearly the notion of design robustness, yielding an extended design family of variants, is a powerful concept that has important implications for companies' long-term design and development strategies. While the (short-term) entry costs for a robust design might be high, the (long-term) strategic benefits can be very considerable indeed.

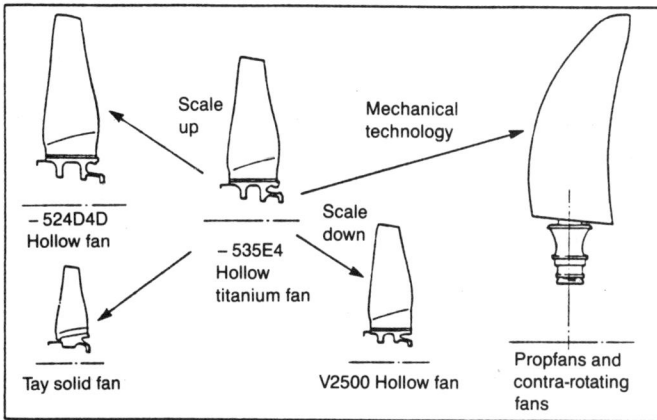

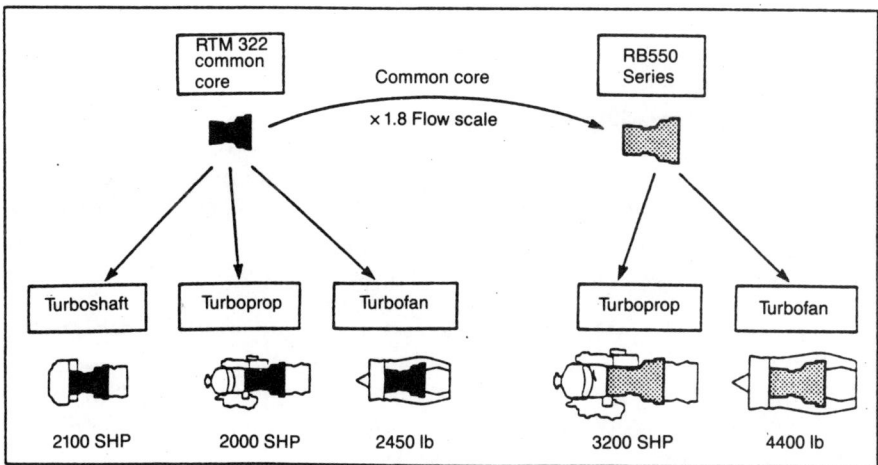

Fig 11.7 Design family economies

5 Economy in technology

Allied to the concept of robust designs is the notion of 'economy in technology' which has been embraced by Rolls-Royce in its aeroengine development programme. According to P C Ruffles, Rolls-Royce's Director of Technology, this approach makes it possible to obtain 'economy in technology' which effectively reduces engine development costs by about 35 per cent. Rolls-Royce is currently developing a new aeroengine family — the RTM 322 — to be produced in a number of versions and scaled to cater for a variety of market requirements and power outputs (see Figure 11.7). The core of the RTM322 will be common to turboshaft, turboprop and turbofan versions. This RTM322 core, when scaled-up by x1.8, becomes the core for the higher thrust RB550 series, which is also planned to be produced in turboprop and turbofan versions, yielding in total two basic aeroengine designs and five variants, ie a sophisticated emergent design family.

6 Discussion

We have introduced a number of concepts — design trajectories, redesign, robust designs and economy in technology — that have profound implications for firms' design management strategies. Perhaps the most powerful of these concepts is that of the robust design which yields an extended family of significant variants. Robust designs offer the manufacturer considerable flexibility in meeting evolving user requirements and the ability to cope with market segmentation as it develops. It also enables manufacturers to combine scale economies in production (high commonality of parts) with economies of scope (high product variety), which represents a powerful competitive combination. At the same time these designs offer the customer greater choice in the range of product attributes immediately available, and greater confidence in the supplier's ability to satisfy new requirements as they emerge.

The basis of design 'robustness' appears to vary across product types. In the case of aircraft (and hovercraft), for example, it depends on the degree of interrelatedness between different critical operating parameters, ie the degree to which one performance parameter can be varied without detrimentally degrading other parameters (robust designs are essentially design compromises). In the case of automobiles, robustness probably depends more on the product/market strategy of the firm than it does on technical factors (Rothwell and Gardiner, 1984). Finally, close and forward-looking interaction between leading-edge suppliers and leading-edge users during product specification can contribute significantly towards design robustness (Gardiner and Rothwell, 1985; Rothwell, 1986).

The advent of CAD and flexible manufacturing systems has greatly facilitated firms' ability to produce robust designs. CAD techniques also allow the testing of different combinations of new and old designs which, if done with older prototyping approaches, might be too costly to explore. For example, Rolls-Royce has proved that it can significantly reduce the overall costs of aeroengine R&D using CAD linked to computer simulation techniques and still produce innovative new and improved designs (Ruffles,

1986). In short, the strategic use of modern computerised design and production techniques offers firms the ability to produce robust designs at reduced costs and with shorter lead-times, with the manifold benefits this confers on both the producer and his customers. In a world in which international competition is intensifying and user requirements are rapidly changing, the ability to produce cost-effective robust designs will be a major factor determining a firm's profitability, flexibility and, in the longer-term, its survivability. The introduction of robust designs requires the commitment by senior executives to a strategic approach to design management.

Chapter 12

The UK information technology industry and the Alvey programme

Ken Guy

1 Introduction

During the course of the 1980s a number of governments implemented policies which offered firms the opportunity of participating in precompetitive, collaborative R&D programmes. These often involved both other firms and public sector research organisations such as universities. Apart from restructuring relationships *between* government, industry and academia, at least in terms of the nurturing of R&D, participation has also had impacts *internal* to organisations within each group.

One government programme of this type which has attracted a good deal of attention is the UK government's Alvey programme for advanced information technology (IT). In 1982 a committee was established to consider the response of the UK to Japanese initiatives in IT. Later that year the Report of the Alvey Committee suggested the establishment of a directorate, to be known as the Alvey Directorate, which was to set up and coordinate a five-year research programme in the enabling technologies of IT. This was initiated in 1983. Total government funding drawn from three ministries amounted to £200 million, with industry contributing a further £150 million.

Industrial participants were funded half by government and academic participants wholly so. Over 100 firms collaborated with a similar number of academic and other research establishments in approximately 200 full collaborative projects and 100 'uncle' projects i.e. research projects undertaken in academia under industrial supervision.

From the perspective of firms, involvement in the programme has a number of potential impacts. In the first instance, with regard to changes *internal* to the firm, participation has the potential to improve the 'knowledge base' of firms via changes in the content and practice of research activities. In terms of public accountability, activity of this nature additional to that which would have been undertaken in the absence of the programme is essential.

Secondly, again apropos of impacts *internal* to firms, participants in the programme were expected in the long run to exploit the research to improve their competitive position and performance. It was the responsibility of firms to exploit improvements in their 'knowledge bases' to enhance their later 'technology bases' and 'product bases'. Without such eventual exploitation on the part of firms, the appropriateness of policies such as the Alvey programme has to be called into question.

Thirdly, participation in programmes such as Alvey can be expected to impact on the overall strategic thinking and positioning of firms. In particular, participation can colour attitudes towards precompetitive, collaborative research and, more generally, towards involvement in government support programmes of this nature. It can also affect the way firms view and structure their subsequent relationships with other firms and with public sector organisations. In other words, participation can affect attitudes and practice vis-à-vis the structural relationships *between* industry, government and academia. It is an open question whether participation can have even more profound impacts on overall firm strategies.

This chapter presents the results of an empirical investigation into the impact of Alvey on industrial participants. It was conducted as part of a much larger programme of work aimed at evaluating the Alvey programme as a whole, primarily from the point of view of assessing the appropriateness and effectiveness of the programme as a support vehicle for the UK IT sector.

The evaluation of Alvey began in 1984 and is scheduled to end in 1990. This chapter is based upon a series of interviews conducted during September/October 1986 with key decision-makers in UK- based firms concerned with electronics and IT. Thirty-five people were seen in 25 interviews within 19 firms. Positions held by interviewees ranged from managing directors through strategic planning directors, finance directors, technical directors and research directors. The people interviewed were of such stature within their own organisations that their individual views can be regarded as representative of important currents within their firms. Collectively, their views must be treated as reflecting the spectrum of opinion within the upper reaches of the industrial community in this sector.

The firms interviewed fell into five categories: large, medium and small UK-owned IT 'producer' firms, all participants in the Alvey programme; a small number of IT 'user' firms, again all involved in Alvey projects; and foreign-owned multinationals with UK R&D and production sites, all but one holding Alvey contracts.[1] The firms accounted for approximately 70 per cent of the Alvey project grants awarded to firms.

Because of the timing of the interview programme — approximately halfway through the Alvey programme's lifetime — it was only possible to identify certain of the impacts one can expect such a programme to have. Specifically, it was possible only to investigate impacts on research practice and on strategic thinking and positioning, and this chapter thus deals primarily with these impacts. It was too early to assess whether and how firms were exploiting Alvey research, and how this exploitation was affecting overall technology and product strategies. Nevertheless, although the results of this phase of the Alvey evaluation did not address the issue of exploitation, the conclusion to this chapter refers to subsequent work within the context of the evaluation which does begin to deal with this issue.

2 Impact on research practice

In this section, Alvey research is located within the context of firms' R&D portfolios. The impact of the programme on the scale, pace and direction of work is then examined.

2.1 Alvey in the overall corporate R&D context

Amongst the IT firms interviewed, the proportion of total annual turnover spent on R&D varied from almost zero to 15-20 per cent. Small software firms came at the lower end of the spectrum, with silicon-based subsidiaries of larger firms at the other. The large 'major' IT companies tended to spend between 5 and 10 per cent of their turnover on R&D.

For many companies, the proportion of total R&D devoted to Alvey projects tended to be very small — no more than about 5 to 10 per cent of the R&D budget. On this basis, therefore, one would not expect Alvey to have or to have had a dramatic effect on overall R&D strategy, never mind company strategy as a whole.

The situation is not so straightforward, however. Alvey work is not distributed over the whole R&D spectrum within most firms. It is concentrated within a limited number of long-term, 'blue-sky' technical areas, many of which are expected to grow into key R&D sectors within the next five to fifteen years. It is therefore important to examine the 'concentration' effect of Alvey R&D support in these key enabling technologies.

Within many firms, Alvey R&D tends to be more 'R' than 'D'. (Major exceptions arise in the area of silicon semiconductor work carried out under the Very Large Scale Integration (VLSI) programme, where a number of firms consider their Alvey work to be more developmental in nature.) For some of the smaller firms specialising in Alvey-related technical areas, especially some of the software companies, Alvey work constitutes a large proportion of the actual research carried out, as opposed to work which is classified as product development. In a few companies, Alvey research is almost the only research being undertaken. The potential ramifications of Alvey funding in years to come are therefore considerable for smaller firms.

In large companies, the existence of R&D conducted in areas not directly related to Alvey technologies tends to disguise the importance of Alvey R&D. When like is compared with like, however, ie when Alvey-funded work is compared with similar work in Alvey-related technological areas, the 'concentration' effects of Alvey are often quite marked. For example, in one large firm which has exploited Alvey funding in VLSI and Intelligent Knowledge Based Systems (IKBS) in particular, Alvey work was said to constitute 30-50 per cent of all IKBS R&D and 30 per cent of VLSI work, with much of the latter classified nearer the 'D' than the 'R'. Again, in companies such as these, Alvey funding is likely to have a crucial effect on future technological performance if the enabling technology areas chosen by Alvey prove to be truly key enabling areas. This is especially so given that some companies stated that Alvey had acted as a catalyst to research in certain areas, and that although Alvey now constituted a small proportion of work in these areas, little of this work would have been attempted if it had not been for initial support from Alvey.

Some companies, often of medium size, have not succeeded in exploiting Alvey in quite the same way. There are a number of firms in which the proportion of Alvey work in Alvey-related technological areas is fairly low.

A common refrain in these quarters is that of missing the Alvey boat, primarily due to an 'outsider' status in the government funding stakes. Typically, companies such as these had never felt truly plugged into the government support infrastructure for IT firms. For example, some firms' dealings with the Ministry of Defence (MOD) and the Post Office(PO)/ British Telecom (BT) had been either negligible or secondhand (via subcontracting arrangements). In another instance, one firm had never really felt part of the IT community: although nearly 40 per cent of its activities could be classified as electronics, its major product group heading lay outside this field. Firms such as these were unable to exploit Alvey when this new funding opportunity arose. They were so distanced from the funding infrastructure that they didn't see the change coming. Moreover, they lacked the experience and contacts to manoeuvre successfully within the newly emerging infrastructure — the 'majors' had a head start.

Amongst the foreign multinationals interviewed, one had no Alvey commitments and the remainder had only marginal commitments — typically just one or two projects. All had initially felt excluded from the programme, manifestly so in its formulation stage and implicitly so in its early implementation phase. No company was aware of an explicit veto on the participation of foreign multinationals — all tacitly accepted that this would be the case and were reinforced in this belief by the number of rumours circulating to this effect within the UK research community. When the chance to participate arose, often at the invitation of the Directorate, the chance to exploit Alvey in the way the UK 'majors' had done was no longer an option. The rationale for participation therefore tended to be political rather than technical. The Alvey programme has a high visibility and membership of an Alvey Club endows 'UK Community' status on its members. One firm summarised the situation by saying that club membership offered few technical promises, but that nonmembership and consequent lack of visibility in the area would be most unwelcome. Similarly, both the 'user' firms interviewed gave 'high visibility' and 'club membership' as reasons for a small, exploratory involvement with Alvey.

2.2 Additionality and impact on research practice

One of the usual conditions for the provision of government support is that of additionality. Government support is made available only if the proposed work is, in some sense, new or additional to work which would have been undertaken in the absence of government support. From the standpoint of public accountability this sounds quite reasonable, but the definition of a workable concept of additionality has caused a few headaches both within government circles and in the business community. Certainly, many of the firms interviewed in this study made a point of relating anecdotes about harrowing encounters in the past with the concept of additionality.

The situation is not straightforward. On the one hand, firms are unlikely to run with projects which are in entirely new technology, product or market areas, ie ones in which they have no track record. On the other hand, projects which fall within the mainstream of their activities and directly in line with overall firm strategy can hardly be called novel. When additionality is equated with novelty, it becomes a slippery, marginal entity. It has become common practice, therefore, to accept that additionality has to have connotations other than novelty at the margins of a firm's mainstream activities. When projects fall within the main thrust of a firm's strategy, additionality now tends to be interpreted in terms of concepts such as acceleration and concentration of effort.

Firms receiving support for Alvey projects have not generally been asked to satisfy additionality criteria. It has been accepted that collaboration *per se* constitutes the crucial element of novelty or additionality. However, when discussing the impact of Alvey on firm strategy during the course of this study, most firms tended to couch their views on the relationship of Alvey to overall company strategy in terms redolent of the additionality debate.

Again and again, firms stressed that Alvey projects had been chosen to fit in with overall company strategy — that Alvey had allowed them to strengthen and build on an existing momentum. For many, Alvey was not seen as a means of changing direction or of entering brand new territories. It was seen as a means of accelerating and broadening existing effort. Naturally, there were exceptions. In particular, one of the 'majors' was adamant that Alvey had allowed it to enter fields it would not otherwise have entered. But even within this firm the bulk of its Alvey projects were concentrated in technical areas which had traditionally been regarded as mainstream activities.

Within the context of fitting in with existing company strategies, Alvey projects were perceived, discussed and negotiated with the following in mind:

– accelerating developments in existing R&D tracks;
– broadening or widening current R&D tracks;
– using Alvey to reduce in-house contributions to work already planned;
– maintaining R&D coverage in areas which might have had to be cut without Alvey support; and
– using Alvey to substitute for in-house monies which could then be used to bolster R&D in higher risk, non-Alvey areas.

Of the above, the first two were cited by the vast majority of firms, some of whom went to great lengths to counter accusations that Alvey monies had been used in any other way. Most of these firms talked of a 'doubling up' of resources. Only two firms — each with very minor Alvey commitments — said that Alvey support and similar support from ESPRIT, the EEC's counterpart to Alvey (*see* Chapter 13), had been used to reduce in-house contributions to work already planned, both of them noting that the monies had been absorbed into general company accounts. Only one firm, albeit one with major Alvey commitments, had stated quite explicitly that Alvey support had allowed it to continue in an area in which it might otherwise have had to make cutbacks. The same firm admitted that Alvey had freed resources which it had then allocated to higher risk research areas.

On the borderline between a strong fit with existing strategies and leaps into entirely new areas, a number of firms talked in terms of 'critical masses'. In other words, Alvey allowed some of the larger firms conducting exploratory R&D in Alvey-related areas to contemplate integrating this work into mainstream company strategy. In this sense subcritical R&D activities achieved a critical mass via Alvey.

Although most of the remarks made about the impact of Alvey on research practice and strategy were positive, there were one or two negative undercurrents. A few of the larger firms noted that whilst they had tried to ensure that Alvey projects fitted in with overall company strategy, collaboration implied a certain amount of flexibility. Concessions had to be made both to the Alvey Directorate and to potential partners. In some instances this had led them to participate in projects which did not fit comfortably with their overall R&D portfolio. Furthermore, one large firm noted that exogenous factors had forced it to beat a retreat in one of the business and technology areas in which it had Alvey projects. These projects no longer fitted in with its long-term plans. Nevertheless, it planned to continue with Alvey projects in this area. Many of the smaller firms interviewed felt that they could not afford luxuries such as these. Conversely, however, some research managers noted that Alvey had allowed them to 'lock-in' to longer-term research projects which they considered crucial, but which were often curtailed due to short-term financial pressures when conducted outside the framework of programmes like Alvey.

3 The impact on strategic thinking and positioning

Alvey funding constitutes just a small proportion of the R&D budgets of most firms. At first sight, therefore, Alvey might appear to be little more than a minor perturbation in resource terms, although its concentration in potentially key areas belies this simplistic conclusion. Nevertheless, in the short-term at least, ie prior to the eventual emergence of Alvey-related products and processes, it might seem unrealistic to expect Alvey to have any major impacts on overall firm strategies.

All of this presupposes that the impacts of Alvey will manifest themselves solely in terms of tangible technologies and products. However, during the course of this study it became clear that Alvey has had a more widespread influence on what can only be termed the culture of the industrial IT community in the UK. In many ways this was to be expected — both novel funding arrangements and the reality of new, collaborative arrangements were bound to alter the established pattern of things. But at a more reified level Alvey appears to have had a marked 'consciousness-raising' impact on strategic and tactical thinking generally.

This chapter has already discussed the generally favourable industrial reaction to Alvey. It is now argued that this reaction has influenced the way firms are positioning themselves with regard to the way they conduct research, the way they interact with government and the way they interpret their role within the IT community.

3.1 Attitudes towards precompetitive research programmes

At the time of the Alvey Report, which recommended the implementation of a precompetitive, collaborative R&D programme, a major point of discussion in the UK was the correctness of the decision to locate Alvey support at the 'precompetitive' end of the R&D spectrum, ie nearer the 'R' than the 'D'. In very crude terms, one school of thought maintained that if the UK electronics and IT industry was to keep its head above water, then it needed all the help it could get at stages later in the product life cycle, ie at the development stage, the production stage and at the marketing and diffusion stages. In particular, the 'market-pull' school tended to favour schemes such as increased public procurement. Conversely, 'technology-push' elements argued that, if the UK were to stand any chance in future markets, it had to unify and build on areas of fragmented strength at the research end of the spectrum in order to build up long-term, leading-edge technological capabilities. Moreover, if scarce resources dictated a choice, this had to be attempted in preference to 'market-pull' alternatives.

The fact that the Alvey programme was set up as a precompetitive programme tends to suggest that a 'technology-push' consensus emerged among the 'first circle' firms, or at least those represented on the Alvey Committee. This interpretation has to be qualified, however. It is nearer the truth to say that whilst the 'technology-push' school had its strong advocates, others took a rather different view of precompetitive research. These different perspectives can still be perceived today, though the experience of Alvey has caused some firms to shift their ground.

Amongst the firms interviewed during the course of this study a number of camps can be discerned. The first camp consists of firms which considered that Alvey had been correct in concentrating on precompetitive R&D in order to unite fragmented resources. Some, notably those lacking centralised R&D facilities, or having no track record at the 'R' end of the spectrum, were simply grateful for the opportunity both to undertake research and to formalise links with the university sector (though some of the smaller software companies had been initially sceptical of their ability to participate, primarily because of the 50:50 funding arrangements). Others — many of whom had representatives on the Alvey Committee — considered that the programme had successfully accomplished the task of uniting fragmented resources, or at the very least was well on the way to achieving this. In brief, the experience of Alvey in this camp had persuaded some and confirmed others in their opinion that a precompetitive programme was a sensible choice.

The most sizeable camp readily agreed with the concept of a precompetitive programme, but for rather different reasons. This camp took the pragmatic view that Alvey could be 'all things to all men', ie that precompetitive research is a misnomer for the range of activities which it now transpires occurred under the Alvey umbrella. Some members of this group even pointed out that use of the label 'precompetitive research' is a politically expedient way of disguising the fact that government support for some of the work carried out in Alvey (and ESPRIT) could feasibly contravene the Treaty of Rome's dictates concerning industrial support programmes. These firms point to some of the 'loony fringe' elements of IKBS, the developmental nature of much of the VLSI whole-process work, the Large Scale Demonstrators and the Alvey Awareness Clubs as activities which span all but the latter stages of the usual product life cycle.

This sanguine view of precompetitive research was often adopted by some of the larger companies — especially those possessed of the necessary muscle to have had some influence over the composition of the programme. Many of these firms only participated in Alvey projects which they considered to have high exploitation potential in the relatively short-term. For firms such as these, the experience of Alvey has consolidated their view that precompetitive research is a licence to participate in almost any kind of R&D activity. It is also noticeable that this camp also contains some of those firms originally doubtful of the relevance of a precompetitive programme to their needs. Actual practice and the malleability of the concept has convinced them otherwise. For this camp, therefore, it would appear that precompetitive research programmes are potentially neither better nor worse than programmes with a more explicit 'market-facing' flavour.

Firms who still maintain that the Alvey programme was fundamentally misconceived constitute a third group. Amongst this group can be counted 'user' firms and some of the firms with only a small number of Alvey commitments or projects clustered in just one or two technological areas. Indeed, a number commented that their involvement would have been greater if Alvey had had a different, more 'product-oriented' focus. However, nearly all of the projects in which they were involved had been chosen for their short-term development potential and could scarcely be called 'blue sky'. Although still opposed to the idea of precompetitive programmes, even firms of this bent had managed to take limited advantage of the actual programme.

In summary, across the firms interviewed, Alvey was responsible for a positive shift in terms of the acceptance of both the concept and the reality of precompetitive research. This does not imply, however, that the balance of opinion favoured yet another precompetitive programme in the context of the UK. The industrial preference for more market-oriented initiatives in the future is considered further in a later section.

3.2 Attitudes to collaboration

There are a good number of arguments as to why collaboration in precompetitive research is theoretically desirable in the UK electronics and IT context. Many of these were cogently presented in the Alvey Report and have been the subject of much discussion and elaboration since then. From the perspective of individual firms the horns of the dilemma are as follows: on the one hand R&D costs in some technical areas are becoming prohibitive and personnel scarce, tendencies which in isolation would encourage selectivity; conversely, industry analysts argue that it is becoming excessively risky to place all of one's eggs in the same basket, and that the flexibility of response which a broad-based research strategy can achieve is becoming vital. One way out of the dilemma, therefore, is to pool resources in collaborative ventures, thus lowering individual costs, accessing scarce skill resources, reducing risks and ensuring flexibility.

During the course of the interviews conducted for the purposes of this study, firms were not specifically asked to provide a succinct rationale for collaboration in precompetitive research. Questions relating to this topic typically focussed on how firms had originally perceived Alvey and how involvement in the Alvey programme had occurred. Firms were not asked directly why they had wished to participate in a collaborative, precompetitive R&D programme. Nevertheless, most firms offered some comments on their behaviour, many of them echoing the 'unification of fragmented resources' argument of the Alvey Report. Common responses referred to the high visibility of Alvey, the chance to make new contacts and to the importance of being seen to be 'a member of the club'. A number also pointed to the collaborative schemes undertaken by the Japanese as examples of government and industry combining to foster both collaboration and competition. The need to find the right admixture to suit UK tastes was stressed, though no one underplayed the difficulties of accomplishing this. It must be said, however, that only a few firms proffered anything resembling a cogent, well argued rationale for their initial entry into precompetitive collaboration. Although it is fair comment to say that this was not asked for directly, one might have expected a coherent argument to be expounded if such arguments had become accepted folklore within the industry. All too often it appeared that lip service was being paid to a series of unconnected statements describing a few positive, partial facets of collaboration. In very few instances were these attributes presented in such a way that they forcefully illustrated the underlying logic of collaboration. Instead, the impression was given that for many firms collaboration was initially accepted, often reluctantly, as the then current funding flavour, a taste of which was unavoidable if government support was to be obtained — a 'necessary evil if one wanted to join the bandwagon'.

Initial acceptance of collaboration may have been tempered with wariness and even a little reluctance, but for the majority of firms interviewed this situation changed appreciably. Experience of collaboration both within Alvey and in other programmes such as ESPRIT enabled them to weigh up the practical rather than the theoretical costs and benefits of participation. For most, the outcome was positive. Table 12.1 lists some of the most commonly perceived advantages and disadvantages of collaboration.

On the debit side, many firms placed the costs of increased administration and travel, and the resources consumed during the preparatory proposal and negotiation phases were common bones of contention. Firms were generally willing, however, to concede that the benefits of collaboration outweighed such costs. Although a good number of firms felt that it was too early to comment on the merits of intended technical outputs, the majority seemed appreciative of factors such as the creation of a community, 'club membership' and their increased links with the university sector. Indeed, this last appreciation emerged as one of the most commonly and forcefully

Table 12.1. The advantages and disadvantages of Alvey collaborations

---

ADVANTAGES

- Collaboration within Alvey has given rise to a stronger research focus on critical enabling technologies;
- Collaboration has increased linkages within the IT community, both between firms and between firms and universities;
- Most firms welcomed the the creation of an Alvey community and the 'club' atmosphere surrounding it;
- The momentum of research has increased and, in some technical areas such as speech and image processing, critical mass is being achieved;
- Access to a wide body of research has justified initial investment costs eg for one firm an investment of £3 million across a broad range of technologies has granted it access to a £25 million pool of research;
- Leadership of collaboration projects is favoured since leverage is enhanced by control over project direction;
- The ability to participate at a number of different levels (eg research project, research centre, research club, awareness club) allows a great deal of flexibility in 'covering the waterfront';
- Collaboration reduces risk and enhances choice;
- Collaboration increases the familiarity of firms with each other and encourages flexible relationships to develop between them; and
- The experience of collaboration within a UK context provides a solid base for other forms of collaboration, especially within European programmes.

DISADVANTAGES

- The administrative costs of collaborative research can be heavy, especially for small firms;
- Negotiation of collaboration agreements and intellectual property rights can give rise to start-up delays and are time- and resource-consuming; and
- Involvement in collaborative research can reduce flexibility of response in the management of the R&D process. For example, compromises sometimes have to be made at the outset of research to appease partners, and later in the day firms find it more difficult to extricate themselves from projects once changes in the business environment demand new strategies.

---

expressed sentiments, many firms valuing their academic links over and above their links with other members of the UK industrial electronics and IT community.

Many firms were also participants in the ESPRIT programme and a few were undertaking Eureka projects (a European, industry-led collaborative programme with a more developmental flavour). Most firms had something to say of a comparative nature. Not unnaturally, the overheads of participation in European collaborations were generally reckoned to be greater than in Alvey, but again these costs tended to be outweighed by other advantages of collaboration. In structural terms, however, there was a preference for the more formal procedures adopted by the ESPRIT administration, especially with regard to project proposals and selection. Only one firm felt that ESPRIT was overly bureaucratic compared with Alvey.

A few companies expressed a preference for ESPRIT over Alvey on strategic grounds. Some firms saw European collaborations in terms of establishing a European presence. Others took 'standards' to be the extra additionality ingredient in European involvements. Netting European suppliers and users into a common standards loop through collaboration was seen as the major long-term strategic advantage of ESPRIT. Many firms also saw their future in terms of links with European firms rather than with UK firms. In fact, these firms had few complimentary things to say about other UK companies in comparison with some of their newly established European partners. Two companies even regretted that Alvey funding had become available prior to ESPRIT funding. These companies felt that they had overcommitted themselves to Alvey and hence limited their ability to take on board all the ESPRIT projects they deemed desirable.

This was an isolated viewpoint, however. A more commonly expressed sentiment was that Alvey had formed a necessary first step on the path to European collaborations and, eventually, European markets. Experience gained via prior participation in the Alvey programme had usefully equipped firms intent on broadening horizons. One firm in particular had used contacts gained via its comparatively small involvement in Alvey (£1 million support) to secure a prime contractorship on an ESPRIT project (ECU 1.5 million support) and a substantial proportion (ECU 5 million support) of a large (ECU 80 million) Eureka project. In so doing it had built up a 50-strong research team from scratch and gained a high profile in Europe — something it felt was vital for any expansion of its European business.

Only two firms came down against participation in European collaborations: one because it could not grasp the rationale for such involvements; the other because it still felt it had a lot to learn from Alvey before it extended its horizons further. Participation in Alvey has helped convince many firms of the value of collaboration in precompetitive research. It has also helped some companies appreciate the value of collaboration and 'strategic alliances':

– with industrial partners in both the UK and in other countries;
– both within public and private ventures;
– with the university sector; and
– in areas other than precompetitive research eg development, production, marketing etc.

As noted earlier, some firms have used Alvey as a springboard into ESPRIT, and the willingness of firms to enter Eureka demonstrates the fact that collaboration of a more market-facing nature is considered palatable. A number of private sector research collaborations have also been effected, and some firms admitted that Alvey had played a part in determining strategy in this area.

For some of the larger firms, 'strategic alliances' with other firms — often from the USA and Japan — have been a matter of course for a number of years and it is unlikely that Alvey has had any direct effect on firm behaviour in this respect. Certainly none of the firms interviewed indicated a direct causal relationship. Nevertheless, a number did stress that Alvey had catalysed strategic thinking generally and had thus indirectly impacted on firm behaviour outside the limited confines of collaboration in precompetitive research.

Alvey has also encouraged firms to strengthen their links with universities. Many had established fruitful new relationships with universities and polytechnics in Alvey projects and were intent on building up these links, whether within the context of formal government-sponsored programmes or not. Overall, increased contact with the academic sector appears to have improved firms' appreciation of the advantages of nurturing such relationships.

On occasion, however, it was evident that some Alvey-arranged marriages had not been made in heaven. Indeed, although both industry and academia appear to have embraced each other willingly, industry has shown signs of greater reserve in the clinches. Interviews and questionnaires conducted in the academic sector during the course of the evaluation have indicated a high appreciation of the benefits of collaboration. In comparison, industrial representatives are still positive but somewhat cooler in their appraisal of the potential of greater university-industry links. Understandably, there was a reluctance to place academic contributions on the critical path of research projects, especially those of a more developmental nature (though most academics felt that their work was crucial to the success of joint ventures), and inevitably there was occasional criticism of the more informal management procedures in operation in the academic sector. However, it must be stressed that despite the above remarks the overall acceptance within industry of the benefits of collaboration with academia was still impressive.

3.3 Attitudes towards government support programmes

The firm interviews revealed an unexpected strength of opinion favouring government commitment to a coherent industrial strategy for the production and diffusion of IT within the UK. Although many of the firms had long been recipients of government moneys from a range of government sources, eg MOD, the PO/BT and a variety of schemes run by the DTI, and might therefore have been expected to welcome some aspects of this funding source pluralism, there were some quite vehement condemnations of the absence of any semblance of coherence either between the policies of the different branches of the establishment or over time within each branch. One firm accused the government of knee-jerk responses. Another bemoaned the fact that it was being urged both to collaborate and compete at the same time. Yet another complained that there was no single forum in which to discuss policy and no identifiable body to formulate such policy. Considerably more identified overlaps with European programmes as both a current and a potential source of concern. The plea for government to take a firm grip on the situation and produce coherent policies for the sector was loud and cogent. Some even went so far as to call for a 'Euro-MITI' to establish a policy framework for Europe.

In this broad context, Alvey was interpreted as a step in the right direction. For some, though, the measure of the step was too little. A few of the firms voicing this opinion had originally argued that the programme should not have had a 'technology-push', precompetitive bias but should have been more market-facing and have had a 'market-pull' element. Others argued that Alvey on its own was a necessary but insufficient policy, and that for real change to have been effected within the industry Alvey should have been just one component of a tightly knit suite of programmes and policies operating at different parts of the product life-cycle, all geared to ensuring that sufficient 'coupling' took place between technologies and the market.

There was an alternative view on offer, however. This was the view put forward by some of the companies suggesting that Alvey had had a radicalising effect on strategic thinking both within their own companies and within the industrial community at large. The suggestion was made that Alvey had been the only appropriate strategy to opt for at the time; that firms within the UK IT industry would not have been able to cope with or exploit anything more comprehensive in nature. Collaboration in research was needed before collaboration in exploitation. Collaboration in the UK was needed before collaboration in Europe. These firms argued that collaboration under Alvey had been necessary to catalyse a cultural change in the community and that the application of anything more powerful in the early 1980s would have meant taking a sledgehammer to the proverbial nut. It was suggested that an impartial observer surveying the IT industry would find it difficult to fault the logic of this argument.

Although a variety of views were to be found concerning the relative appropriateness of the Alvey programme in the early 1980s, there seemed to be a general agreement that new initiatives were needed post-Alvey. In this context there was universal agreement on the timeliness of the IT86 initiative.[2] Moreover, there was a surprising degree of unanimity as to the government policies which would be welcomed by the community. Admittedly, some of those interviewed had actually sat on the IT86 Committee since the early part of the year and could therefore be expected to speak with one voice, but similar recommendations emanated from most other quarters.

As might be expected given the scale of support for a coherent industrial strategy, the desirability of further government initiatives affecting the IT sector was a dominant theme running through discussions. It must be said, however, that some firms despaired of the then current government either providing adequate fiscal support or selecting the correct mix of policies.

Many firms felt that it was wrong to regard the Alvey programme as a 'pump-priming' exercise and that three types of follow-on initiative were necessary if the Alvey strategy were to succeed. In the first instance, at the research end of the spectrum, the argument was made that a coordinated 'package' of support measures continued to be essential in many of the Alvey-related precompetitive, enabling technology areas. Four main reasons were advanced:

— as noted in the Alvey Report itself, work in some areas was unlikely to reach fruition within a ten year framework let alone the five year lifetime of the Alvey programme. It was therefore remiss to staunch the flow of funds after five years;

— many smaller firms had exploited Alvey to build up a research capability, often for the first time. Few felt that such capability could be maintained in the absence of continued government support;

— R&D is a continuous process. Thus, even as research activities become more developmental in nature, other related research work comes on-stream and becomes eligible for funding; and

— although funding for future work on enabling technologies could be organised by different agencies under different initiatives, this might undermine the sense of purpose which had been built up in the so-called Alvey community. Many prized this new found atmosphere but felt that it still needed to be nurtured carefully. Cultural reformation, it was stressed, takes time.

The second type of support initiative which it was felt should follow on from the Alvey programme was one which countenanced support nearer the market for work which would build upon the foundations laid by Alvey. For many of the firms interviewed, Alvey was seen as having successfully united fragmented resources. In so doing it had increased the size of the 'technical pool of knowledge' — or reoriented it in more 'relevant' directions — to such an extent that exploitation of this pool had become the priority of the day, whereas uniting it had been the priority at the time of the Alvey Report.

Of course, if this interpretation is correct, then it has to be granted that the Alvey programme achieved a significant degree of success. Alternatively, it could be argued that the Alvey Report's interpretation of the state of affairs in the early 1980s was incorrect: that the 'pool' was actually much larger or much more 'relevant' than had been estimated and that the impact of Alvey had thus been marginal. It is a measure of the high regard in which the Alvey programme was held that no firm would accept this latter view.

At the outset of the Alvey programme, the hope in some quarters was that government support at the enabling technology end of the spectrum would provide sufficient impetus for firms to self-finance subsequent exploitation without any further government assistance. Indeed, this was the picture painted by representatives of the industry in the Alvey Report itself. The plea for support nearer the market end of the spectrum might therefore seem to warrant a charge of effrontery. A strong argument justifying this apparent volte-face would seem to be required.

Many of the firms interviewed felt no such need to justify their stance. These firms pleaded that they were not asking for direct product support for themselves. The types of support at the market end of the spectrum which they were advocating had more of the flavour of 'market-pull' or procurement initiatives — many of them offering financial inducements to end-user firms to install 'advanced prototypes' provided by the IT sector. These firms argued that whereas they did not necessarily require direct government support, indirect assistance in the form of incentives to users was appropriate. The Achilles heel had become the market rather than the industry itself. In this sense, few firms felt that they had reneged on the spirit of the proposals put forward in the original Alvey Report. The third policy imperative to be stressed on numerous occasions called for UK initiatives to be tightly integrated with European programmes, especially those designed to establish standards and to encourage market unification. For many this implied that European collaborations should take place nearer the development end of the product life-cycle than at the precompetitive end of the spectrum.

The experience of Alvey led firms to lend strong support to a future programme which would replicate much of Alvey but which would also expand the concept in the direction of greater user involvement and European integration. This in itself speaks volumes about both the strengths and weaknesses of Alvey and the strategic desire to participate in government programmes. It must be said, however, that the interviews did not elicit any truly convincing arguments as to why government should support an expanded programme of the type described above. Even the arguments put forward for the component which would replicate Alvey-type precompetitive research are insufficient to explain why firms should not support this work themselves. This is not to say that such arguments do not exist — many good ones do — but none were forcefully expressed during the course of the interviews. And when it came to arguments in support of government-funding as opposed to self-funding of more 'market-facing' initiatives, sound arguments were even less in evidence. Alvey may have strengthened the desire of firms to participate in government-support programmes, but it is questionable whether it has improved industry's ability to make a case for this support.

3.4 Overall strategic awareness

At one extreme, more than a few firms were ready to admit that prior to Alvey their 'strategic awareness' had been limited. Some of these were adamant that Alvey had been a major — if not the major — factor stimulating them and causing them to rethink overall company strategy. Others were not so willing to attribute direct causality in this way, but were willing to ascribe to Alvey a significant contributory role. For example, one firm had already decided to found a centralised research establishment prior to Alvey, but the existence of Alvey support in the very areas it had already earmarked as important for its own development helped boost confidence that its strategy was correct. Alvey moneys also played a significant part in getting the centre off the ground. Not unexpectedly, many of the companies emphasising the importance of Alvey to strategic thought were major recipients of Alvey support.

Apparently at the other extreme were companies which denied that Alvey had had any impact on overall firm strategy. Generally speaking, those firms with only one or two Alvey projects fell into this category. However, on further questioning it became apparent that Alvey had certainly impacted on what may be termed 'tactical' thinking. For example, some firms lying outside the 'first circle' of electronics and IT 'majors' considered that they had been ill-prepared and badly positioned vis-à-vis the government support infrastructure to fully exploit Alvey at its inception. They were determined to rectify the situation henceforth by positioning themselves within any newly evolving infrastructure. In some cases they had sought to become actively involved in the policy debate surrounding post-Alvey initiatives.

Similarly, foreign multinationals and 'user' firms had seen fit to benefit from the high visibility afforded to Alvey participants and the sense of community which club membership conferred. Alvey's consolidation of an indigenous electronics and IT community has made exclusion from this club undesirable. Foreign multinationals are particularly conscious of this and appear grateful for the opportunity to play some part, however small, in initiatives such as Alvey.

Alvey has impacted strategic and tactical thinking in a number of ways. For some the act of thinking through the position of Alvey work within the context of existing firm strategies has helped them translate tacit agreements as to the nature of these strategies into more explicit, articulated policies. Alvey has helped firms decide on the relevance of particular technology areas to their overall business stratagems. It has helped others rethink and restructure the way R&D fits into a firm. Furthermore, as earlier sections made clear, it has certainly caused almost all firms to rethink their attitudes to precompetitive and collaborative research programmes.

In the period since Alvey was first mooted in the UK there have been a number of major changes in the IT sector, all of which are likely to have affected company strategies and strategic awareness within firms. Internationally, a corollary of the rise of Japan and the continuing strength of the USA in many market sectors has been a declining market share for the UK IT industry. On the home front, changes in procurement policies by the MOD and the deregulation, liberalisation and privatisation of BT have markedly altered the environment in which many UK IT firms operate. All have been stirred, if not shaken, by these changes. Against this background, the precise role of Alvey in the formulation and reformulation of strategic directions must remain in doubt. However, from the responses provided by interviewees it is difficult to escape the conclusion that Alvey has helped remove some very parochial blinkers. Many firms confirmed that involvement in Alvey had helped them to appreciate both their position on a world stage and the position of the UK electronics and IT industry more generally.

4 Conclusions

From the point of view of firms there can be no doubt that the Alvey programme has contributed positively to the strengthening of the 'knowledge base' of both individual firms and the UK IT sector as a whole. Although it is extremely likely that many firms would have carried out similar R&D projects in the absence of Alvey, it is doubtful whether they could have been conducted at the same pace or on the same scale.

The programme has also had a strong formative effect on potential relationships between the various parts of the IT community. The benefits of working with both universities and rival firms in collaborative, precompetitive research have been demonstrated, whether within the context of government-inspired programmes — both national and international — or outside these. Collaboration at the precompetitive end of the spectrum has also provided a foretaste of, and encouraged some to indulge in, collaborations at other parts of the spectrum.

In terms of government-industry relations, participation in both the formulation and implementation of the programme helped firms to appreciate the benefits of being close to the policy-making nexus, first from the point of view of being able to influence future strategies, and secondly from the position of benefiting from them. Even given this, however, and even though firms were clearly able to see the advantages of programmes like Alvey and the desirability of future programmes which both built on Alvey and incorporated additional features, it was not apparent from the strength of the arguments being presented in late 1986 that industry was fully capable of making a case to government for either extended support or a more intimate involvement in the policy-making process.

Subsequent developments support this conclusion. In November 1986 the IT86 Committee presented its recommendations to government. A reply was expected in the Spring of 1987. It did not arrive until January 1988. It backed some of the IT86 recommendations, notably continued support for precompetitive research and a greater emphasis on participation in European programmes such as ESPRIT II, but on the whole the government response disappointed the IT industry by its lateness, by its advocacy of a reduction in the overall amount of government support, and by its non-inclusion of the 'market-facing' elements suggested by the IT86 Committee. The industry was pervaded by an overwhelming sense of disillusionment with its own ability to successfully mount an effective lobby for extended government support for the IT sector. Alvey may have strengthened industry's resolve to benefit from government support and to participate in the evolution of strategies for the sector, but just desire has not brought its just desserts.

Alvey has been a high-profile programme which has attracted considerable attention from other parts of the world. Participation in a programme with such a global dimension has played a part in raising the strategic sights of industry from near to far horizons as the globalisation of the IT industry continues apace. It has also prompted some companies to re-evaluate the way in which R&D 'fits' within firm structures, processes and strategies. However, such strategic rethinking is by no means universal and it is still uncertain whether it has, or will be, translated into effective action.

The need for firms to refocus internally on the management of R&D is apparent from an inspection of Alvey exploitation track records. Although at the time of the survey on which this chapter is based it was too early to say much about the exploitation of Alvey research, subsequent and current work within the evaluation programme is tending to indict management procedures for dealing effectively with the exploitation, though not the conduct, of R&D. There have been many instances of successful exploitation of Alvey research, and more which look as though exploitation will follow in due course, but it is becoming apparent that more effective exploitation could have been enhanced by greater internal attention to the way in which companies structure the process of internal technology transfer. In short, the efficacy of links between research and production functions within companies leaves much to be desired, especially within the larger firms involved in Alvey, and this applies not only to Alvey research but to all research conducted within firms. Almost invariably, the more successful instances of the exploitation of Alvey R&D are characterised by their initial formulation as part of coherent strategies which are market-led in the sense that interest in projects within production divisions is stimulated at a very early stage, often at the time of their genesis. Too often the projects which look like stagnating are those conceived and conducted in relatively isolated research environments, and which, once completed, are only then brought to the attention of the relevant groups within organisations in a position to take the work further. There are exceptions, of course, but these tend to reinforce the general rule rather than contradict it.

The issue of the effective management of R&D within the context of overall firm strategy is very relevant in any discussion of appropriate government support policies for an industrial sector. For example, in a case such as Alvey one has to weigh the benefits accruing from an undoubted expansion of the industrial 'knowledge base' with the more limited success firms have had and are likely to have in transforming this expanded 'knowledge base' into 'technology' and 'product' bases. Is there any point in increasing the 'knowledge base' and stimulating new collaborative research arrangements between firms and between industry and academia without complementary policies designed to attack the problem of the inefficient management of the output side of the R&D process? Can and should government attempt to evolve and implement policies which infringe such traditional areas of industrial sovereignty?

In the case of Alvey sufficient 'exploitables' to justify the programme's existence are likely to emerge in the near to medium-term. The industry is also likely to benefit in the long run from the general increase in overall strategic awareness catalysed by Alvey. But unless these firms exploit this heightened awareness by turning the spotlight inwards and re-evaluating and restructuring internal procedures for the effective utilisation of in-house R&D, it is increasingly likely that future government programmes similar to Alvey will start to produce diminishing returns. Even government policies designed to abet this restructuring process will prove futile unless firms in the UK IT sector grasp this nettle of their own volition.

Notes

1 This latter firm was included to provide some feel for the reasons for non-participation in Alvey.
2 During 1986 the IT86 Committee was constituted to review future policy for the IT sector. The round of interviews on which this chapter is based was undertaken prior to the publication of its recommendations.

Chapter 13

Corporate strategies and collaboration: the case of ESPRIT and European electronics

Margaret Sharp

1 Introduction

The 1980s have witnessed a major volte-face in European industrial policies. While the 1960s and 1970s could well be called the Age of the National Champion, the 1980s may earn the title the Age of Collaboration. Within Europe the decade of the 1980s has indeed seen the demise of the national champion and the emergence of a new generation of European-based multinationals with sights firmly fixed on competing within a global framework.

The purpose of this chapter is to explore these developments within one sector, that of electronics, and to consider the part played in these developments by the European Commission's collaborative programmes, and especially that of ESPRIT (European Strategic Programme in Research in Information Technology). Its contention is that ESPRIT has played a seminal part in changing attitudes and strategies amongst Europe's top electronics firms and, in this respect, has acted as a catalyst for the rationalisation that is currently taking place. But it also casts doubt on how far collaboration is a permanent phenomenon, suggesting on the contrary that it is a transitional phase in the process of adjustment and realignment by the firm to fundamental changes in underlying technologies.

2 The European electronics industries of the 1970s and early 1980s

The state of the European electronics industry in the 1970s is perhaps best illustrated by Tables 13.1 and 13.2 taken from a McKinsey Report on the European IT Industry written in 1983. Table 13.1 depicts the deteriorating trade balance of the countries of the European Community. From a modest balance in 1975 (when all three trading areas, the EEC, the US and Japan were net exporters to the rest of the world) the position had slipped to a deficit of over $4 billion by 1980, with that deficit predicted to rise to over $9 billion by 1990. The actual figures, quoted in the final column, show that the position has been as bad, or even rather worse, than predicted.

Table 13.2 illustrates the typical position of European industries in the IT field in 1980-81 showing that even in fields such as integrated circuits and computers, where the ostensible share of European production was relatively high, a good part of it came from US and (to a much lesser degree) Japanese subsidiaries located in Europe.

Table 13.1. Information technology trade balance ($ billion, constant 1980, except 1986)

	1975	1980	1990 (estimate)	1986 (actual $bn)
		$ 1980 dollars		
EEC	1.7	–4.1	–9.7	–14.0
Japan	5.5	15.3	17.6	18.0
US	4.2	5.3	4.5	–1.0

Source: McKinsey (1983); 1986 figures from European Commission

Table 13.2. European market shares in 1980 by origin of company

	Integrated Circuits		Computers	
	Total %	% produced in Europe	Total %	% produced in Europe
EEC	31	34		
Japan	5)		–	
	)	20		
US	64)		66	50

Source: McKinsey 1983.

One of the main areas of deficit within the IT sector was in semiconductors (SC), and developments in this sector illustrate well what was happening to European electronics. As Chapter 5 describes, the European SC industry has been dominated since the mid-1960s by foreign companies. In the 1950s firms such as AEI and Marconi (both subsequently part of GEC), Philips and the Società Generale Semiconduttori (SGS) were substantial producers of transistors, dominating their respective national markets. But the development in the US of the integrated circuit in the 1960s, gave the US firms most closely associated with its development — Texas Instruments, Fairchild, Motorola, Signetics and National Semiconductor — a technological lead which enabled them to exploit overseas markets both directly via exports, and indirectly via branch plants (subsidiaries) abroad.

A variety of motives led these firms to establish European subsidiaries. First was the fast expansion of European markets at that time with overall GDP growth rates averaging 5 per cent a year and particularly rapid expansion of the new consumer electronics (television sets, tape recorders, hi-fi, transistor radios). There was also fast expanding use of computers for such tasks as routine invoicing, wage and salary accounts. All this meant that components were in high demand, and expanding markets demanded new production capacity. Moreover, at that time a European location offered cost advantages for these US firms, particularly for the more routine, labour-intensive assembly operations. There were also direct trade advantages in local production: it avoided tariff protection (the common external tariff has remained unchanged at 17 per cent since the early 1970s) and gave advantage in public purchasing contracts, particular defence industry contracts, where local purchase of components was demanded.

The early 1970s brought the first major recession for this industry, which has since become marked by periodic crises of shortage and glut. The US firms survived better than their European counterparts — they had the advantage of the buffer of major military contract work in the US and, as the more substantial producers, of being able to spread overheads. They also used the opportunity to cut prices aggressively vis-à-vis their European competitors in an attempt to gain market share. It had the desired effect. Many European competitors — firms such as Plessey and SGS — concluded that the main 'commodity' SC markets (the markets for mainstream memory chips) were not for them, and retreated to the relative safety of the custom chip market — niche markets where products were bespoke and prices appropriately inflexible.

This process of realignment is described by Sciberras (1977). He concludes that after the shakeout of the early 1970s, the industry effectively divided itself into two non-competing segments — the Big League firms which maintained a presence in the 'commodity' SC sectors; and the Little League firms which had withdrawn to niche markets. What was more, the leagues were essentially self-perpetuating. 'The dominant US multinational firms in the industry are able to obtain the elimination of competition by pricing at a level which ensures volume economies, through pre-emption of mass standard device markets, and, at the same time, long run profits'. (Sciberras, 1977, p273).

What Sciberras documents are the learning curve advantages which accrue in markets such as SCs. Firms already in the market have knowledge and experience which enable them continuously to undercut potential new entrants to the market. The cumulative benefits of a substantial market presence thus help to perpetuate existing market dominance. His thesis was that by the latter half of the 1970s the European SC market was effectively segregated into Big League and Little League firms, with the US multinationals dominating the Big League. Of European firms only Philips really had claim to Big League status; Siemens' output was relatively large but much of it went for internal (captive) use. Thomson continued to manufacture, but at relatively low volume and because of French government insistence that they maintained a presence in mainstream memory chip manufacture. The three British firms, GEC, Plessey and Ferranti all pulled out as mainstream manufacturers, as did SGS, the only major Italian SC firm (Dosi, 1982).

Sciberras' thesis held for the best part of ten years. From the mid-1970s to the mid-1980s, the US multinationals continued to dominate the European industry seemingly unchallenged. Worldwide, however, their position was challenged by the rise of the Japanese SC firms. Spearheaded by the MITI-organised VLSI (Very Large Scale Integration) programme in the late 1970s, the main Japanese manufacturers — Hitachi, Toshiba, NEC, Matsushita — effectively broke into the market by using the same tactics their US counterparts had used in the early 1970s. They concentrated their research on VLSI techniques of production, broke into the market ahead of their US competitors, cut prices in anticipation of volume sales and effectively pre-empted the market. The shake out that has taken place in the mid-1980s in the SC markets has seen many of the US firms pull out of the mainstream memory chip market just as their European counterparts did in the 1970s. And like their European counterparts they sought refuge in the seemingly 'safer' markets of the more specialised microprocessors and semi-custom chips (Application Specific Integrated Circuits or ASICs).

The rapid rise of the Japanese is effectively illustrated in Table 13.3 which lists the ten top suppliers of integrated circuits worldwide between 1973 and 1985. Notice that there were no Japanese producers in the top ten in the 1970s, and that the only European producer was Philips, which entered the top ten as a result of its acquisition of Signetics in 1978. Table 13.4 illustrates dramatically the effect on world markets of Japan's entry as a big league player. The dominant memory chip of the early 1980s was the 64K RAM, introduced in 1982. Normally such a chip could expect a two to three year life before the next generation of chips — in this case the 256K RAM — would begin to eat into market share. The Japanese strategy had been to enter the market on a substantial scale with the 64K RAM, establishing market openings and distribution systems, but to use the 256K RAM as the means of overtaking US competitors. This they introduced at the end of 1983, barely two years after the launch of the 64K RAM, and within one year its price had dropped from the 'premium levels' of $100 or more to below $10, sinking at one point in 1985 to below $2. Since that time, a somewhat unhappy pact between the Japanese and the US has held prices above the $2 mark, but even at this level the mainstream US manufacturers maintain they are selling

Table 13.3. The top ten producers of integrated circuits 1973-1985

1973	*1979*
1 Texas Instruments (US)	1 Texas instruments (US)
2 Motorola (US)	2 National Semiconductor (US)
3 National Semiconductor (US)	3 Motorola (US)
4 Fairchild (US)	4 Intel (US)
5 Signet (US)	5 Fairchild (Schlumberger - French)
6 American Microsystems (US)	6 Philips (Netherlands)*
7 Intel (US)	7 Mostek (United Technologies - US)
8 RCA (US)	8 Advanced Micro Devices (AMD-US)
9 Rockwell (US)	9 RCA (US)
10 Mostek (US)	10 Harris (US)
1983	*1985*
1 Motorola (US)	1 NEC (Japan)
2 Texas Instruments (US)	2 Texas Instruments (US)
3 NEC (Japan)	3 Hitachi (Japan)
4 Hitachi (Japan)	4 Motorola (US)
5 Toshiba (Japan)	5 Toshiba (Japan)
6 National Semiconductor (US)	6 Philips (Netherlands)*
7 Intel (US)	7 Fujitsu (Japan)
8 Fujitsu (Japan)	8 Intel (US)
9 AMD (US)	9 National Semiconductor (US)
10 Philips (Netherlands)*	10 Matsushita (Japan)

*Includes Signetics acquired in 1978

Source: Dosi (1982) and *Financial Times*

Table 13.4. Prices for 256K DRAM chips (average over year in $)

1983	120
1984	20
1985	3 (lowest point below $2)
1986	2.5
1987	3
1988	8

Source: Financial Times 24 October 1985 and 6 May 1988

below cost. With R&D costs for current generations of memory chip at $100 million, and a further $100 million or more required for investment in production facilities, minimum 'front-end' costs are now in the region of $200 million. It requires substantial sales to recoup such costs within a matter of eighteen months! (With the recovery in world markets in 1987-88 prices have begun rising again as the market moves into an era of famine, but too late for most manufacturers to recoup the losses on their 256k chip production.)

What was happening in SCs illustrates well what was happening more generally to European electronics. Caught behind the leading edge of technology, the industry lagged its main competitors in the US and Japan and retreated into niche markets where it was substantially protected by public purchasing, particularly telecommunications and defence contracts. In other words as national champions they were largely immune from international competition and could maintain reasonable profitability by concentrating on their traditional home markets.

Over time, however, the knock-on effects of a technological lag in a mainstream area such as SCs begin to show. SCs are an important component in downstream products such as telecommunications

Source: McKinsey (1983)
Fig 13.1 Vicious circle of decline in European IT

switchgear, computers, radar equipment, video recorders, even TV sets. Initially it did not matter that the European manufacturers bought-in SCs for these products: the problem was that as they fell progressively behind leading-edge technologies, so they lost touch with how best to *use* the new generations of SCs. It was not just a question of not being competitive in the SC markets, but over time this affected competitiveness in many of the other downstream product markets. Siemens, for example, got a rude shock in 1978 when they discovered that their EWS-A telecommunications switching system was badly out of date. The Nimrod affair in the UK likewise demonstrated GEC's difficulty in keeping abreast of computer based technologies linked to radar and avionics equipment. Figure 13.1 from the 1983 McKinsey report sums up the vicious circle of decline in which European electronics found itself in the early 1980s. It was this type of analysis which pervaded Europe and encouraged the deep Europessimism which took hold at that time.

3 Community initiatives in electronics and ESPRIT

Collaborative activities in electronics at a European level were slow to get off the ground. The 1960s saw an inconclusive attempt to get Siemens, Bull, Olivetti and Elliott Automation (subsequently the core of ICL) to work together, and an abortive consortium comprising ICL, Philips, CII, AEG-Telefunken, Saab and Olivetti came together in 1969 to bid for the ESRO (European Space Research Organisation) computer needs. The latter consortium collapsed under pressure from the German government, largely because of the exclusion of Siemens. But the subsequent attempt to bring Siemens, CII and Bull together under the Unidata umbrella collapsed when the French government negotiated a separate deal with Honeywell behind the backs of the German government and Siemens! (Sharp and Shearman, 1987).

While hopes for the success of Unidata were still riding high in 1974, the EC Council of Ministers passed a resolution on data processing which backed a medium term programme on the application, development and production of data processing systems. But this collapsed with the failure of Unidata and left nothing but a series of small and isolated Commission initiatives. Community industrial policy was dominated at this time by the collapse of Europe's older industries — steel, shipbuilding and textiles — and problems in areas such as chemicals and man-made fibres, and little thought was given to the relatively trouble-free new industries which were, in any case, given preferential treatment by their respective national governments.

By the end of the decade, however, attitudes had changed. Active intervention gave way to scepticism as to how far governments could or should prop up failing industries, and there was a new interest in structural adjustment and the growth of new industries. In 1977, Vicomte Davignon took over the Commission's industrial portfolio (DG III), at the same time as DG XII (research and development) put in hand its forward looking FAST

(Forecasting and Assessment in Science and Technology) studies. The latter included a module on the information society, and successive reports underlined Europe's weakness in these sectors, even though individually European governments were supporting their own firms with substantial subsidies and active promotional programmes.

The contrast between the relative failure of the separate European initiatives and the success of MITI's coordinated and collaborative VSLI programme was stark, and the lesson did not go unheeded. Under Davignon's guidance the Commission began to develop a more strategic approach to the IT sector. The broad outline of a programme for microelectronic technology was produced in 1979-80 and agreed by the Council in November 1981. The Commission then took the unorthodox step of inviting representatives from the major companies to establish a working group and to draw up the detailed programme which was to develop into ESPRIT.

Davignon played a vital role in developing the ESPRIT programme. In his evidence to a 1985 House of Lords Select Committee on the European Communities, he outlined the three factors which had motivated his attempts (House of Lords, 1985, p169). In the first place, he had been struck by the 'very distinctive difference of performance' between the industries of the US, Japan and the EC. Secondly, he had felt that the time had come for Community competence to be upgraded to reflect more accurately the state-of-the-art; and, third, he had been aware of the fact that no real incentive existed for cross-border collaboration. Any Community-level solution therefore needed a new approach to policy development. Up to that time the Commission had tended to work with research directors and their equivalents and initiatives had come unstuck because they had been unable to carry those higher up the hierarchy. Davignon determined to liaise with only the very highest levels of company management, to define priority areas with them and thus secure their commitment.

Over the period 1979-80 Davignon had therefore invited the heads of Europe's leading electronics and IT companies to a series of Round Table discussions. The 'Big Twelve', as they came to be known, comprised ICL, GEC and Plessey from Britain; AEG, Nixdorf and Siemens from Germany; Thomson, Bull and CGE from France; Olivetti and STET from Italy; and Philips from the Netherlands. Davignon received a more favourable response than the Commission had received from their lower-level counterparts in earlier years. A technical committee was established which set up a number of panels and workshops and discussions continued for a couple of years. Initially the thought was that they would establish a series of Airbus-style joint companies to manufacture products within Europe. Such activities, however, proved difficult to organise from the top down, whereas the concept of carrying out a major collaborative research programme seemed a more appropriate activity for organisation on a Community basis (House of Lords, 1985, p35). Discussion therefore began to focus on the precompetitive end of collaborative research, a stance which from the Commission's viewpoint also neatly avoided the issue of competition policy.[1]

The first outline proposal for ESPRIT was produced in September 1980. The idea was to develop a European strategic programme based on the collaboration between the major European companies and their smaller counterparts, and universities and research institutes. By May 1982 these had been worked into a full proposal and the Commission's paper 'Towards a European Strategic Programme for Research and Development in Information Technology' (CEC, 1984) was put to the Council, and subsequently to the Versailles European Summit in June 1982. The response was favourable and by December 1982 the Commission had the go-ahead for the first pilot phase costing ECU 11.5 million (£7.5 million).

The pilot phase was a deliberate part of the Davignon strategy. Given the doubts he encountered from the participants in his Round Table, in particular over the capacity of the Commission to mount an effective programme which would not become bogged down in bureaucratic delays, his strategy was the 'toe in the water' one — see how the pilot phase goes before you have to commit yourself. A special task-force, including many recruited from industry, was set up to handle applications and to cut through the Brussels red-tape. The call for proposals went out in February 1983, and contracts began to be signed in May that year. By September, 38 projects had been launched which were later to be incorporated into the main part of the programme. Over 80 per cent of the first round of contracts went to the twelve Round Table companies (comprising, it has to be said, 70 per cent of the industry). The majority involved participants from two to three member states. Of the total number of organisations associated with the pilot phase, 27 were located in Britain, 21 in Germany, 10 in the Netherlands, 8 in Belgium, 4 in France and 2 in Italy. Examples of the projects were: the Thomson-CGE partnership with Plessey and GEC in the development of an advanced interconnect for VLSI with the Universities of Newcastle, Southampton and Montpellier; the collaboration between Siemens, System Designers Ltd, CIT Alcatel and Philips on software production and maintenance management systems; and that between Olivetti and Nixdorf in broad-based office communication systems.[2]

Encouraged by the success of the pilot phase, the Commission rapidly pushed ahead with its full plans. Those comprised a 10-year programme (1984-1993) with a first-phase budget of ECU 750 million (approximately £500 million). The first five-year phase was to concentrate on the development of generic technology in three areas (microelectronics, advanced information processing and software technology) and two fields of application (office systems and computer integrated manufacturing). These plans were put to the Council in November 1983, but held up until February 1984 by British and German reservations over budgetary costs.[3]

The first call for proposals under the full programme went out in March 1984 and met with a huge response (441 serious submissions). The 201 projects eventually selected for the programme's first phase involved 240 firms (57 per cent of these from firms with less than 500 employees) and 210 research institutions. Three-quarters of the research projects involved collaboration between firms and academic research units. As of January 1987, the total cost was ECU 1.36 billion (approximately £900 million).

A crucial feature of ESPRIT has been the openness and degree of commitment it has required of the firms linked into it. Project proposals have to be submitted in reply to open invitations. Each project must involve at least two independent industrial partners from separate member states. Costs are generally co-financed by the Community and industry on a 50/50 basis. Research results are shared between all the participants in any given project who are free to apply them commercially, and preferential access is then granted to other ESPRIT participants outside that project. These guarantees are cornerstones of the whole ESPRIT process.

The Council decision adopting the full ESPRIT programme required its progress to be reviewed as soon as 60 per cent of the first phase budget had been committed. This point was reached by the end of 1984 and a three person Review Board was set up under Dr Pannenborg, ex-head of Philips, which reported in October 1985. By and large, ESPRIT was given a clean bill of health. The Review Board concluded that the programme had been successfully established and was well on its way to meeting its original objectives. Certain changes in the selection procedure and evaluation of proposals were suggested, together with improvements in project management and additional channels of communication. For future development the Board pointed to a continued emphasis on the precompetitive aspect of research, a consolidation and restructuring of research areas and, finally, the addition of focussed demonstration projects with a large user-involvement (CEC, 1985).

These suggestions have been incorporated in the second phase of the programme originally scheduled to start in 1987 but delayed by the problems over the agreement of the Framework Budget (of which ESPRIT was a major part).[4] Phase II is roughly double the size of ESPRIT I with a budget of ECU 1.6 billion (£1.1 billion). The Review Board's suggestions for streamlining the programme into three main areas of research — microelectronics, IT processing systems and application technologies — were accepted, as were the greater focus on what is called 'demand driven' aspects of the programme, for example the greater emphasis on the ASIC technology. The Review Board's call for demonstration projects is incorporated into what are called 'Technology Integration Projects' (TIPs), the aim of which is to pull the various strands of work together to show their usefulness to one another. For example, work on desktop workstations is being linked to the more theoretical work on parallel architectures and, if successful, this combination will considerably enhance the processing and presentation capabilities of the workstations.

Meanwhile the Task Force, brought into being by Davignon to launch the original ESPRIT programme, has been wound up and reabsorbed into the Commission structure. (It had always sat somewhat unhappily outside it, but had achieved what Davignon had aimed at — namely showing that the Brussels bureaucracy could move quickly and flexibly). Its functions are now fulfilled by DG XIII (Information Technology and Telecommunications) which handles ESPRIT and the telecoms programme, RACE (Research in Advanced Communications and Electronics) and BRITE (industrial technologies), while DG XII (Research and Development) handles the programmes on biotechnology (BAP and CUBE) the two education and training initiatives (COMETT and DELTA), and the older COST programme promoting innovation in small and medium-sized firms which has recently seen a new lease of life.

4 European electronics in the mid-1980s - Renaissance?

We need at this juncture to return to general developments in European electronics. The final column in Table 13.1 makes it clear that Europe's position in the later 1980s is not that strong. In particular Europe is as dependent as ever on non-European companies for its major supplies of components. Under the surface, however, major changes have been taking place.

The 1980s have seen the Japanese SC manufacturers follow their US counterparts in setting up production facilities in Europe. The first company to come was Hitachi (already well established in consumer electronics) with a plant at Munich in 1980; Fujitsu went to Ireland in the same year; NEC had a small assembly plant in Ireland from 1976, but expanded with a major new plant in Scotland at Livingston in 1982; Toshiba went to Braunschweig in West Germany in 1982. The factors attracting the Japanese firms were much the same as those attracting the US firms in the 1960s — the growth potential of the European market and its relatively low penetration to date by Japanese producers, the continuing 17 per cent tariff and the attraction of being in close proximity to major consumer electronics subsidiaries. One of the main reasons, however, why Japanese producers have set up subsidiaries has been fear of exclusion through voluntary export restraint or similar restrictions. Given the continuing threat of antidumping action by the EC authorities, this is a justified fear. The sites chosen for location were influenced in part by proximity to users (Hitachi), in part by the ready availability of two important inputs — skilled labour and clean water (NEC, Toshiba) and in part by the availability of substantial regional development aid (Fujitsu, NEC, Toshiba).

The Japanese had, of course, already made major inroads into the consumer electronics field. Indeed, one of the marked differences between the Japanese firms setting up subsidiaries in SCs in the 1980s and their US counterparts in the 1970s was that the Japanese firms were all major, integrated electronics concerns with interests ranging from SCs, through computers and office automation to factory automation and consumer electronics (*see* Hobday, Chapter 5). It is perhaps worth looking briefly at what had been happening in this sector.

The history of Japanese inward investment in consumer electronics is well known. Japan made its postwar industrial recovery by initially developing products for export to consumer markets such as textiles, toys and, with the advent of the transistor, cheap pocket radios. From radios, the industry moved on to tape recorders (and up-market hi-fi) and televisions and by the end of the 1960s was dominating the production of small, black and white TVs, moving into the colour TV (CTV) market. The European market for

CTV was protected by the PAL system which had been developed by the Germans and was adopted as the European industry standard. The PAL licensing system posed major problems for Japanese firms. First, it was not the system used in Japan and therefore the Japanese manufacturers were not able to enjoy the benefits of a large home base on which to build; secondly, the terms of the licence required no more than 50 per cent of output to be exported. In addition, by the early 1970s the Europeans had begun to protect their own producers from competition from Japan and other South East Asian countries. In the UK, for example, imports of CTVs over 20 inches were prohibited, and a subsequent voluntary export restraint agreement negotiated with Japan in 1973 limited Japanese exports to a 10 per cent share of the market.

For most of the 1970s the European consumer electronics industry remained relatively passive in the face of the threat from the Far East. The industry was highly fragmented and incapable of withstanding the fierce price competition from the standardised products of the Japanese. As competitive pressures built up, many European firms abandoned products at an early stage, partly perhaps because of erroneous market assessments, such as the failure to foresee a continuing market for portable monochrome TVs in the late 1970s. Production of hi-fi audio equipment kept going longer, thanks to numerous small firms that retreated into specialist market niches, but eventually many of these were overtaken by the technical and price performance of Japanese products. Consequently, the European industry became increasingly dependent on a single product, TV, which because of its protected position, was spread among a large number of independent producers (Brech and Sharp, 1984).

The Japanese response to the protection afforded by the PAL licensing system to CTVs, and the increasing threats of further protection through voluntary export restraints, was to set up manufacturing plants in Europe, building on the sales organisation it had already established to service its exports (see Baba, Chapter 3). The first company to establish itself in the European market was Sony with plants in Wales (1973) and West Germany (1975), followed by Matsushita (1976 - Wales), Mitsubishi Electric (1979 - Wales), Aiwa (1980 - Wales; 1981 - France) and JVC (joint venture with Thorn and Telefunken to manufacture video recorders in 1982).

By the early 1980s the pressure had shifted from CTVs, where the European market had become more or less saturated, to Video Cassette Recorders (VCRs). The notorious Poitiers incident illustrates well the element of hysteria that had by then crept into the European reaction to developments.[5] It seemed, however hard the Europeans tried, that it was impossible to stem the tide of Japanese products from flooding on to the market. In Britain there was increasing concern at the redundant plant and the unemployment caused by the withdrawal of British operators from the market. In the early 1980s Sanyo were therefore persuaded to take over the old Pye TV works at Lowestoft, and Toshiba and Hitachi constrained to work in joint ventures with Rank (at Plymouth) and GEC (Hirwaun, South Wales) respectively. Neither of these joint ventures was to prove satisfactory and in both cases the British partner withdrew, leaving the Japanese manufacturer to continue. This involved a major rationalisation at both plants, with the inevitable redundancies, and subsequent adoption of Japanese labour management techniques — one union, no-strike agreements, pendulum arbitration and single status plants. But Japanese management has also brought substantial new investment to each plant and a turn round in productivity and output trends (Cawson et al, 1986).

The entry of these same firms — strong, integrated concerns with interests across the whole range of electronics — might well have been seen as sealing the fate of the European industry. The industry could have fragmented still further, with the European firms quitting all mainstream markets for the safety of the niche markets. Surprisingly this has not been the case. On the contrary, far from quitting, the European players have, in the course of the last three years, rallied and pushed themselves back into mainstream markets.

The effort has been spearheaded by the Philips-Siemens megaproject announced in 1984, a joint project aimed at giving both firms the capability to produce the 1 Megabit (1000K RAM) chip and the 4 Megabit chip (4000K RAM). Both are now entering production, admittedly two years *after* the Japanese launch; nevertheless the project is seen as having lived up to expectations and there are plans afoot for the two companies to accelerate their research into the next generation (16 Megabit) of SCs (*Financial Times*, 15 Mar 1988). In a similar vein, in 1986 Thomson bought up the ailing US SC firm Mostek and then in 1987 announced the merging of its SC interests with SGS-Ates with a view to producing chips of the megabit generation. SGS-Ates, a subsidiary of the Italian telecommunications company STET, having more or less pulled out of the market in the 1970s, has been steadily increasing its role in the 1980s, not least through a link forged with, first, Zilog and subsequently AT&T in the US. Only the British firms — GEC, Plessey and Ferranti — stuck firmly to their Little League strategies. But there are signs of change. Plessey, for example, in 1987 opened a £50 million SC plant in Plymouth, which enhances its ability to compete in the semi-custom chip market and has recently bought out the SC interests of Ferranti in a much needed move to rationalise UK SC interests. The British have also been behind the establishment of a new SC firm — European Silicon Structures, ES2 — aimed as a cross-European venture in the custom chip area (*see* Hobday, Chapter 5).

Philips, Siemens and Thomson, however, provide the key to what has been happening to European electronics.

Philips, the Dutch company which established its multinational status in the interwar years, is the most important manufacturer of consumer electronics in Europe. With 170 plants in 60 countries, Philips had survived the war and flourished in the postwar years as a highly decentralised organisation. Subsidiaries, such as the UK company Mullard, had only tenuous links with the parent company and behaved, and indeed were treated, as indigenous companies in their host country. As a consequence, they benefited from public purchasing contracts and other favours bestowed generally by national governments upon national firms. But the resultant management structure was fragmented, cumbrous and conservative, which in many ways negated Philips admirable record on R&D and innovation. Time and again the company seemed incapable of exploiting the product opportunities thrown up by their R&D department, a prime example of this being their failure to exploit the potential of the video recorder and the fiasco of the V-2000 range which they did produce. Moreover, the whole ethos of the company, with its emphasis on establishing close and friendly relations with government made it highly protectionist. Its reaction to competitive threats to established market positions was to seek help from government — indeed it was heavy Philips lobbying which secured EC quotas on video cassette recorders in 1981, and more recently Philips has played a leading role in securing the 19 per cent 'infant industry' tariff on compact disc players.[6]

Philips' reaction to Japanese and Far Eastern threats to its markets is now, however, not just protectionist. It argues that it needs the protection to give itself breathing space in which to turn the company around. (And it also argues, with some validity, that while Japanese markets remain so impenetrable, it is only fair to provide European electronics firms with some protection.) But the main emphasis is now on 'turning the company around', with the old, fragmented decentralised structure now replaced by a highly centralised structure based on product divisions. Consumer electronics are central to the new strategy. Asked why, like their US (and British) counterparts, the company had not cut its losses in consumer electronics and left the whole area to the Japanese, the answer was that consumer electronics was too central to Philips' organisation for the company to be able to 'dump it'. Over 50 per cent of the output of its components division, for example, goes into the full range of Philips consumer electronics. The businesses are too interlocked for Philips to be able to drop one large sector such as consumer electronics. Its strategy is, therefore, to make a comeback with its consumer electronics division. The purchase of Grundig was a first step in this direction. It has belatedly shifted into making VCR machines to the VHS standard, linking up with Matsushita. £100 million has been sunk in its new CD player plant at Hasselt in Belgium — the world's largest CD production centre — and it is making a determined effort to get into the North American market through the acquisition of GTE's television interests.[7]

There are similarities between the Philips response to the Japanese threat to its consumer electronics base and that of Siemens, even though for Siemens consumer electronics forms a much smaller part of its overall product base. As one Siemens executive explained:

> Consumer electronics is that part of business which uses a high volume of semiconductor products. So the Japanese get two things if you give over your market to them — first they get control of the consumer products, then they move into manufacturing the microelectronics that go with them.[8]

Siemens' strategy, like that of Philips, is not to do as their American counterparts have done, and cut their losses and run away from consumer electronics, but to keep firmly in the market.

It would appear that this is now also the strategy of Thomson, although for several years there was speculation that Gomez, chairman of Thomson since 1982 and renowned for selling off loss making subsidiaries, would sell off Thomson's consumer products division. But, just as it has been reinforcing its SC interests by its purchase of Mostek and its joint venture with SGS, so Thomson has been building up its consumer electronics interests. In 1982 there was the abortive bid for Grundig which was blocked by the German cartel office; in 1983 was the 'compensatory' prize of Telefunken; then in 1987 came two surprise moves — first the purchase from Thorn EMI of their Plymouth plant which was the last remaining British manufacturer of TV sets in Britain, (this actually has some logic since Thomson and Thorn were already linked through the J2T joint venture with the Japanese Victor Corporation to manufacture JVC video cassette recorders), and subsequently in July the purchase of (US) General Electric's RCA television and audio equipment businesses to give it a 23 per cent stake in the US market. Commenting on the RCA purchase, Gomez said that he sees the acquisition as an opportunity for the European consumer electronics industry to counter attack against the Japanese.

We lost the first round in the 1970s in the colour television, video cassette rcorder and compact disk markets because we did not have the necessary volumes or costs. What Thomson is now seeking is to be among the winners in the second round (*Financial Times*, 24 July 1987).

5 Conclusion: ESPRIT and the realignment of the European electronics industry

By 1988, therefore, we see a major realignment of the European electronics industry taking shape around three main poles — Philips, Siemens and Thomson — all now firms with integrated capabilities ranging from mainstream SC production through office automation to consumer electronics. Siemens also has extensive capabilities in telecommunications (where similarly European activities have been coalescing around three firms — Siemens, Ericsson and CGE (CIT-Alcatel)). Much of this realignment has taken place within the last two years and it is too early to tell how successful it will be. It can be argued that it was a necessary, though not sufficient, condition for the renaissance of the European electronics industry. Certainly the realignment and rationalisation that has taken place, however, has engendered a new mood of optimism in the industry, captured by the bullishness of some of the quotations given in the last section.

What role has ESPRIT played in all this? Outwardly surprisingly little. Its ECU 3 billion (£2.1 billion) total expenditures (including the industrial contribution) spread over the five years 1984-89 is small compared with the investments being poured into the IT sectors by firms such as Siemens and Philips. Moreover, concentrating as it does on precompetitive research, the emphasis is not so much on products that can be brought to market as on developing the tools and techniques to enable those products to be made. There are successes — prime among which is the use of the Inmos transputer in the Parsys super computers, developed jointly with the French — and the work on developing software standards for manufacturing and office automation systems has been invaluable in helping to open up these markets to European manufacturers.

Psychologically, however, ESPRIT has played a vital role in three important respects. First, ESPRIT has provided an important *channel for cooperation*. The need for cooperation should be set in the context of the early 1980s — the fragmented European industry gradually waking up to the realisation that it had allowed the US and then the Japanese multinationals to acquire a seemingly dominant technological lead; the increasingly high cost of R&D and initial set up costs in most high-tech sectors, combined with the uncertainties of the shortening product cycle; and the threat posed by the impending entry into the European arena of AT&T once deregulation opened the door to such entry. The tide of Japanese inward investment into consumer electronics had illustrated how limited was the value of protection when capital was freely mobile. There was no alternative but to meet the threat head-on, which in turn meant rapidly acquiring technological capabilities not possessed in-house. Links with US and Japanese firms made sense technologically, but not strategically, since the objective was to decrease rather than to increase technological dependency. The figures speak for themselves. In 1983 the European Commission recorded 32 US-EC link-ups in firms in the IT sector, to six internal Community link-ups. By 1986, they were almost in balance; 49 US-EC link-ups to 46 internal Community link-ups. Some would, of course, have taken place without the existence of ESPRIT; but there is little doubt in the minds of many participants that the existence of ESPRIT (and other programmes such as BRITE and EUREKA) has encouraged the European route (Dawkins, 1988).

Second, ESPRIT has provided *a mechanism for creating* amongst top level decision takers in this industry *convergent expectations* about the future, and about the sort of measures needed to meet the competitive threat from the US and Japanese multinationals. The power of such convergence should not be underestimated for it becomes self fulfilling — if all decision takers make investment decisions in the light of common expectations, production will expand as expected! The Japanese VLSI and Fifth Generation Programmes are based upon this principle; MITI effectively act as a mechanism which ensures that all firms acts on a common set of expectations which then have a tendency to become self fulfilling. In the case of ESPRIT, Davignon's Round Table fulfilled this same function. For the first time, Europe's fragmented electronics industry confronted the threat of competition together. They discovered that there was among them 'convergent expectation' that competition would get tougher, that tariff or export constraint protective barriers were ineffective given the free mobility of capital, and that national champions protected by public purchasing ran the risk of being out of touch with market developments. Thus these major European companies came to recognise that to compete successfully even *within* Europe they needed to set their sights on global markets and global competitiveness. In this context, the national champion becomes irrelevant.

Third, ESPRIT has created an *important constituency pressing for the completion of the internal market* and the abolition of all remaining internal barriers to trade, such as divergent standards and regulations. Once the major electronics firms had discarded their 'national champion' role, it was logical that they should begin to look to Europe as their 'home base' and to see the divergent European standards, for example, on data transmission, as major hindrances to their effective operation in those markets. This has been reinforced by the very successful programmes within ESPRIT aimed at establishing Europe-wide standards for IT products. For example, it has created a set of software (called Communications Network for Manufacturing Applications (CNMA)) which allows different types of robots to work together within an automated factory, which in turn prevents the phenomenon that is seen so often with IT products, of tying customers into one particular range of equipment. A similar software has been developed for office systems (Office Document Architecture) which enables documents to be passed from one computer to another without loss of formatting etc. Recognising the advantages of these common standards has put companies such as Siemens, Bull and ICL into a constituency which recognises and promotes the virtues of the single European market.

Finally, ESPRIT has for many firms provided an important *learning process in collaboration*. The history of successful collaborations, such as Air Bus Industrie, illustrates only too well the fact that collaboration is a slow process of building up mutual trust and respect among partners. Collaborations cannot be created and expected to be successful overnight. For many European firms there has been no experience of collaboration with other European firms, for European operations were frequently directed from a home base, whereas US and Japanese operations were conducted through local licensees who often became natural partners in any collaboration. For many such firms ESPRIT has been the first experience of collaboration with other European firms. The fact that over 1000 applied in Spring 1988 to participate in the second phase of the programme starting January 1989 is testimony to the positive response the experience has provoked.

As a postscript, it is worth considering whether there is not, in addition, one more lesson to be learned from the experience of European electronics. Is collaboration merely a transitional phase in the strategic game-play? At a time when technology is moving fast, creating great uncertainty both in a technological and a commercial sense, when skills are scarce and the product cycle is shortening, collaboration makes commercial sense. It provides a quick and efficient way of acquiring new expertise and of sharing costs and risks. Over time, however, as new technologies mature these advantages lessen, and the advantages of internalising these operations and their profits increase. The European electronics industry, as we saw, has begun to internalise some of these linkages through a process of merger and consolidation. Could it be that writing in ten years time we shall see the hectic collaborations of the 1980s as a purely temporary phase in global development?

Notes

1 Collaborations for precompetitive research are given block exemption under EC competition policy rules whereas collaboration for competitive research and development (defined as being R&D undertaken by the firm and necessary for the launch of a new product) require case by case exemptions.

2 (CEC, 1984). A full list of the ESPRIT projects through its various phases of development can be obtained from DG XIII of the European Commission, rue de la Loi 200, B-1049, Brussels.

3 At this point in its development ESPRIT got caught up in the perennial dispute over the financing of the Common Agricultural Policy and Britain's appropriate budget contribution.

4 The Commission put forward a composite four year forward plan for R&D in the Community, called the Framework Programme, in the spring of 1986. The original Commission proposals envisaged an expenditure of ECU 10.3 billion (£7.7 billion) for the 4 year period 1987-91 but this was rapidly scaled down to ECU 7.7 billion (£5.2 billion). Even this reduced budget was politically unacceptable to Britain, W Germany and France, and was further scaled down to ECU 6.7 billion (£4.8 billion). This was still, however, unacceptably high for Britain, which argued in favour of a budget of no more than ECUs 4.2 billion (£2.9 million). The issue once again got caught up with the financing of the agricultural deficit and, subsequently, with the British general election, after which Britain finally, after almost 18 months of argument, agreed to settle for a figure of ECU 5.8 billion (£4.1 billion). ESPRIT is the major programme within the Framework Programme but it also covers BRITE (industrial technology), BAP (biotechnology), RACE (telecoms) and COMMETT (training).

5 In October 1982, faced by a major trade deficit on IT equipment and accelerating imports of VCRs from Japan, the French decreed that all VCRs would have to pass through the Customs point at Poitiers, a small town in central France with only one customs official! The incident made France the laughing stock of the international trade world at the time, but it did, in fact, signal a turning point in French attitudes to inward investment since from that time onwards France made it known that it preferred Japanese investments to their flooding the market with some particular product.

6 Interview with Cor van der Klugt, President of Philips by Guy de Jonquieres (*Financial Times*, 25 April 1986).

7 See previous note.

8 Interview with Karlheinz Klaske, chief executive of Siemens by Terry Dodsworth (*Financial Times*, 29 June 1987).

Chapter 14

Conclusions: realising technological opportunities

Mark Dodgson

1 The broad industrial relevance of technology strategy

Chapter 1 examined some of the reasons why corporations should consider technology strategically. This chapter will pull together some of the insights reported in earlier chapters into the nature of, and influences upon, technology strategy.

Before discussing the current significance of technology strategy, it is important to emphasise that, as Jones argues, technology is but one element determining corporate and sectoral competitiveness. Its contribution to competitiveness may be considerable or it may be insignificant, and this varies over time. In the automobile industry, for example, technology has not over the past few decades been a particularly important element affecting firms' competitive positions, but may well become so in the near future. In subsequent discussion, therefore, it is not assumed that technology is the primary determinant of competitiveness, or that any role it does play is likely to remain constant.

With this in mind, technology strategy has been seen to be a useful and relevant concept in all the wide range of industries and industrial sectors discussed in this book. Leading firms producing products as diverse as automobiles, woollen clothes, semiconductors and chilled chicken have been shown to possess technology strategies. This is so because these firms' products depend on technology for a number of important characteristics — from cost to quality and performance — which differentiate them from competing products in the market place. Technology, through which this competitive advantage is attained, is facing a period of radical change, and this provides further incentive for firms to view technology with a strategic perspective.

It is impossible unequivocally to assert that there is a strong positive correlation between the existence of a technology strategy and corporate success (growth, profitability, high market share etc). Research attempting to prove the existence of such a relationship has not, and probably could not, be undertaken. Nevertheless, this book has provided a considerable amount of evidence showing that significant advantages are attained by firms with appropriate technology strategies. This applies to both modern and traditional sectors. Hobday and Baba in their chapters on the semiconductor and colour television industries, and Belussi and Senker in their chapters on the Benetton clothing company and the food retailing industry show that competitiveness depends to a great extent on strategies for achieving comparative advantage in product and production technology.

2 How common are technology strategies?

Despite the value in viewing technology strategically, not all companies are doing so. In the US, poor comparative technological performance has stimulated a string of books urging firms to adopt a strategic perspective. The titles of these books are informative: *Restoring our competitive edge* (Hayes and Wheelwright, 1984), *The competitive challenge: Strategies for industrial innovation and renewal* (Teece, 1987), *Strategies for technology-based competition: meeting the new global challenge* (Link and Tassey, 1987). The language of 'restoration' and 'renewal' to meet a new 'challenge' imply a lag in the behaviour of US companies compared with their competitors. Hobday and Baba show this to be so in the semiconductor and colour television industry. Baba typifies US company strategies as involving low R&D expenditure, short-term profit taking, and international investment without significant investment in product and process development. By contrast, both these chapters highlight the success many Japanese corporations have enjoyed through their strategies for technology-based growth.

The UK situation is similar to that in the US. During the late 1970s and early 1980s, the deep economic recession led UK companies into a massive rationalisation programme. The number of employees in manufacturing industry declined from 7.2 million in 1976 to 5.2 million in 1986. In their 1985/86 Annual Reports 25 out of 50 of the largest UK companies claimed that they were rationalising by concentrating on their core businesses. The concentration on core businesses and technologies in part reflected the belief that comparative advantage lies in the ability of firms to use their technical know-how, and accumulated managerial and scientific/engineering skills only in a limited number of areas; and that in the past, a great many problems have arisen from firms' inability to manage diverse portfolios of businesses (Peters and Waterman, 1982). It is also probable that as most of the careers of the members of the board of directors in UK companies developed during a period of rationalisation, few have any experience of technology-based growth.

On the other hand, some UK companies have re-evaluated their technological efforts. For some, such as Glaxo, GKN and STC, this has involved a steadily increasing commitment to R&D between 1976 and 1986 (R&D expenditure measured as a percentage of sales). Occasionally, as in the case of GKN, this has involved an organisational restructuring by creating technological companies or divisions. For others it has resulted in an increase in the use of some of the tactics for realising technology strategies: collaborative research and strategic alliances, building university linkages, encouraging spin-offs and corporate venturing, intrapreneurship and strategic acquisitions.[1]

The diversity in the strategies adopted by UK companies pose an important question: why are some companies adopting a 'back to basics' strategy while others choose to diversify to deal with technological turbulence and seek to realise the potential advantages to be derived from convergent technologies? To answer this question, account must be taken of the dynamics of technological development, organisation structure and firm size. Also very important, as many chapters in this book have shown, are managerial capabilities.

3 Factors affecting the development and realisation of technology strategies

3.1 Technology

Firms are obviously affected by the directions and speed in which technology is developing. As Nelson (1988) argues, in many industries the process of technological advance has a strong internal logic, and that '...firm behaviour, and industry structure, may be moulded by the way technology is unfolding, at least as much as the character of innovation depends on firm behaviour and market structure' (Nelson, 1988, p220).

It is necessary, therefore, for firms to monitor and comprehend the ways their core technologies are developing. The chapter by Pavitt et al develops our understanding of the relationship between firms and technological development. They show that technological opportunities and threats vary widely according to companies' core business, and the ways that companies are organised. Developing a typology of firms, distinguishable as supplier-dominated, scale-intensive, specialised suppliers and science-based, Pavitt et al argue that the technological position of each firm is strongly conditioned by the nature and extent of its accumulated technology. There is an increasing trend towards technological diversification: upstream into production technologies for scale intensive and supplier-dominated firms; upstream, horizontal and downstream for chemical firms; and horizontal for mechanical, instrument and electrical-electronic engineering firms.

The very different nature of technological threats and opportunities facing different industries questions the validity of theories of technological development based on the changing importance of technology throughout product life cycles. Baba shows that Japanese colour television firms are concerned with technological competitiveness in products and production throughout product life cycles. Technology strategy, he argues, is based on the assumption of decreasing long-run average costs through the introduction of microelectronics, and has focussed on product differentiation. Thomas and Miles, in their chapter on new interactive services (NIS), contend that the development of such networks shows characteristics of 'reverse product cycles'. In such a model, firms use information technology (IT) first to improve processes, and following a learning process then sell their assimilated expertise in the form of products (Barras, 1986). Further empirical research is required to ascertain how applicable this model is to other new, high technology industries, such as biotechnology.

3.2 Organisation and size

Flexibility enables organisations to deal with periods of rapid change. Successful firms are often those that continually redefine the concept of their business across industry boundaries (Ghazanfar, McGee and Thomas, 1987). The difficulty of doing this is, of course, extreme. As Doz, Anglemar and Prahalad argue: '...conscious choices of organisational differentiation - in anticipation of the requirements of a new business rather than a response to a crisis in managing it - remain difficult, and probably relatively rare' (1987, p7).

Pavitt et al contribute to the debate on the relationship between corporate strategy and structure. By comparing SPRU data on technological diversification with other data on output diversification, the authors found greater diversification in technology than in output. They explore two reasons as to why this is so: company need to maintain a presence in technologies to prevent opportunistic entry by competitors, and the complex nature of contemporary technological interdependencies. Both imply a need on the part of companies to remain aware of the technological behaviour of other companies; that is, to view technology strategically.

They also consider the question of size. Companies employing fewer than 1000 employees have major technological opportunities, the authors contend, particularly with specialised strategies in mechanical engineering and instruments. Those with more than 1000 employees are virtually all divisionalised, with the size of innovating divisions having diminished between 1945 and 1983. Divisionalisation also improves the congruence between the core business of the innovating division and the innovation. They conclude that whilst divisionalisation can create the small size of unit conducive to effective implementation, it cannot absolve management from the continuous task of matching technological opportunities with organisational forms and boundaries.

Smaller firms have fewer organisational rigidities than large multidivisional firms. Dodgson and Rothwell argue that technology-based small and medium-sized firms have increased in importance in European industry, and describe how some highly successful smaller firms overcame the major problems of technological and organisational growth. Their identification of the importance of an effective innovation strategy is confirmed by Belussi as she charts the development of Benetton from a small, traditional firm into the world's largest supplier of woollen clothes.

Small, high technology, entrepreneurial firms have provided an alternative model of innovative efficiency for large firms. Many large firms are now using novel organisational structures of 'intrapreneurship' and spin-off companies (Burgelman, 1986). Such strategies are, however, limited to few companies in Europe. It is also apparent that few large European companies address their relationships with small firms in a particularly strategic manner, and that companies that do: like the French company Elf Aquitaine, are very much in a minority (Dekker, 1988; Turbil, 1986).

4 Management and technology strategy

In this book it is argued that there is scope for realignment of firms' technological efforts given radical change and impetus provided by management. This argument is based on two major premises. First, that management pay due attention to developments external to the firm, and attempt to match internal strengths with external opportunities. Second, that internal strengths often lie within accumulated technical competence and know-how. The development of much contemporary technology involves a global, complex set of interrelationships between firms — from the R&D process to competition in the market place. Few, if any, firms have the resources and expertise to generate novel technologies entirely in-house. Most often technology is developed in conjunction with, or in response to, activities of other firms. However, firms can only take advantage of these external opportunities if they have some autonomous strength.

In any analysis of the variation in strategies between firms, it is of course essential to understand the role played by management. A number of studies have found that strategic change is most often attained through changes in the most senior management posts (Doz and Prahalad, 1987; Tushman and Anderson, 1987). Dodgson and Rothwell's chapter argues the key factor underlying the success of a sample of leading, technology-based European small and medium-sized firms was the strategic awareness of the top managers. Hobday highlights the resurgence of European semiconductor firms under the tutelage of new US-trained managers.

While functional and divisional management can play an important role in the formulation technology strategy, it is crucial to analyse the role played by corporate management, and in particular the chief executive officer. Sharp provides a revealing insight when she describes how an EC-promoted collaborative European response to international IT competitition was engendered only when EC officials gained the support of the leaders of the largest IT firms. Previous efforts, concentrating on R&D directors, had failed to gain the required levels of commitment.

A central function of technology strategy is to foster the knowledge of the importance of technology thoughout the firm. Jones highlights the success Japanese automobile firms have enjoyed through a strategy of encouraging technological improvements derived from the shopfloor. He argues that the knowledge and cumulative experience required constantly to improve production systems lies with those whose daily life revolves around them. Encouraging such feedback, and ensuring that it is effectively used to make improvements, is a key management skill, and an important aspect of strategy.

A number of other aspects of the strategic management of technology are considered in the book. Thomas and Miles highlight the problems of managing complexity. They describe some of the specific problems facing companies introducing NIS, such as difficulties in appropriating returns from investment through the use of traditional means such as patenting and copyright. Various problematic consequences of the extreme technological complexity of NIS are drawn out, including those of convergence and the current early ('preparadigmatic') stage of development of the technology. The authors argue that this complexity provides an opportunity for competitive advantage if it is managed effectively.

K

By comparing the development of BT's Prestel system and Telecom Gold, Thomas and Miles ascribe the success of the latter to flexibility in its design and to close contact with users, both lessons learnt from the failure of Prestel. The strengths and weaknesses of various strategies are described: lock-in; service bundling and total packaging; specialisation and niche marketing; and the importance of matching strategy and available skills is emphasised. The question of entrance barriers is raised; and it is argued that the present trend towards vertical integration of networks and services reflects an attempt to raise entrance barriers.

Senker and Brady, in their criticism of the model of management rationality proposed by neoclassical economics, describe an alternative model where managers have discretion to decide whether to innovate or not, and rather than adopt a lowest cost approach to manpower, can complement technological development with strategies based on improving training and worker skills. The ability to attain and retain the skills required to improve products and production processes within firms is a key function of management. This, as Thomas and Miles show, also applies in services, where the convergence of previously discrete technologies, and the provision of new services, depends critically on the ability of managers to create novel skills. In the sample of firms described by Dodgson and Rothwell one of the factors accounting for the success of the firms, and a major management skill, was the retention and stimulation of key staff through matching the progress of individual careers with the development of the firm.

The chapter by Gardiner and Rothwell highlights the importance of the strategic management of the highly complex process of industrial design. Using concepts such as design trajectories, design families, robust designs and economy in technology, the authors argue the benefits to be attained from good management practice. Examples as diverse as Black and Decker's heat gun, Canon's laser copier and Rolls Royce's RB211 aero engine, illustrate the ways strategically managed technological accumulation, generation and diffusion can provide competitive advantage.

Whether it is the novel skills of managing technological complexity, or the more commonplace management of more routine matters, an essential prerequisite for effective strategy development is management learning. Dodgson and Rothwell describe the importance of top managers continually learning new skills as firms grow. Belussi describes the importance of management learning for the successful development of Benetton. Baba's chapter provides an interesting example of management learning in Japan. He shows that initially in the colour television industry, there were only a few 'entrepreneurial' firms like Sony and Matsushita which were aggressive in their R&D and marketing strategies; the majority of firms were content being 'followers'. However, as the success of the leading firms became apparent, the others copied and strategies converged.

The organisational context in which technology is used is also an important focus for management learning. Jones describes the way US automobile firms invested heavily in manufacturing technology to 'catch up' with Japanese productivity levels, only to find that rather than investment in mechanical systems, greater advantage is to be obtained through consideration of human factors concerned with work organisation.

Technology strategy is an important focus for management learning. It is this central element of technology strategy that blurs the distinction made between the content, context and process of strategy by some business academics (Pettigrew, 1987). In many successful companies, the content of their technology strategies involves a process of continual monitoring, learning and re-evaluation with continuous feedback from action and experience to subsequent decisions. There are essential elements of learning-by-doing and learning-by-using (Rosenberg, 1982). The content and process of an effective technology strategy, rather than interacting in a mechanistic fashion, merge and are indistinct.

5 Some characteristics of successful strategies

5.1 Accumulated competences

In her study of food retailing, Senker argues that established in-house technological expertise is a prerequisite to the adoption of a technology strategy. Only those retailers with a long tradition of investment in technical expertise can build a competitive strategy with a technological dimension. This provides the basis for her criticism — also expressed by Pavitt et al — of Porter's approach to technology strategy: he makes no allowance for the importance of accumulated skills within firms.

Nelson and Winter's (1982) argument that strategic capabilities are limited by firms' past experiences and innovation 'routines', are confirmed by Cantwell's (1989) study of international sectoral patterns of technological advantage. He argues that countries and regions are likely to have their greatest scope for future innovation and growth in areas closely related to those in which their firms have been successful in the past. There are advantages for firms in building upon existing competences and skills. While radical changes in strategic direction are attainable, they are more easily realisable, and more likely to be successful, if they pay due attention to the competences, skills and know-how existing within the firm.

The significance of accumulated technological competences is questioned by Hobday. He cites the examples of new start-ups in the semiconductor industry in Europe, and the prevalence of strategic alliances, as examples of opportunities provided to firms without established technological strength. Just how important these developments are, and whether they can address more than limited market niches, has yet to be seen. Nevertheless, Hobday's observations are important. It is not purely accumulated technological competences that provide the basis for successful diversification, but it is also accumulated management skills, market knowledge, and the experience within organisations allowing their untraumatic transformation in line with changing market requirements.

This argument is developed further by Belussi. She argues that Benetton's impressive technological development is strongly influenced by accumulated technological competence. Furthermore, she contends that the growth of the firm can only be understood in the context of its history and socio-economic environment. Emphasis is placed, therefore, on a number of key influences on the company's pattern of growth: on traditional forms of subcontracted work organisation, on skills and working practices in the local region, and on the recent growth of an entrepreneurial culture.

5.2 Complementary assets

The importance for successful innovation of collaboration and interaction amongst the various functions within a firm, particularly R&D, production and marketing, is well known (Rothwell et al, 1974; Cooper, 1980). These considerations have been emphasised recently by Teece (1987a), and both he and Porter (1985b) have highlighted how distribution channels are important assets. The chapters by Jones, Baba, Hobday and Belussi have shown how important it is for an effective technology strategy to incorporate both products and production processes. Throughout this book it has been asserted that technology strategy cannot be considered in isolation from the other facets of corporate activity; including: finance, investment and marketing. Successful technological innovation, be it in semiconductors, NIS, clothing or foodstuffs, depends on the ability of firms to access non-technological assets, and to use them effectively.

One particularly important — though rarely seriously analysed — complementary asset is the skills of the people developing and using technology. Senker and Brady provide examples of mismatches of emphasis in firms between technological and 'human' factors. Just as technological development can be a lengthy process, so too is the process of attaining the requisite skills within firms to promote it. Just as technology needs to be considered strategically, so too does human resource development.

5.3 Externalities

Technological collaboration between firms, and between firms and infrastructural scientific organisations is now a common feature in industry. Some of the reasons why this is so have been described: the complexity and composite nature of technology, and the high cost and risk associated with its development. The ability successfully to access and integrate external sources of knowledge helps overcome these problems, can overcome skill deficiencies, and provides a potential source of comparative competitive advantage. Jones argues that automobile producers will increasingly have to recruit managers and engineers from other industries to access external expertise, and to interact well with their key suppliers. This process involves considerable managerial skill: in identifying, and recruiting to overcome, important skill deficiencies; in choosing partners, in defining the boundaries of each firm's activities; and in ensuring that the benefits of collaboration are achieved and shared equitably. These skills are utilised to greatest effect in the pursuit of technology central to firms' future development; that is, external relationships and collaboration have to be viewed in a strategic framework.

5.4 Globalisation

The global nature of technological competition is discussed in the automobile industry by Jones, the colour television industry by Baba, and the semiconductor industry by Hobday. Hobday describes the changing strategies and competitiveness of firms in the global 'triad': Japan, US and Europe. Japanese corporations are characterised by vertically integrated business structures, access to long-term finance, a high commitment to R&D and strong organisational links between design and production functions. Hobday argues that these factors provide them with comparative advantage in product and production technology. The response of US corporations to the loss of market share to the Japanese has involved collective and greater R&D, strategic alliances and the use of the law as a competitive weapon. In turn, the European semiconductor industry has been stimulated by a number of recent strategic alliances and by the formation of small semiconductor companies. A more recent response to increased competition has seen Japanese corporations increase large-scale global investment and still greater investment in R&D. The importance of strategic foreign investment is also highlighted in Baba's chapter.

6 Some lessons for management and policy-makers

It is hoped that one of the main contributions of this book is the provision of empirical evidence showing the value for many firms in developing and using an effective technology strategy. From the evidence presented it appears that not all companies are aware of this value, and for those that are there are great differences in their ability to develop cogent strategies. This difference is particularly marked when comparing Japanese with UK and US firms.

The nature of technology strategies in a number of very different sectors has been discussed, and some of the factors which constrain the direction of particular strategies have been described. Some characteristics of successful strategies have been identified: they have long-term horizons, link well with other facets of corporate development, build upon existing skills and competences, are often international in focus, and can be stimulated and implemented best by managers prepared to learn from past successes and failures. Most of the factors identified as being important are well known to the 'innovation studies' and 'management of technology' literature. This book provides some much-needed empirical evidence in support of these contentions. Although many of these characteristics of technology management appear self-evident and simple, perhaps the key to success is managing to do these in a coordinated and strategic fashion, and to do them well. Certainly a major contributor to success is the ability of managers to learn from their own, and their competitors', successes and failures.

As technology is currently such an important factor in the competitive position of many of the firms and sectors discussed in this book, so, obviously, is its management. As we have seen, managing technology strategically involves the development of new competences and skills, including: technology assessment; building and obtaining benefit from collaborative links, and integrating these with internal expertise; and integrating technology strategy with other aspects of corporate strategy. Jones argues that in the future a premium will be placed on those managers and engineers whose technological knowledge extends beyond their national boundaries. The evidence presented in this book on the complex and international nature of much contemporary technology points to the increased importance for firms of the effective management of technology.

Sharp and Guy have provided evidence of the ways public policies can directly influence the behaviour of private corporations. Such policies are by no means uncontroversial: governments which espouse the logic and virtues of market forces rest uneasily with interventionist policies, and private corporations are occasionally embarrassed by accusations of subsidy and unfair competition. Nevertheless, as Sharp and Guy argue, public intervention in the guise of the Alvey programme and ESPRIT has had a marked effect on the behaviour of companies. Alvey has encouraged firms to examine the benefits of collaboration, and ESPRIT has built up an awareness amongst European firms of the need for a European response to US and Japanese competition. Both have encouraged management learning in companies.

There are numerous reasons why there should be an awareness amongst public policy makers of the nature of corporate technology strategies. First, the performance of key firms determines technological competitiveness in important industrial sectors. Second, awareness of corporate technological activities alerts public policy makers to deficiencies in breadth, depth and time scale of national efforts. Third, it may reveal the necessity for rationalising, or at least reducing duplication in, research activities. Fourth, it enables better analysis and prioritisation of public sector R&D.

There is also often a need on the part of firms to inform public policy makers of their technology strategy. As Guy shows, firms need to collectively and coherently present reasoned cases for intervention, and failure to do so may result in no support being offered. Governments are unlikely to support long-term technological developments in firms without those firms explaining their commitment to, and the strategic importance of, those developments.

7 Concluding comments and suggested future research agenda

No single volume could attempt to encompass all of the themes currently discussed under the umbrella title: corporate technology strategy. Thus some topics such as the influence of corporate cultures, and the management of the R&D function, are not discussed. Nor are the important questions considered of the extent of rationality in managerial technological decision making, or of intra-organisational political influences on strategic development (Pettigrew, 1985). The book instead contributes a compilation of a series of empirical studies in an area of research infamous for its complexity and paucity. These empirical studies collectively add considerable weight to our understanding of the importance, nature and variation of corporate technology strategies. They provide the basis for questioning or supporting a wide range of perceived theory and wisdom. They furthermore add to our understanding of managerial discretion in strategically managing technology, on the role technology plays in extending the boundaries of the firm, and the reflexive influence of public technology policies and private corporations' strategies.

7.1 A future research agenda

Throughout this volume, the individual chapters pose a battery of highly topical areas for future research. Some of these will be elucidated.

The following are in no particular order.

A common theme throughout the book has been the need for firms to understand the strategies of their competitors. Firms need to establish their technological position vis-à-vis other firms. As such some empirical indicator of relative performance and potential is required. While there is certainly value in using conventional indicators such as R&D expenditure and patents, these are problematic, not least because of two factors addressed in the book: first, the extent to which R&D is externalised, and second, the problems of using patents in new technologies such as NIS. More research is required to develop efficient methods of monitoring the technological activities of competitors.

Very little is known about the processes of technological learning within firms; how technical know-how is generated, assimilated and distributed throughout the firm, and how strategies are developed and altered in response to this learning. Related to this are a series of questions about the location and organisation of technical functions, in order to: learn from outside; diffuse knowledge internally and across divisions; and redefine organisations and their missions.

There is little doubt that information and communications technology will have a profound effect on the ability of corporations to operate on a global basis. Which corporations, using which strategies, will realise the potentials is still a matter of conjecture, and much research needs to be undertaken in this area.

Greater research is needed to examine the factors affecting the relative success of 'leaders' and 'followers' in technological innovation.

More needs to be known about the phenomenon of inter-firm technological collaboration. Is it likely to remain a permanent feature of corporate behaviour, or is it, as Sharp argues, a temporary response by companies to assist the process of industrial readjustment? Should governments, as some appear to be doing, uncritically accept the benefits of collaboration, without first understanding the effects they are likely to have on sectoral competitiveness and consumer choice?

There are by now numerous examples describing the benefits of technological collaboration between large and small firms. Systematic study of the nature of these complementary links, the strategies that induce them, and sectoral and national differences which encourage them is, unfortunately, absent.

Particularly high on any observer's list of priorities for research is the relationship between military expenditure and corporate technology strategies. The influence of the extent and type of R&D commissioned by the military on corporate technology strategies needs to be mapped. Opportunity costs for civil R&D in corporations highly reliant on the massive military R&D undertaken in countries such as the US and UK need to be explored, as do transfers between military and civil applications. Research has highlighted the ways that high military R&D has adversely affected civil technological development, it is similarly important to establish the differences in strategies and performance of military and non-military R&D performers.

Notes

1 The evidence supporting this contention is piecemeal. There have been some studies showing increasing activity in corporate venturing (NEDO, 1986), spin-offs and 'intrapreneurship' (Lloyd and Seaford, 1987) and increased university/industry collaborative research (Rothwell, Dodgson and Lowe, 1988). However, there is very little data on the increasing use of strategic alliances and acquisitions, and inter-corporate collaborative research apart from reports in the financial press.

References

Abernathy, W. (1978), *The Productivity Dilemma: Roadblock to Innovation in the Automobile Industry*, Johns Hopkins University Press, Baltimore.

Abernathy, W.; Clark, K. and Kantrow, A. (1983), *Industrial Renaissance: Producing a Competitive Future for America*, Basic Books, New York.

Altshuler, A.; Anderson, M.; Jones, D.; Roos, D. and Womack, J. (1984), *The Future of the Automobile*, Allen and Unwin, London.

Amendola, G. (1988), The Diffusion of Synthetic Materials in the Automobile Industry: Towards a Major Breakthrough?, DRC Discussion Paper, Science Policy Research Unit, Sussex, June.

Ansoff, I. (1968), *Corporate Strategy*, Penguin, Harmondsworth.

Ansoff, I. and Stewart, J. (1967), Strategies for a Technology-Based Business, *Harvard Business Review*, November-December.

Aoki, M. (1986), Horizontal vs. Vertical Information Structure of the Firm, *American Economic Review*, Vol. 76, December.

Archibugi, D. (1986), Sectoral Patterns of Industrial Innovation in Italy: An Analysis of Italian Patenting in the US, Technical Report, CNR, Rome.

Arnold, E. and Guy, K. (1986), *Parallel Convergence: National Strategies in Information Technology*, Pinter, London.

Arrow, K. (1962), The Economic Implications of Learning By Doing, *Review of Economic Studies*, June.

Baba, Y. (1985), *Japanese Colour TV Firms' Decision-Making from the 1950s to the 1980s: Oligopolistic Corporate Strategy in the Age of Microelectronics*, DPhil dissertation, University of Sussex, 1985.

Bagnasco, A. and Trigilia, C. (1984) (eds), *Società e Politica nelle Aree di Piccola Impresa, Il caso di Bassano* Arsenale Editore, Venice.

Bain, J. (1968), *Industrial Organization* Wiley, New York.

Baranson, J. (1981), *The Japanese Challenge to U.S. Industry*, DC Heath, Lexington.

Barna, T. (1962), *Investment and Growth Policies in British Industrial Firms*, NIESR Occasional Paper XX, Cambridge University Press.

Barras, R. (1986), Toward a theory of innovation in services, *Research Policy*, Vol.15, pp.161-173.

Baumol, W. (1959), *Business Behaviour, Value and Growth*, Macmillan, New York.

Beaumont, J. (1982a), *The Multiple Grocery Trade. A Brief History*, Institute of Grocery Distribution, Watford.

Beaumont, J. (1982b), *Aspects of a Changing Relationship Between Food Manufacturing and Distributors in the U.K.*, Paper presented to the OECD Conference, The Adjustment and the Challenges Facing the Food Industries in the 1980's, Paris, 11th-14th January.

Beesley, M. and Rothwell, R. (1987), Small Firm Linkages in the United Kingdom, in Rothwell, R. and Bessant, J. (eds), *Innovation, Adaptation and Growth*, Elsevier, Amsterdam.

Belussi, F. (1987), *Benetton: Information Technology in Production and Distribution - A Case Study of the Innovation Potential of Traditional Sectors*, Occasional Paper No. 25, Science Policy Research Unit, Sussex.

Berle, A. and Means, G. (1932), *The Modern Corporation and Private Property*, Macmillan, New York.

Berry, C. (1971), Corporate Growth and Diversification, *Journal of Law and Economics*, Vol. 14, pp371-83.

Bessant, J.; Guy, K.; Miles, I. and Rush, H. (1985), *IT Futures*, NEDO Books, London.

Bigadikke, E. (1979), *Corporate Diversification, Entry, Strategy and Performance*, Harvard University Press, Cambridge, Mass.

Birley, S. (1982), Corporate Strategy in the Small Firm, *Journal of General Management*, Vol. 8, No. 2, pp82-6.

Booz Allen and Hamilton Inc. (1985), *Diversification: A Survey of European Chief Executives*, London.

Brady, T. (1989), New Technology and Skill Shortages: Problems of Measurement, in de Montmollin, M. and Hingel, A. (eds), *Information Technology, Competence and Employment*, John Wiley.

Brady, T. (1988), *Advanced Ceramics: Research Innovation and the Implications for Skills and Training*, Manpower Services Commission.

Brech, M. and Sharp, M. (1984), *Inward Investment: Policy Options for the UK*, Chatham House Paper No. 21, Routledge and Kegan Paul, London.

Bresson, C. de (1986), Technological Clusters: Poles of Development, Department of Economics Working Paper 87-102, Concordia University.

Brusco, S. (1975), Economie di Scala e livello tecnologico nelle piccole imprese, in Graziani, A. (ed), *Crisi e ristrutturazione nell' economia italiana*, Einaudi, Torino.

Brusco, S. (1982), The Emilian Model: Productive decentralisation and social integration, *Cambridge Journal of Economics*, No.2.

Burgelman, R. (1986), Managing Corporate Entrepreneurship: New Structures for Implementing Technological Innovation, in Horwitch, M. (ed), *Technology in the Modern Corporation*, Pergamon, New York.

Burgelman, R. and Sayles, L. (1986), *Inside Corporate Innovation: Strategies, Structure and Management Skill*, Free Press, New York.

Business Week (1986) 30 June, p22.

Canon (UK) (1986), *Canon Laser Copier*.

Canon (Japan) (1986), The Canon Story 1986/87.

Cantwell, J. (1989), *Technological Innovation and Multinational Corporations*, Blackwell, Oxford.

Caves, R. (1964), *American Industry: Structure, Conduct, Performance*, Prentice Hall, Englewood Cliffs.

Caves, R. and Porter, M. (1977), From Entry Barriers to Mobility Barriers: Conjectural Decisions and Contrived Deterrence to New Competition, *Quarterly Journal of Economics*, Vol.91, pp241-61.

Cawson, A.; Shepherd, G. and Webber, D. (1986), *Government Industry Relations in the European Consumer Electronics Industry: Contrasting Responses to Competitive Pressures in Britain, France and the Federal Republic of Germany*, Working Paper No. 6, ESRC Government-Industry Relations Project, University of Sussex, School of Social Sciences.

CEC (1984), Commission of the European Communities, Official Documents on the ESPRIT Programme, Ref COM(84)608, CEC, Brussels.

CEC (1985), Communication from the Commission to the Council and the Parliament concerning a Review to Assess the Initial Results of the Programme ESPRIT, Ref COM(85)616 Final, CEC, Brussels.

Centre de Prospective et d'Evaluation-CPE (1985), Rapport sur L'Etat de la Technique, *Sciences et Techniques*, Paris.

Chandler, A. (1962), *Strategy and Structure: Chapters in the History of Industrial Enterprise*, MIT Press, Cambridge, Mass.

Chandler, A. (1977), *The Visible Hand: the Managerial Revolution in American Business*, Harvard University Press, Cambridge, Mass.

Channon, D. (1982), Industrial Structure, *Long Range Planning*, Vol. 15, No. 5, pp78-93.

Clark, K. (1988), European Product Development Practice in a World Perspective, IMVP paper, MIT, Cambridge, Mass.

Cohen, W. and Mowery, D. (1984), Firm Heterogeneity and R&D: an Agenda for Research, in Bozeman, B., Crow, M. and Link, A. (eds), *Strategic Management of Industrial R&D*, DC Heath, Lexington.

Constable, J. (1986), Diversification as a Factor in UK Industrial Strategy, *Long Range Planning*, Vol.19, No.1, pp.52-60.

Constable, J. and McCormick, R., (1987), *The Making of British Managers*, British Institute of Management, London.

Cooper, R. (1980), *Project NEWPROD*, Quebec Industrial Innovation Centre, Montreal.

Cooper, R. (1983), A Process Model For Industrial New Product Development, *IEEE Transactions in Engineering Management*, Vol. EM-30, No.1, February, pp2-11.

Coopers and Lybrand (1985), *A Challenge to Complacency: Changing attitudes to training*, MSC/NEDO, London.

Correale, G. and Gaeta, R. (1982), Mutamenti Strutturali nell' Industria Tessile – abbiglimento mondiale. Posizione competitiva e strategie multinazionali delle aziende italiane, *Economia e Politica Industriale*, No.52.

Cranston, M. (1984), *Consumers and the Law*, 2nd Ed., Weidenfeld & Nicolson, London.

Cusumano, M. (1985), *The Japanese Automobile Industry*, Harvard University Press, Cambridge, Mass.

Cyert, R. and March, J. (1963), *A Behavioural Theory of the Firm*, Prentice Hall, Engelwood Cliffs.

Davies, K.; Gilligan, C. and Sutton, C. (1984), *The Changing Nature of the Grocery Retailing Sector in Great Britain: A Preliminary Investigation*, Sheffield City Polytechnic, Dept of Economics and Business Studies, Discussion Paper 18, August.

Dawkins, W. (1988), Keeping Europe on the IT Map, *Financial Times*, 18 May.

Dekker, D. (1988), Large Company Involvement with SMEs: A European Survey, paper presented at EC conference Partnership Between Small and Large Firms, Brussels, 13-14 October.

Didrichsen, J. (1982), The Development of Diversified and Conglomerate Firms in the United States, 1920-1970, *Business History Review*, Vol. 46, No.2, pp202-19.

Dodgson, M. (1987), High-growth, Technology-based Small and Medium-sized Firms in Europe, in Rothwell, R. and Bessant, J. (eds), *Innovation, Adaptation and Growth*, Elsevier, Amsterdam.

Dodgson, M. and Rothwell, R. (1988), Small Firm Policy in the UK, *Technovation*, Vol.7, No.3, pp.231-247.

Doi, N. (1985), Diversification and R & D Activity in Japanese Manufacturing Firms, *Managerial and Decision Economics*, Vol.6, No.3, pp147-52.

Dore, R. (1987), *Taking Japan Seriously*, The Athlone Press, London.

Dosi, G. (1982), Technological Paradigms and Technological Trajectories. A Suggested Interpretation of the Determinants and Direction of Technological Change, *Research Policy*, Vol.11, No.3.

Dosi, G. (1984), *Technical Change and Industrial Transformation*, Macmillan, London.

Dosi, G. (1986), Institutions and Markets in a Dynamic World, DAEST/SPRU mimeo.

Dosi, G. (1988), The Nature of the Innovative Process in Dosi, G. et al (eds), *Technical Change and Economic Theory*, Pinter, London.

Dosi, G.; Freeman, C.; Nelson, R.; Silverberg, G. and Soete, L. (eds) (1988), *Technical Change and Economic Theory*, Pinter, London.

Doz, Y.; Angelmar, R. and Prahalad, C. (1987), *Core Technologies and New Business Development in Large, Complex Firms*, paper presented to the INSEAD conference on the management of technology in large, complex firms, INSEAD, Fontainebleau, 1-2 September 1987.

Doz, Y. and Prahalad, C. (1987), A Process Model of Strategic Redirection in Large Complex Firms: The Case of Multinational Corporations, in Pettigrew, A. (eds), *The Management of Strategic Change*, Blackwell, Oxford.

Earl, M. and Runge, D. (1987), *Using Telecommunications-Based Information Systems for Competitive Advantage*, Oxford Institute of Information Management Research, Discussion Paper.

Economist (1980), Europe's Processed Cuisine, Vol. 276, No. 7145, pp88-89.

Electronics, various issues.

Electronics and Power, various issues.

Electronics Times, various issues.

Ergas, H. (1983), *Restricting Japan - Who Benefits?*, (third draft), mimeo.

Feeny, D. and Brownlee, C. (1986), *Competition in the Era of Interactive Network Services*, Oxford Institute of Information Management Research, Discussion Paper.

Financial Times, various issues.

Foster, R. (1987), *The Attacker's Advantage*, Pan Books, London.

Freeman, C. (1982), *Economics of Industrial Innovation* (first edition 1974), Pinter, London.

Freeman, C. (1987), *Technology Policy and Economic Performance: Lessons from Japan*, Pinter, London.

Freeman, C.; Clark, J. and Soete, L. (1982), *Unemployment and Technical Innovation: a Study of Long Waves in Economic Development*, Pinter, London.

Freeman, C.; Pavitt, K. and Soete, L. (1982), Innovative Activities and Export Shares: Some Comparisons between Industries and Countries, in Pavitt, K. (ed), *Technical Innovation and British Economic Performance*, Macmillan, London.

Freeman, C. and Perez, C. (1986), *The Diffusion of Technical Innovations and Changes of Techno-economic Paradigm*, paper presented at the Venice Conference on Innovation Diffusion, March.

Freeman, C. and Perez, C. (1988), Structural Crises of Adjustment: Business Cycles and Investment Behaviour, in Dosi, G. et al (eds) *Technical Change and Economic Theory*, Pinter, London.

Freeman, C. and Soete, L. (1985), *Information Technology and Employment*, Science Policy Research Unit mimeo.

Freeman, C. and Soete, L. (1987), *Technological Change and Full Employment*, Blackwell, Oxford.

Freeman, C.; Young, A. and Fuller, J.K. (1963), The Plastics Industry: A Comparative Study of Research and Innovation, *National Institute Economic Review*, No.26.

Friar, J. and Horwitch, M., (1986), The Emergence of Technology Strategy, in Horwitch, M. (ed)., *Technology in the Modern Corporation*, Pergamon Press, New York.

Galbraith, J. (1963), *American Capitalism*, Penguin, Harmondsworth.

Galbraith, J. (1972), *The New Industrial State*, (second edition), Penguin, London.

Gardiner, J. (1984a), Design Trajectories for Airplanes and Automobiles During the Past Fifty Years, in Freeman, C. (ed), *Design, Innovation and Long Cycles in Economic Development*, Design Research Publications, London.

Gardiner, J. (1984b), Robust and Lean Designs with State of the Art Automotive and Aircraft Examples, in Freeman, C. (ed), *Design, Innovation and Long Cycles in Economic Development*, Design Research Publications, London.

Gardiner, J. and Rothwell, R. (1985), Tough Customers: Good Designs, *Design Studies*, Vol. 6, No. 1, pp7-17.

Gershuny, J. and Miles, I. (1983), *The New Service Economy*, Pinter, London.

Ghazanfar, A.; McGee, J. and Thomas, H. (1987), The Impact of Technological Change on Industry Structure: the Case of the Reprographics Industry in the United Kingdom, in Pettigrew, A. (ed), *The Management of Strategic Change*, Blackwell, Oxford.

Gold, B. (1981), Changing Perspectives on Size, Scale and Return: An Interpretative Survey, *Journal of Economic Literature*, Vol.18, March.

Grant, R.; Jamine, A. and Toker, S. (1986a), *Diversification Strategy and Firm Performance in British Manufacturing Industry*, Centre for Business Strategy, Working Paper No. 9, London Business School.

Grant, R.; Jamine, A. and Thomas, H. (1986b), *Diversification and Profitability: A Study of 305 British Manufacturing Companies, 1972-84*, Centre for Business Strategy, Working Paper No. 25, London Business School.

Graves, A. (1987), *Comparative Trends in Automotive Research and Development*, paper presented to the First International Policy Forum of the International Motor Vehicle Programme, Ontario, May.

Graves, H. (1988), *Design Houses and the Introduction of New Technology: A Case Study*, IMVP paper, MIT, Cambridge, Mass.

Gregory, G. (1986), *Japanese Electronics Technology: Enterprise and Innovation*, Wiley, Chichester.

Griffiths, R. (1984), *Future Trends in Retailing*, Paper presented to BAAS Conference, Norwich.

Gruppo di Lavoro IRES (1984), Struttura e scelte strategiche del Gruppo Benetton, *Oltre il Ponte*, No.7.

The Guardian, various issues.

Hamel, G.; Doz, Y. and Prahalad, C. (1986), *Strategic Partnerships: Success or Surrender? The Challenge of Competitive Collaboration*, Centre for Business Strategy, Working Paper No. 24, London Business School.

Hamilton, W. (1986), Corporate Strategies for Managing Emerging Technologies, in Horwitch, M. (ed), *Technology in the Modern Corporation*, Pergamon Press, New York.

Harvard Business School (1985), Istituto studi direzionali, *The Benetton Case-study*, mimeo.

Harvey Jones, J. (1988), *Making it Happen: Reflections on Leadership*, Collins, London.

Hassid, J. (1975), Recent Evidence on Conglomerate Diversification in UK Manufacturing Industry, *The Manchester School*, Vol. 43, No. 4, pp372-95.

Hayes, R. and Wheelwright, S. (1984), *Restoring Our Competitive Edge: Competing Through Manufacturing*, Wiley, New York.

Hladik, K. (1985), *International Joint Ventures*, DC Heath, Lexington.

Hobday, M.G. (1986a), *Technological Monitoring, Families, and Leads and Flags for VLSI Semiconductor Technology - A Methodological Exploration*, Science Policy Research Unit, mimeo.

Hobday, M.G. (1986b), *Digital Telecommunications Technology and the Third World - The Theory, the Challenge, and the Evidence from Brazil*, D. Phil. thesis, University of Sussex, SPRU.

Hobday, M.G.(1987), *Alvey and the International Semiconductor Industry*, Science Policy Research Unit, mimeo.

Horst, T. (1974), *At Home Abroad*, Ballinger, Cambridge, Mass.

House of Lords (1985), House of Lords Select Committee on the European Communities, ESPRIT session 1984-5. Eighth Report, HMSO, London.

Hughes, K. (1987), Technological Opportunity and R&D Diversification in the Conglomerate Firm, University of Manchester, mimeo.

IEEE Spectrum (1986), June issue.

Institute of Manpower Studies (1984), *Competence and Competition*, NEDO/MSC, London.

International Trade Administration, *Presentation to the US Department of Commerce*, April 1983, p. 70.

Jaffe, A. (1989), Characterising the Technological Position of Firms, with Application to Quantifying Technological Opportunity and Research Spillovers, *Research Policy* (forthcoming).

Johnstone, B. (1986), Untitled, *New Scientist*, 1 May.

Jones, D. (1987), Brownfields, Transplants and New Entrants: The Overcapacity Problem, DRC Discussion Paper No.55, Science Policy Research Unit, Sussex.

Jones, D. (1988), Measuring Technological Advantage in the Motor Vehicle Industry, IMVP paper, MIT, Cambridge, Mass.

Kamien, M. and Schwartz, M. (1982), *Market Structure and Innovation*, Cambridge University Press, Cambridge.

Kaplinsky, R. (1984), *Automation*, Longman, Harlow.

Kay, N. (1974), *The Emergent Firm*, Macmillan, London.

Kay, N. (1979), *The Innovating Firm. A Behavioural Theory of Corporate R&D*, Macmillan, London.

Kay, N. (1982), *The Evolving Firm; Strategy and Structure in Industrial Organisation*, Macmillan, London.

Keen, P. (1986), *Competing In Time: Using Telecommunications for Competitive Advantage*, Ballinger, Cambridge, Mass.

Kim, L. and Lee, J. (1987), Korea's Entry into the Computer Industry and its Acquisition of Technological Capability, *Technovation*, Vol.6, pp277-293.

Klein, B. (1977), *Dynamic Economics*, Harvard University Press, Cambridge, Mass.

Knickerbocker, F. (1983), *Oligopolistic Reaction and Multinational Enterprise*, Harvard University Press, Cambridge, Mass.

Kodama, F. (1986a), Japanese Innovation in Mechatronics Technology, *Science and Public Policy*, Vol. 13, No.1, pp44-52.

Kodama, F. (1986b), Technological Diversification of Japanese Industry, *Science*, Vol. 233, 18 July, pp291-96.

Koepp, S. (1986), Feeling the Crunch from Foreign Chips: Semiconductor Makers Fight Back, *Time*, 3 Nov, pp26-27.

Krafcik, J. (1988), The Triumph of the Lean Production System, *Sloan Management Review*, Vol.30, No.1.

Kuhn, T.S. (1962), *The Structure of Scientific Revolutions*, University of Chicago Press, Chicago.

Link, A. and Tassey, G. (1987), *Strategies for Technology-Based Competition*, DC Heath, Lexington.

Little, A.D.(1977), *New Technology Based Firms in the UK and the FRG*, Anglo-German Foundation, London.

Littler, D. and Sweeting, R. (1984), Business Innovation in the UK, *R&D Management*, Vol.14, No.1.

Lloyd, S. and Seaford, C. (1987), *New Forms of Enterprise: From Intrapreneurship to Spin-Off*, Small Business Research Trust, London.

Mackenzie, F.W. (1985), *Microelectronic Components: The Issue for Europe*, Centre for Business Strategy, London Business School, mimeo.

McKinsey Inc. (1983), *A Call to Action: The European Information Technology Industry*, Report to the Commission of the European Community, January.

Maidique, M. and Zirger, B. (1984), A Study of Success and Failure in Product Innovation: the Case of the US Electronics Industry, *IEEE Transactions on Engineering Management*, EM-31.

Maidique, M. and Zirger, B. (1985), The New Product Learning Cycle, *Research Policy*, No.14.

Malerba, F. (1985), *The Semiconductor Business: The Economics of Rapid Growth and Decline*, Pinter, London.

Mangham, I. and Silver, M. (1986), *Management Training - Context and Practice*, Economic and Social Research Council, London.

Marris, R. (1963), A model of managerial enterprise, *Quarterly Journal of Economics*, Vol.77, No.2.

Marris, R. (1964), *Theory of Managerial Capitalism*, Macmillan, London.

Marshall, A. (1961), *Principles of Economics*, Ninth (Varorium) edition, Macmillan, London.

Metcalfe, J. (1986), Technological Innovation and the Competitive Process, in Hall, P. (ed), *Technology, Innovation and Public Policy*, Philip Allan Publishers, Oxford.

Miles, I. (1988a), *Home Informatics*, Pinter, London.

Miles, I. (1988b), Information Technology and the Services Economy, in Zorkosky, P. (ed), *Oxford Surveys in Information Technology*, Vol.4, Oxford University Press, Oxford.

Miles, I. and Gershuny, J. (1986), The social economics of information technology, in Ferguson, M. (ed), *New Communications Technologies and the Public Interest*, Sage, London.

Molina, H. (1986), The US Revalues its Electronics Patents, *New Scientist*, 1 May, pp41-42.

Mowery, D. (1983), The Relationships Between Intrafirm and Contractual Forms of Industrial Research in American Manufacturing, *Explorations in Economic History*, No.20.

Mowery, D. (1987), *Alliance Politics and Economics: Multinational Joint Ventures in Commercial Aircraft*, Ballinger, Cambridge, Mass.

Narin, F. and Noma, E. (1985), Is Technology Becoming Science?, *Scientometrics*, Vol.7, Nos. 3-6, pp.369-381.

NEDO (1986), *Corporate Venturing: A Strategy for Innovation and Growth*, NEDO, London.

NEDO (1987), *Education and Training in IBM United Kingdom Ltd*, NEDO, London.

NEDO (1987), *Education and Training in Lucas Industries*, NEDO, London.

Nelson, R. (1988), Preface to Part IV: Innovation and the Evolution of Firms, in Dosi, G. et al (eds), *Technical Change and Economic Theory*, Pinter, London.

Nelson, R. and Winter, S. (1977), In search of a useful theory of innovation, *Research Policy*, No.1.

Nelson, R. and Winter, S. (1982), *An Evolutionary Theory of Economic Change*, Belknap Press, Cambridge, Mass.

New York Times, 6.1.87.

O'Dochartaigh, A. (1974), *Grocery Own Labels - A Review*, IPA, London.

Park, Y. (1987), *The National System of Innovation in Korea with an Introduction to the Semiconductor Industry*, University of Sussex, SPRU, M.Sc. thesis.

References

Patel, P. and Pavitt, K. (1987), The Elements of British Technological Competitiveness, *National Institute Economic Review*, No.122, pp.72-83.

Pavitt, K. (1984), Sectoral patterns of technical change: towards a taxonomy and a theory, *Research Policy*, Vol.13, No.6.

Pavitt, K. (1986a), Chips and Trajectories: How Does the Semiconductor Influence the Sources and Directions of Technical Change?, in Macleod, R. (ed), *Technology and the Human Prospect*, Pinter, London.

Pavitt, K. (1986b), Technology, Innovation and Strategic Management, in McGee, J. and Thomas, H. (eds), *Strategic Mangement Research: A European Perspective*, Wiley, Chichester.

Pavitt, K. (1987), *Comment* on Tushman, M. and Anderson, P., Technological Discontinuities and Organization Environments, in Pettigrew, A. (ed), *The Management of Strategic Change*, Blackwell, Oxford.

Pavitt, K. (1988), Uses and Abuses of Patent Statistics, in van Raan, A. (ed), *Handbook of Quantitative Studies of Science and Technology*, Elsevier, Amsterdam.

Pavitt, K.; Robson, M. and Townsend, J. (1987), The Size Distribution of Innovating Firms in the UK: 1945-1983, *Journal of Industrial Economics*, Vol.XXXV, No.3, pp297-316.

Pavitt, K. and Soete, L. (1980), Innovative Activities and Export Shares: Some Comparisons between Industries and Countries, in Pavitt, K. (ed), *Technical Innovation and British Economic Performance*, Macmillan, London.

Pavitt, K. and Thomson, A. (1987), The Successful Management of Technology, *Technology, Innovation and Society*, Vol.3, No.3.

Peck, M. and Wilson, R. (1982), Innovation, Imitation and Comparative Advantage: The Performance of Japanese Color Television Set Producers in the US Market, in Giersch, H. (ed), *Emerging Technologies: Consequences for Economic Growth, Structural Change, and Employment*, J.C.B. Mohr, Tubingen.

Penrose, E. (1959), *The Theory of the Growth of the Firm*, Blackwell, Oxford.

Peters, T. and Waterman, R. (1982), *In Search of Excellence: Lessons from America's Best Run Companies*, Harper and Row, New York.

Pettigrew, A. (1985), *The Awakening Giant: Continuity and Change in Imperial Chemical Industries*, Blackwell, Oxford.

Pettigrew, A. (1987), *The Management of Strategic Change*, Blackwell, Oxford.

Pfeffer, J. (1987), Bringing the Environment Back In: The Social Context of Strategic Management, in Teece, D. (ed), *The Competitive Challenge*, Ballinger, Cambridge, Mass.

Piore, M. and Sabel, C. (1984), *The Second Industrial Divide*, Basic Books, New York.

Pisano, G. and Teece, D. (1988), *Collaborative Arrangements and Global Technology Strategy: Some Evidence from the Telecommunications Equipment Industry*, Berkeley Business School International Business Working Paper No. 1B-10.

Porter, M. (1979), The Structure within Industries and Companies' Performance, *Review of Economics and Statistics*, Vol.61, pp214-27.

Porter, M. (1980), *Competitive Strategy: Techniques for Analysing Industries and Competitors*, The Free Press, New York.

Porter, M. (1983), The Technological Dimension of Competitive Strategy, *Research on Technological Innovation Management and Policy*, Vol.1, JAI Press Inc., pp. 1-33.

Porter, M. (1985a), Technology and Competitive Advantage, *Journal of Business Studies*, Winter, pp. 60-78.

Porter, M. (1985b), *Competitive Advantage: Creating and Sustaining Superior Performance*, Free Press, New York.

Porter, M. (1987a), Changing Patterns of International Competition, in Teece, D. (ed), *The Competitive Challenge*, Ballinger, Cambridge, Mass.

Porter, M. (1987b), From Competitive Advantage to Corporate Strategy, *Harvard Business Review*, May-June.

Rees, G. (1969), *St. Michael: A History of Marks & Spencer*, Wiedenfeld & Nicolson, London.

Riddle, D. (1986), *Service-Led Growth*, Praeger, New York.

Robson, M. and Townsend, J. (1984), Users Manual for ESRC Archive File on Innovations in Britain since 1945: 1984 Update, Science Policy Research Unit, Sussex.

Robson, M.; Townsend, J. and Pavitt, K. (1988), Sectoral Patterns of Production and Use of Innovations in the UK: 1945-1983, *Research Policy*, Vol.17, No.1, pp1-14.

Rosenberg, N. (1976), *Perspectives on Technology*, Cambridge University Press, Cambridge.

Rosenberg, N. (1982), *Inside the Black Box: Technology and Economics*, Cambridge University Press, Cambridge.

Rosenberg, N. (1984), *The Commercial Exploitation of Science by American Industry*, Stanford University.

Rosenberg, N. and Frischtak, C. (1985) (eds), *International Technology Transfer*, Praeger, New York.

Rosenbloom, R. and Cusumano, M. (1987), Technological Pioneering and Competitive Advantage: the Birth of the VCR Industry, *California Management Review*, Vol. XXIX, No.4.

Rothwell, R. (1977), The Characteristics of Successful Innovators and Technically Progressive Firms, *R & D Management*, Vol. 7, No. 3.

Rothwell, R. (1986), Innovation and Re-innovation: A Role for the User, *Journal of Marketing Management*, Vol.2, No.2.

Rothwell, R. and Dodgson, M. (1987), Technology-based Small Firms in Europe: The IRDAC Results and their Public Policy Implications. Paper presented at Second International Technical Innovation and Entrepreneurship Symposium, Birmingham, 1-4 September, published in conference proceedings.

Rothwell, R.; Dodgson, M. and Lowe, S. (1988), *Technology Transfer Mechanisms: Part 1 - the UK, Part 2 - the US, France, Japan, West Germany and the European Community*, Report to NEDO.

Rothwell, R.; Freeman, C.; Jervis, P.; Robertson, A. and Townsend, J. (1974), SAPPHO updated - project SAPPHO phase II, *Research Policy*, Vol.3, pp.258-291.

Rothwell, R. and Gardiner, J. (1982), *The Role of Design in Competitiveness*, paper presented at International Conference on Design Policy, Royal College of Art, 20-23 July, published in conference procedings.

Rothwell, R. and Gardiner, J. (1983), The Role of Design in Product and Process Change, *Design Studies*. Vol. 4, No. 3.

Rothwell, R. and Gardiner, J. (1984), Design and Competition in Engineering, *Long Range Planning*. Vol. 17, No. 3, pp 78-91.

Rothwell, R. and Gardiner, J. (1985), Invention, Innovation, Re-innovation and the Role of the User: A Case Study of British Hovercraft Development, *Technovation*, Vol.3, pp 167-186.

Rothwell, R. and Zegveld, W. (1985), *Reindustrialisation and Technology*, Longman, Harlow.

Routh, G. (1975), *The Origin of Economic Ideas*, Macmillan, London.

Ruffles, P.C. (1986), Reducing the Cost of Aero Engine Research and Development, *Aerospace*, Vol.13, No.9, pp10-19.

Rullani, E. and Zanfei, A. (1984), Benetton: Invenzione e Consolidamento di un Sistema Internazionale, *Bolletino Ospri*, No.1.

Rumelt, R. (1974), *Strategy, Structure and Economic Performance*, Graduate School of Business Administration, Harvard University, Cambridge, Mass.

Sabel, C. (1982), *Work and Politics*, Cambridge University Press, Cambridge.

Sabel, C. and Zeitlin, J. (1982), Alternative storiche alla produzione di massa, *Stato e Mercato*, No.5.

Sayer, A. (1986), New Developments in Manufacturing: The Just in Time System, *Capital and Class*, No. 30.

Scherer, F. (1980), *Industrial Market Structure and Economic Performance*, (second edition), Rand McNally, Chicago.

Scherer, F. (1986), *Innovation and Growth: Schumpeterian Perspectives*, MIT Press, Cambridge, Mass.

Schonberger, R. (1982), *Japanese Manufacturing Techniques: Nine Hidden Lessons in Simplicity*, Free Press, New York.

Schonberger, R. (1986), *World Class Manufacturing: The Lessons of Simplicity Applied*, Free Press, New York.

Schumpeter, J. (1934), *The Theory of Economic Development*, Oxford University Press, London.

Schumpeter, J. (1950), *Capitalism, Socialism and Democracy*, Allen and Unwin, third edition, London.

Sciberras, E. (1977), *Multinational Electronic Companies and International Competitiveness in the Television Industry*, OMEGA, Vol.10, No.6.

Segal, Quince and Wickstead and ISI (1986), *New Technology Based Firms*, SQW, Cambridge.

Senker, J. (1988), *A Taste for Innovation: British Supermarkets' Influence on Food Manufacturers*, Horton Publishing, Bradford.

Senker, P.; Vandevelde, M.; Beesley, M. and Hutchin, T. (1988), *Electronics on the Shopfloor*, EITB Research Report RC21, Watford.

Sharp, M. and Shearman, C. (1987), *European Technological Collaboration*, Chatham House Paper No. 36, Routledge and Kegan Paul for the Royal Institute of International Affairs.

Shaw, B. (1985), The Role of the Interaction Between the User and the Manufacturer in Medical Equipment Innovation, *R&D Management*, Vol.15, No.14.

Sheriff, A. (1988), *The Competitive Product Position of Automobile Manufacturers: Performance and Strategies*, IMVP Paper, MIT, Cambridge, Mass.

Simon, H. (1961), *Administrative Behaviour*, (second edition), Macmillan, New York.

Soete, L. (1985), Electronics, in Soete, L. (ed), *Technological Trends and Employment*, Gower, Aldershot.

Stiglitz, J.E. (1986), *Learning to Learn, Technological Change and Economic and Social Structure*, mimeo.

Teece, D. (1982), Towards an Economic Theory of the Multiproduct Firm, *Journal of Economic Behaviour and Organisation*, Vol. 3, No. 1, pp39-63.

Teece, D. (1986), Profiting from Technological Innovation: Implications for Integration, Collaboration, Licensing and Public Policy, *Research Policy*, Vol.15, pp.285-305.

Teece, D. (1987a), Profiting from Technological Innovation: Implications for Integration, Collaboration, Licensing, and Public Policy, in Teece, D. (ed), *The Competitive Challenge*, Ballinger, Cambridge, Mass.

Teece, D. (1987) (ed), *The Competitive Challenge: Strategies for Industrial Innovation and Renewal*, Ballinger, Cambridge, Mass.

Teece, D. (1987b), Capturing Value from Technological Innovation: Integration, Strategic Partnering, and Licensing Decisions, in Guile, B.R. and Brooks, H. (eds), *Technology and Global Industry*, National Academy Press, Washington DC.

Teubal, M. (1982), The R & D Performance through Time of High Technology Firms, *Research Policy*, Vol. 11, No. 6, pp333-46.

Thomas, G. and Miles, I. (1988), *New Interactive Services in the UK*, Report to the Leverhulme Trust, (Science Policy Research Unit mimeo, currently under revision for book publication).

Townsend, J.; Henwood, F.; Thomas, G.; Pavitt, K. and Wyatt, S. (1981), *Science and Technology Indicators for the UK - Innovations in Britain since 1945*, Occasional Paper No. 16, Science Policy Research Unit.

Tse, K.K. (1985), *Marks and Spencer*, Pergamon Press, Oxford.

Turbil, J-P. (1986), How Elf Aquitaine Provides Technological Assistance to Small and Large Firms, *Long Range Planning*, Vol.19, No.3.

Tushman, M. and Anderson, P. (1987), Technological Discontinuities and Organization Environments, in Pettigrew, A. (ed), *The Management of Strategic Change*, Blackwell, Oxford.

Utterback, J. and Abernathy, W. (1975), A Dynamic Model of Process and Product Innovation, *Omega*, Vol. 3, No. 6, pp639-56.

Utterback, J. and Kim, L. (1986), Invasion of a Stable Business by Radical Innovation, in Kleindorfer, P. (ed), *The Management of Productivity and Technology in Manufacturing*, Plenum, New York.

Utton, M. (1979), *Diversification and Competition*, Cambridge University Press, Cambridge.

Van Mesdag, M. (1985), Europe's Brand Squeeze, *Management Today*, March, pp.70-73 and 114.

Vernon, R. (1966), International Investment and International Trade in the Product Cycle, *Quarterly Journal of Economics*, Vol. 80, No. 2, pp190-207.

Vernon, R. (1979), The Product Cycle Hypothesis in a New International Environment, *Oxford Bulletin of Economics and Statistics*, Vol.41, November.

von Hippel, E. (1976), The Dominant Role of Users in the Scientific Instruments Innovation Process, *Research Policy*, Vol.5, No.3, pp212-239.

von Hippel, E. (1982), Appropriability of Innovation Benefit as a Predictor of the Source of Innovation, *Research Policy*, Vol.11, No.2, pp. 95-115.

Watts, B. (1982), *Structural Adjustment in the United Kingdom Food Manufacturing Industry Over the Past Twenty Years*, Paper presented to the OECD Conference, The Adjustment and the Challenges Facing the Food Industries in the 1980's, Paris, 11-14 January.

Williamson, O. (1975), *Markets and Hierarchies: Analysis and Antitrust Implications*, Free Press, New York.

Williamson, O. (1979), Transaction Costs Economics: The Governance of Contractual Relations, *Journal of Law and Economics*, No.22.

Williamson, O. (1981), The Modern Corporation: Origins, Evaluation, Attributes, *Journal of Economic Literature*, Vol.13, December.

Williamson, O. (1985), *The Economic Institutions of Capitalism: Firms, Markets, Relational Contracting*, Free Press, New York.

Williamson, O. (1986), *Economic Organisation: Firms, Market and Policy Control*, (English edition), Wheatsheaf Books, Brighton.

Wilmot, R. (1985), Wanted: An Industry That Is World Class, *Financial Times*, 26 June.

Womack, J. (1988), *The European Motor Vehicle Industry in the World: Some Strategic Considerations*, IMVP paper, MIT, Cambridge, Mass.

Wyatt, S. (1984), The Role of Small Firms in Innovative Activity, Science Policy Research Unit mimeo.

Yates-Mercer, P. (1985), *Private Viewdata in the UK*, Gower, Aldershot.

Yoffie, D. (1983), *Power and Protectionism: Strategies of the Newly Industrializing Countries*, Columbia University Press, New York.

Zeitlin, J. (1984), *Strutture industriali e distretti industriali in prospectiva storica*, paper presented at the conference Piccola Citte e Piccola Impresa, Florence, 16-18 February.

Index